Running For The Hansons

*An Insider's Account of the
Brooks-Sponsored Marathon
Training Group Made Famous
by Olympian Brian Sell*

a book by
Sage Canaday

Edited by Robert Louis Scribner

Vo2max Productions, LLC.
Rochester, Michigan

Vo2max Productions, LLC
email: sage@vo2maxproductions.com

To order additional copies please visit:
www.Vo2maxProductions.com

Library of Congress Cataloging-Data:
LCCN: 2011929666
Published May 2011

ISBN: 978-0-9832941-1-5

A book by Sage Canaday
Edited by Robert Louis Scribner

Front and back cover photo credit:
Joe Baldwin & MichiganRunner.com

Printed in the United States of America

Acknowledgments

I'd like to thank my family for their ongoing support of my "selfish" running endeavors. I'd also like to thank my teammates at Newberg High School, my teammates at Cornell, and my teammates at Hansons. You guys are not only my teammates, but also my friends in life outside of running. On days I didn't feel like going the extra mile you guys encouraged me forward; during tough workouts you guys pushed me to new levels of pain. Also, a special thank you to my editor Robert Scribner, who went over drafts of the original manuscript, fixed my errors, and helped make the book possible. I'd like to thank my major sponsor Brooks Sports for having faith in me as an athlete and for providing me with lots of shoes and gear. Finally, I'd like to thank all my coaches: my high school coach Bruce Sinkbeil (who also taught me calculus), Cornell distance coach (and LetsRun.com co-founder) Robert Johnson, and Keith and Kevin Hanson. All of these people had a major role in allowing me to continue running and without their support this book would not exist.

Thank you.

- Sage Canaday

Preface

I looked directly to my left and saw Olympians Ryan Hall and Meb Keflezighi toe the starting line. A coveted front row spot! I definitely didn't belong here - this was like playing in a major league baseball game when you are used to playing catch in the backyard. A swift breeze flowed over my left shoulder, coming from the Northwest. Good! There was some element of a tailwind. It was a perfect day for running fast, 52 degrees and sunny. I anxiously stared at the downward sloping road ahead, slightly distracted by the hundreds of spectators, fans, loved-ones and video cameras on both sides. Behind us, over twenty-three thousand runners nervously stood, crammed like sardines between ropes which separated them into waves. We had all been patiently waiting, visualizing this very moment of truth: Race Day.

For some this was a culmination of years of training, a lifetime dream that was coming true. For others it was going to be a trip down memory lane, a glorious rebirth filled with pain and suffering but laced with ecstasy. Regardless, for everyone it was going to be a feat of endurance. For the last three months, I had trained specifically to run these 26.2 miles. Yet I now reminded myself of all the thousands of miles I had run in my life to get here. The vomit-inducing workouts and races on hot asphalt tracks in middle school; the NCAA Cross Country Championship in college; the thousands of monotonous running hours in between; the forgotten summers and winters; a blur of roads and trails whose names I didn't even remember…it had all come down to this.

It was April 19, 2010: Patriots Day in Hopkinton, Massachusetts. We were about to run the 114th BAA Boston Marathon.

Contents

Appendix:

Introduction

I arrived in Rochester Hills, Michigan on August 27, 2009. I was slightly out of shape, and at 5'11" and 158 pounds, an overweight wannabe national class marathon runner. My dream was to see how fast I could run 26.2 miles. I had heard this was the place to be to make that dream a reality. A slew of quality runners were already on the roster, including one of my idols, 2008 Olympic Marathoner Brian Sell. I was ecstatic to be running with such accomplished teammates. This had been a dream of mine since high school. I had finally made it to a level I never thought I could achieve in running. As a funded athlete, I could live the running lifestyle and have a shoe brand sponsor to boast about, courtesy of Brooks Sports Inc. I was fresh out of college and swimming in student loan debt, yet resistant to conform to typical career paths out in the "real world." Kevin and Keith Hanson saw potential in me and gave me the opportunity of a lifetime. This was it…you are only young once! I was willing to make some sacrifices to pursue what most in society would view as a silly and selfish pipe dream. But I didn't care. I had lived the last decade of my life obsessing about running…plus, the 2012 U.S. Olympic Marathon Trials loomed.

Meet The Men's Team

When I joined Hansons at the end of August 2009, the men's roster consisted of the following athletes:

(Editor's note: The women's team is not listed here because the author did not know them very well. Segregation of the men's and women's teams is discussed later in the story. A complete, updated Hansons-Brooks athlete listing is included at the end of the book).

Nick "Snick" Arciniaga
College: Cal State Fullerton
Hometown: Orange County, CA

Nick started off his running career with some speed. He had a 1:56 800m personal best in high school…a time that really didn't get you much in a competitive state like California. At Cal State Fullerton he had a decent, but not flashy college career, with a 14:23 track 5k to his credit despite training recklessly at 110 miles per week for years. Before joining Hansons, Nick debuted at the 2006 Chicago Marathon and cranked out a 2:16:58. During his first year at Hansons he ran another 2:16 for 10th place (1st American) at Boston in 2007. Resistant to injury and single-mindedly tough, Nick always goes the extra mile.
PRs 5k: 14:22, 10k (road) 29:46, Marathon: 2:16:13

Luke "Grizzly Bear/Mr. Pants" Humphrey
College: Central Michigan
Hometown: Sydney, Michigan

Luke was one of the "grumpy old men" on the team when I came in. Unlike most of the guys in the program, Luke works outside of the store in a hospital doing cardiac care. An experienced marathoner now, he previously had 50 second 400m speed in high school. Luke stayed in-state for college and ran on the Central Michigan cross country team that placed 9th at DI NCAAs in 2002. He ran 14:15 for 5k on the track in college. After joining Hansons he quickly flourished and ran 2:15:23 at Boston in 2006, before following it up with a 2:15:22 at Chicago that fall. He seeks to PR by a more significant margin before the next Olympic Trials.

PRs: 5k: 14:15, 10k: 29:04, Half Marathon: 1:04:05, Marathon: 2:15:22

Paul "Precious" Jellema
College: Southern Indiana
Hometown: Dyer, IN

Paul was a talent coming of out high school. He was 11th at the Foot Locker Midwest Regional meet as a junior the same year that Dathan Ritzinhein dominated. After suffering from several femoral stress fractures throughout his career, Paul has had to keep his mileage at a relatively modest 70 to 90 miles a week. He is the store manager at the Hansons Utica store, and his wife is expecting.

PRs: 10k: 28:58

Chad "Nails" Johnson
College: Minnesota
Hometown: Chetek, WI

Chad appeared on the cover of *Wired* Magazine in an article about building the "Ultimate Runner." He was a national champion jump-roper (really), and state champion in the high jump in his early prep days. After a brief, initial stint with Hansons, he ran for the original Nike Oregon Project in Portland, OR and was coached by the legendary Alberto Salazar for several years. As a speedy track guy, Chad has run the equivalent of a 4:00 mile, and got 8th in the Olympic Trials 5k in 2004. He was also the national champion at 25k on the roads in 2001. Now he is the "old guy," back on the Hansons team looking for a comeback streak of performances before retirement. He is also now engaged to Hansons female star Melissa White, and they are busy planning their wedding and racing schedule.

PRs: 1500: 3:42, 3k: 7:55, 5k: 13:36, 8k: 22:33, 10k: 28:29, Half Marathon: 64:01, Marathon: 2:15:03

Mike "Little Tokyo" Morgan
College: Nebraska Wesleyan
Hometown: Lincoln, NE

Mike ran for DIII Nebraska Wesleyan and never broke 30:00 for 10k on the track in college despite being All-American three times. Before those feats, his best performance was as a high school runner in the state of Nebraska, where he was 14th at the state meet in cross-country. After a gig as a liquor salesman upon college graduation, Mike continued to run on his own for a year before joining Hansons. The "little guy" on the team, Mike likes to prove himself everyday by leading almost every easy run, and pushing the pace on workouts. Mike hammered his way to a 2:15:11 marathon debut at Chicago in 2006, one of the top 30 fastest American marathon debuts of all time. He has made US national teams in both the half marathon and marathon; he was 23rd in the world in the latter. He has suffered multiple stress fractures, and has lost the ability to claw back with his big toe. However, this does not stop him from dreaming big (i.e., a sub 2:12 marathon) and piling on the 140+ mile weeks that it will take to get him there.

PRs: 5k: 14:29, 10k (road) 29:47, 10 miles: 48:06, Half Marathon: 1:04:04, Marathon: 2:15:11

Pat "Rizzo" Rizzo
College: North Central
Hometown: Schaumberg, Ill

Rizzo has Sicilian blood in him, and it shows when he makes his mean pasta sauce. In college at North Central he was part of a dynasty DIII distance running program (a fact he is very proud of). After joining Hansons as a "B-level" athlete who had to pay his own rent initially, Rizzo flourished, improving from a 2:20 to a 2:17, 15th place finish at Boston in the spring of 2009. However, it wasn't always easy for Rizzo: as an adolescent he wore braces, and a freak allergic reaction to metal almost caused him to go completely deaf. During a previous training segment leading up to the Boston Marathon, Rizzo was hit by a car while training with his teammates in Rochester and critically injured. He is the most vocal, open and honest member of the team, and highly valued as a person his teammates can depend on.
PRs: 5k: 14:29, 10k: 29:38, Marathon: 2:17:05

Brian "Selbo" Sell
College: St. Francis
Hometown: Woodberry, PA

Brian is the guy that really put the Hansons Program on the map. He is (and will always be) the blue-collar runner who worked his butt off and accomplished his Olympic dream through guts, tremendous self-discipline, and durability. He is the epitome of what the runners in the program stand for and want to become. I've devoted a whole chapter to this book explaining his background in running and what it took to become an Olympian. For many young runners (myself included), Brian is a hero, and seeing that individuals aspire to follow in his footsteps of self-improvement is one of the reasons I was motivated to write this book. When I came into the program, Brian was already becoming more of a family man, with another child on the way. He enjoyed talking about flying radio-controlled model airplanes and riding motorcycles. He was planning his next stage in life, but first he was going to experience the NYC marathon for the first time…his last marathon wearing the Hansons singlet.

PRs: 3k: 8:07, 3k SC: 8:52, 5k: 13:59, 10k: 28:28, Half Marathon: 1:02:35, Marathon: 2:10:47

Clint Verran
College: Eastern Michigan
Hometown: Lake Orion, MI

The local guy and original team member, Clint has seen it all. As the oldest guy on the team he has had his share of injuries, successes, and race experiences. Clint started out as a solid runner in the state of Michigan, as the 1992 high school state champion in cross country. He later took his running to Eastern Michigan, where he ran 14:15 for 5k and 8:51 for the 3k steeple on the track. He also won the MAC cross country conference meet in 1995. After joining the initial Hanson team, Clint thrived, making multiple US national teams at both the half and full marathon distances, where he placed as high as 17th and 22nd in the world respectively. After being one of the youngest finishers at the 2000 Olympic Marathon Trials, Clint came back and got 5th in 2004, narrowly missing making the US Olympic team. He ran his marathon PR at Boston in 2006, where he placed 10th with a 2:14:12. Now, nearing retirement, Clint operates his own successful physical therapy business outside of Lake Orion, MI.

PRs: 3k: 8:02, 5k: 13:51, 10 miles: 47:53, Half Marathon: 1:04:00, Marathon: 2:14:12

Todd Synder
College: Michigan
Hometown: Ann Arbor, MI

Another local boy, Todd has been a name in Michigan running for a while. There was a period of nearly 2 years in high school where he didn't lose a single race to any other kid in the state. In college, he ran at the University of Michigan where he placed 10th at the DI NCAA Cross Country Championships in 1998. When he's not looking after his two toddler-aged kids, he shreds an American-made Fender Stratocaster (guitar). He's coming off of a 2:19 run at Boston in 2009, and recently suffered from a fall on his bike which broke his arm.
PRs: 20k: 1:01:51, Marathon: 2:19:55

Christian "Doogie" Wagner
College: Wisconsin
Hometown: Columbus, Indiana

Big talent. Christian won the outdoor high school national 2-mile championships in 2003, outkicking Nef Araia and Galen Rupp for the win in a negative split 8:53. As a Badger, he trained with the likes of Matt Tegenkamp and Chris Solinsky to name a couple. He was a part of the NCAA Cross Country Championship Badger team, and earned All-American honors in track at 10000m.
PRs: 5k: 13:59, 10k: 29:00

And me:

Sage "Fat Boy" Canaday
College: Cornell University
Hometown: Sheridan, Oregon

I was a 4:30 miler in high school, and I never qualified for the Oregon state meet in track. I didn't think I'd continue to run in college until I was a senior in high school. However, in the fall of 2003, I had a "solid enough" final season of cross country, where I finished within 300m of Galen Rupp at the state meet. A few years later I improved significantly in college under the coaching of LetsRun.com co-founder Robert "Rojo" Johnson. After qualifying for the 2008 US Olympic Trials in the marathon as a junior at Cornell, I had another solid cross country season where I was the Ivy League Conference Runner-Up (24:41 at Van Cortlandt Park) and an individual qualifier for NCAAs. The following track season I won my first and only outdoor conference title in the 10k. In my final year of college I struggled all track season and didn't place again at conference. Coming into Hansons, I am the "fat and slow" new guy who must learn to adapt to post-collegiate training and racing.

PRs: 5k: 14:29, 10k: 29:47, 20k: 1:03:11, Marathon: 2:21:43

US Olympic Marathon Trials.
November 3rd, 2007

Before you start a journey forward, sometimes you are tempted to glance back at the tracks you left behind, the footprints of memories. You check your rearview mirror for perspective in order to catch your bearings. Perhaps you are afraid that someone or something is chasing you? There is the residue of regret from previous learning experiences that influences your present choices and the way you currently live your life. Was it a past relationship that has soured your perception of love? Maybe there was a class that you remember miserably failing because it pulled your GPA down a couple tenths of a point? Scars from the past haunt your focus on the future as you weigh the risks of new goals and dreams that you must continue to fight for.

Life becomes a delicate balance of shifting paradigms, time-management, and attitude. Some would say it's just your cycle of karma; what goes around comes around; things happen for a reason. When the catalyst of change occurs, your character is shaped and tested. Your mind sometimes gets stuck in that kind of nostalgic moment, that tipping point when you finally overcame some adversity and shifted direction in life. You remember working hard, really buckling down. You remember the big paydays, the big sacrifices, and the drama of your real-life, personal narrative. It sometimes unfolds like a scripted movie in your head. Sometimes what you dream about late at night finally does come true, what were goals for the future suddenly become a present reality that you can lavish in.

For me that year was 2007, the best running year of my life. For 12 months I set PRs in every event from the 800m to the marathon from 21 to 22 years of age. My love life sucked and my college GPA took a turn for the worst

- but man, I was running fast and feeling good! However, that year wasn't just a glory year in running for me - it was a glory year for the Hansons-Brooks Distance Project. It was the year that the "team MVP," Brian Sell, succeeded in his ultimate goal in running and became an Olympian. It all reached a climax at the 2008 US Olympic Marathon Trials.

* * *

New York City. It was a chilly and dim morning near Times Square. Video cameras and the vehicles yielding them drove beside and in front of us. A group of 120 or so men were running at roughly 11 miles per hour towards Central Park. It was the start of the 2008 US Olympic Marathon Trials, and I was right in the mix of it…well, at least for the first couple of miles. As we entered Central Park, I was running next to guys like 2004 Olympians Abdi Abdirahman, Meb Keflezighi, Alan Culpepper, Dathan Ritzenhein, and Dan Browne. Then of course there was former world record holder and 2:05 marathoner Khalid Khannouchi. There was also this guy named Ryan Hall, who had just run a 2:06 marathon earlier that year and who had also become the first American to crack 60:00 in the half-marathon. I ran off to the side, guilty to admit I wanted some camera time, but also timid that I might accidentally trip some of these real contenders and prevent them from making the Olympic Team. I knew before I had even toed the starting line that I was not going to finish this race because I was running cross country for Cornell University that fall and we had NCAA Regionals coming up the very next weekend. Running a hard 26.2 miles and then racing a cross country 10k with the intention of qualifying for NCAAs was simply out of the question. So I had vowed that the purpose of this Olympic Trials would be to gain experience, and that I'd return on my own terms in 2012. Perhaps by then, when I would be 26 years old, I might be able to actually compete for a top 15 finish. It was our first lap of four around Central Park's hilly 6-mile loop. I pulled alongside some runners sporting flashy colored singlets in hues of solid red and yellow. Their jerseys stood out like no other club team or shoe-brand sponsor. These were not slick Nike singlets; instead, they were made by Brooks! I knew exactly who these guys were…they were members of the Hansons-Brooks Distance Project. I had followed this group closely since the last Olympic Trials in 2004. I had secretly dreamed of having a career like their top guy Brian Sell. Now, I was running a race with them! "Keep your distance…don't trip Brian!" I kept thinking to myself as I sheepishly ran alongside the main pack. I knew how much this race meant to him, how he had trained specifically with this day in mind for the last 4 years. A lot of the runners competing in this race may have trained hard and thought about making the Olympic Team, but I was willing to bet that few had sacrificed, toiled, and worked as hard as Brian Sell. That is why I feel his story is unique. His path to success at this moment wasn't a paved road filled with candy canes and chocolates but rather a rocky road full of bittersweet setbacks, long and cold miles, and painful memories from the 2004 marathon trials. Such adversities had challenged his very will to even continue in the sport.

* * *

For the Hansons the race was total team domination. The crowds of spectators lining the park seemed to really like these guys and their unique, matching uniforms! Plain white cotton T-shirts with the Hansons singlet printed on the front and back were being handed out to the crowds by the dozen. Some family members and friends had giant head cutouts with the various athletes' faces printed on them. Shirtless fans were running around in the near-freezing fall weather with their bare chests painted in the iconic yellow, red, and black colors of the Hansons-Brooks' team logo. Of the 104 athletes that finished the Olympic Marathon Trials, 12 of them wore the Hansons-Brooks singlet. The Hansons had 10 athletes in the top 50, and even more remarkably 5 of those finishers were in the top 20! That meant a quarter of the nation's top 20 marathoners hailed from the same program in Rochester Hills, Michigan! The sea of orange, yellow and red swarmed around the finish line, much like a large cross country team running as a pack amongst a cluster of various, unattached and unaffiliated jerseys from all the other individuals.

The Hansons runners all ran a smart pace; they ran with conviction. A look of shear determination was apparent in their eyes and etched across their weary faces. The road here was long and arduous for everyone - but this band of brothers had collaborated in all of their misery. They made their sacrifices together, as a collective. They shared in their pain, and in their triumphs. Brian Sell may have been the only one to make the Olympic Team that day, but his teammates had all played a part in helping him achieve such a rewarding goal. It was a team of underdogs, a bunch of misfit college runners, and many didn't even run DI in college. Few had earned All-American certificates, and some had never even made it to an NCAA final. They were runners who may have had a passion for running since high school, but never made the Foot Locker Nationals or broke 9:30 for 2 miles. They had continued to live out their running career beyond college, to pursue their dreams in running simply because they loved the sport and could not get enough of it. It came down to a matter of seeing how far one could fulfill his potential in some aspect of his life by doggedly pursuing it without respite for several years in the prime of early adult life.

"This, this group! These guys have it made!" I thought to myself. They train like crazy! They are like animals; madmen! What is up there in the water in Rochester, Michigan? I had to find out. I wanted to know "the secret," to run a national class marathon time. I wanted to capture some of that intensity. I wanted to examine and outline the process that drove such motivated self-starters like Brian Sell from a measly 10:00 2-miler in high school to a 2:10 Olympic Marathoner. I wanted to pick their minds, and to physically experience the stress of such a training regimen. I wanted to run with reckless abandon and drop crazy fast, sick times! Luckily my college coach, Robert Johnson of LetsRun.com fame, got me in touch with Kevin and Keith Hanson when I was a junior in college. By the end of 2007 my plan to run post-collegiately for such a group lingered in the back of my mind. When I graduated from Cornell in the spring of 2009 I was ready to take my chances out in Michigan. The following is my first-hand account of the Hansons-Brooks Distance Project, what it is like to live the lifestyle, to train with an Olympian, and to ultimately dream big.

Hansons fans decked out at the 2008 Trials
(Photo credit: MichiganRunner.com)

Premise: Summer 2009, a Gameplan

After spending a full summer in the college town of Ithaca, NY immediately following my graduation from Cornell in May of 2009, I was more than ready for a full-fledged move into the post-collegiate scene of running. Winning the local Ithaca Festival Mile in 4:29 just didn't have the same ring to it as "training for the Olympic Trials Marathon." Earlier in the summer I had sent an email to Keith and Kevin Hanson about my interest in their program, and after about a week of silence they emailed me back and invited me to come out on a visit.

I first ran the Utica Boilermaker 15k (where I placed just out of the prize money in a dismal 47:24, which was 16th place overall), and then a couple days later I hopped on a plane for Detroit. I'll later go into the details about my recruiting trip, but it was pretty uneventful and typical for a Hansons recruit. More importantly, during my 2-day stay in Michigan, it sounded like the Hanson brothers would be willing to offer me a spot on their team. A couple days after my visit I got an email saying I was accepted into the program!

Of course I couldn't say no. I had been warned by several of the ex-Hansons runners I had met over the years that I shouldn't join for various reasons. However, I figured even if things didn't work out, at least I could say that I tried. I knew that I'd regret not giving post-collegiate running a shot, and I knew I'd regret it if I didn't ever run for Hansons when I had a chance. I had thought about this very moment for years. Sometimes you just have to make your own decisions in life and risk not knowing where they may take you. Despite my disastrous 5th year senior college track season, this program and the major shoe company Brooks Sports, Inc. were going to give me a shot to run at the professional level. I was finally going to live out my dream of racing marathons and focusing on being an athlete.

Running had gotten me to places that I felt like I didn't belong; she had gotten me VIP status at races, and local newspaper articles had written about me because of her. She had taught me that there were financial incentives available, even to "slow elites" like me who weren't all-stars in high school or college. There was no other aspect in my life that I had reached a higher level of success in. I was never the smartest kid in the class, but I knew that I was the fastest at times. Running had been too good to me over the duration of our love-hate relationship, and there was no way in hell I was going to let her down now!

After going home to Oregon for a week to see my family in early August, I hopped on a plane back to New York to pack up all my belongings and say goodbye to my college friends. Over the course of 5 years I had accumulated quite a bit of junk at the old "track house." There was a pile of old running clothes and favorite textbooks high enough that it would be impossible to fly on a plane without paying a fortune in baggage fees. Since I needed a car for Michigan anyway, I decided to go up to Syracuse, New York (about a 1 hour drive from Ithaca) to buy a used car on a whim. The small towns in upstate New York didn't have much of a selection, so I decided to take my chances in the "ghetto" of The 'Cuse. I had my Cornell teammate Zac Hine drive me to a really shady-looking used car lot that I had found online to look at some prospective vehicles. A greasy salesman named Jeff tried to put a $2600 value on the '98 Chevy Prizm I had been eyeing on CarFacts. The Prizm was a nauseating Burgundy color. However, since the finish was tarnished and chipped in places, I decided the ugly, maroon-ish paint job wasn't going to be a deal breaker. I talked Jeff down to $2000 over the course of an hour and bought the car just like that. I'm sure I over-paid dearly for such a beater, but you can't expect much from a used car lot on the east side of Syracuse. Plus, I was desperate and needed to drive all my cargo and myself to Michigan ASAP!

The Prizm made the 9-hour trip from Ithaca, NY to Rochester Hills, MI without breaking down. It was a big relief, as the car was packed to the brim with my belongings as I sped through Canada in the hot summer sun; the death-trap proved it wasn't a total lemon despite the non-functional air conditioning. When I arrived at one of the Hansons team houses around 10 PM, I was greeted by Nick Arciniaga and Christian Wagner (both of whom were about to go to bed). Tired and weary from my journey, I passed out in one of the three empty rooms contained by the single floor house. I learned later that it was a room where the infamous Trent Briney (who got 4th at the 2004 Olympic marathon trials) had lived. I was told that we would be running at 7:15 AM. It was going to be a shock to my usual system that revolved around the summer laziness of sleeping in.

After a couple of days in Michigan I had already started working in the Hansons Running Shop stores, adjusted somewhat to running in the morning, and had met all the guys on the team. I also got some of my first sponsored running gear in the form of the Brooks Launch, a light-weight training shoe, as well as some Brooks t-shirts and shorts.

* * *

For my first couple weeks at Hansons I didn't have a training schedule so I just ran the mileage that the other guys were doing. I shadowed Nick a lot in fear of getting lost out on a run and not being able to find my way back to the house. It was going to take a while for me to get used to all the new running loops and foreign surroundings. Nick was putting in big miles. After a summer "speed segment" where he ran the Bix 7-miler and the Peachtree 10k road races (both USATF national championships), he was back to marathon training, gearing up for the New York City Marathon (which was also serving as the 2009 US National Marathon Championships) in November. Brian Sell was also training for the race.

My other housemate, Christian Wagner, was fresh out of college like me, although that is about where the comparisons would end between us. Since Christian was a Badger, he had already run on an "elite" NCAA Championship team. He knew what running hard and fast was all about. Christian had a lot of speed; he had that "pop" in his stride. It was apparent to Kevin and Keith that he'd start off by focusing on the track and trying to get his 10k and 5k PR's down low enough to qualify for the US Track Championships in June 2010. Christian's schedule had him racing a 10k track race that fall and then running some indoor 3ks and 5ks in the winter, concluding with a track 10k in the spring, and then the USATF Outdoor National Championships in the summer.

The other guys on the team had their fall seasons all planned out a "gameplan," as Kevin Hanson would say:

Mike Morgan was training to run a 2:12 pace at the 2009 California International Marathon in December.

Luke Humphrey was on the same training plan as Christian (AKA a "speed segment"), which involved a fall track 10k, some indoor track races, and an attempt at a sub 29:00 10k in the spring. He would also do a few half marathons in the winter.

Chad Johnson was training to run the 2009 Detroit Free Press Marathon, which is an October event. He has yet to win a marathon, and this could be his very first!

Pat Rizzo was training to run Chicago, which is also in early October. He has targeted a 2:15 goal pace, and seeks to place well in the race.

Paul Jellema was coming back from injury, and seeks to run a half marathon in the fall before leaving the program.

Todd Synder was injured and just starting to run again. No racing plans anytime soon.

Eventually, Keith and Kevin mapped out a game plan for my next 9 months of running: I was going to run some local road 10ks in the fall in preparation for the 2009 Rock 'n' Roll Las Vegas Half Marathon in December. After that I was going to run the 2010 Walt Disney World Half Marathon in January. Following Disney, I was to take a week break from running and then start a 3-month training segment for the Boston Marathon in April 2010!

Initially I was a little disappointed, because I really wanted to jump straight into a marathon that fall and PR. However, I realized that their plan would allow me to adjust to the training more gradually, and that it was probably the right thing for me to follow. I just couldn't wait to put on that Brooks singlet and tear up the roads! Vegas and Disney sounded like awesome, fun places to go for racing, and what better stage to debut as a national-class, US post-collegiate than at a major marathon like Boston. However, my excitement and enthusiasm needed to be repressed, as the races are the reward for countless hours and miles spent in preparation training. I still needed to be hardened to the monotony of running thousands of steady, uneventful miles; of running on stiff, sore legs at a pace just a little too fast for any lack in concentration. I was merely a newbie, an ignorant (and arrogant) young and inexperienced post-collegiate athlete about to be "fed to the fishes." I was going to have my patience tested. It was like being a freshman all over again.

An Easy Day
September 8th, 2009

I almost shit myself today. Every runner fears the feeling of such a workout (or race) wrecker. Common and crude sounding as it may be, such distress is a reality that we must confront from time to time. However, in my 12 years of running I have never succumbed to nature's urges and crapped in the bushes while out on a run. I think that is unusual. That kind of record must put you in some kind of elite, prestigious club, right? There is a significant amount of pride that is accompanied with a feat like that, and giving in to that record would be revealing weakness. I asked myself, "What would you do if it was mile 22 of a marathon and you felt this urge?" All this time I have trained myself to "can it," or save it for later. There is a sick sense of joy in some of the unusual struggles that you often want to challenge yourself in as a runner. Sometimes you just are trying to be a masochist. Today was different; I lost my no-shit-on-the-run virginity.

Like any other day here at the Hansons I was up relatively early for my required morning run with the group. This run starts at one of the Hanson's team houses on Driftwood Road by 7:15 AM. We leave at that time so that we can make it to meet the rest of the team at a duck pond in the municipal park of downtown Rochester by 7:30. It's like running a 1.5-mile warm-up, but since I'm running with Nick Arciniaga we usually bolt out the door at close to 6-minute mile pace. This occurs 7 days a week, year-round, with the exception being on workout days and some Sundays when we will meet elsewhere at an earlier time.

I could tell by 7:40 that my first dump of the morning hadn't done the trick. I started regretting my previous evening dinner of Taco Bell and the very late-night (i.e. 10:30) single bottle of beer that I caved in deciding to have.   Momentous gases were accumulating into an uncomfortable pressure despite that fact that I was running exceptionally "slow" at about 7-minute pace with Chad and Paul 70 minutes into the morning run. I was really hurting and broke away from them at the intersection of Tienken and Rochester Road. Unfortunately for me this intersection is on the far side of town, a couple miles away from our "track house" on Driftwood. Now, I already kind of run like I have a stick shoved up my ass, but at this point that form became exaggerated. As I ran thru downtown Rochester, I squeezed my butt cheeks together and grimaced…I wasn't going to make it home this time! I ran past a Dairy Queen: Ah, my safe haven! However, it was one of those Dairy Queens that didn't have a bathroom for customers. It wasn't open this early anyway; wishful thinking on my part. Fuck it! In a last ditch effort I made it to a gravel road right before the Bloomer house (the other Hanson team house) and tore off into the bushes. The only reason I didn't make it to the Bloomer house was because the gravel road makes a rather steep uphill spike at that point and the effort of running uphill would've made me crap my Brooks HVAC running shorts. I'll spare you the details, but as you may have guessed, it wasn't a solid. So long to my 12-year-old, no-shit streak.

The Program

A Brief History

At the turn of the Millennium the opportunity to continue training full-time as a post-collegiate distance runner was bleak at best. The few training groups, like the Nike Farm Team out in California, were fairly exclusive and isolated to the west coast.

Unlike the 1970s when American distance running was booming with the Boston Track Club and individuals like Bill Rodgers, Frank Shorter, Steve Prefontaine, and Alberto Salazar, the late 1980s, '90s, and turn of the century represented demise. In 2000 only Rod DeHaven was able to represent the United States at the Olympic Marathon, because he won the trials without running under the Olympic time standard. Also, only 104 runners in the US surpassed the relatively weak benchmark of 2:22:00. This number served as a representation of how US distance running had taken a turn for the worse. In contrast, at the 1983 Boston marathon 76 Americans broke 2:20 in a single race!

Distance running in the United States was hurting after 1990. Could we blame this on the invention of sophisticated 8-bit Nintendo video game systems? Was the training methodology too biased towards low mileage and high-intensity interval running? Back in the '60s and '70s high school runners were putting in triple digit weeks. The Gerry Lindgrens and Jim Ryuns were talented runners that ran blazing times...but they also put in more work than most high school runners. What had happened to the hard work ethic of younger generations in terms of willingness to achieve athletically in a sport such as distance running? Had technology and opportunities in society led the youth of the '80s and '90s to become soft?

* * *

"Revitalizing American distance running." "Putting US distance running back on the map." "Capturing the benefits of group training." These are phrases typically used in magazine articles and online posts explaining what the Hansons Distance Project is all about. The stories explain the '90s demise in US distance running, and how two brothers in Michigan had an answer for that: organizing a group of American, post-collegiate distance runners that would live together in a house, work together, and run together. The brothers would coach this group and support the athletes financially so they wouldn't have to pay for rent or health care. The theory was that it would be easier to train as a group because individuals looking to improve would push each other to faster and faster performances. Instead of worrying about making money at a full-time job and running 100+ mile weeks, the athletes would only work part-time to ensure that they had time to focus on running. The brothers were going to fund this team, this project, with money generated from their running stores.   Of course, the brothers' last name was Hanson and the running stores were the Hansons Running Shops outside of Detroit, Michigan. This was the framework for the program's inception.

* * *

The Actual Project: Formation and Early Athletes

The Hansons Distance Project started in 1999 when Kevin and Keith opened their doors to the first wave of athletes, including Clint Verran, a local runner. Also on the original team were Jim Jurcevich and Kyle Baker. Within a couple of years runners like Jeff Campbell, Richie Brinker, Donnie Franzen, and Joe Gibson would also make waves as some of the early athletes in the growing program.

Aside from small groups of elite runners training together in places like Boulder, Boston, Gainesville and Flagstaff, there really wasn't much of an opportunity for post-collegiate, diamond in the rough runners to continue at a high level in the sport. Clint Verran recalls, "At the time there was really nothing out there for a 28:30 guy. Unless you scored a big time contract from a shoe company, you were on your own."

Keith and Kevin saw a void in the sport, and decided to fill it by providing for a team of store-sponsored runners. The "Hansons Running Shop Team" was something that locals could recognize; it was a good form of advertising for the stores. Before the team, Keith and Kevin were running all the local road races to generate interest in their business venture (and of course, because they loved running and winning!).

"There was a stretch of time when Keith and Kevin were winning all the local road races in the area," Clint remembers. Clint speaks of how such an idea to develop a post-collegiate team went hand-in hand with the development of selling running shoes and promoting the sport.

> "[Keith and Kevin] know running…running is their thing…they entered the business when Macomb County didn't have any running shops. There is a market of over 3 million in the Detroit Metro Area. It coincided with a time when their business was booming and they needed some employees in the store."

The success and expansion of the running shops meant that the program could also grow: "They decided they would give these runners housing and take care of their basic needs."

It was a win-win situation, and the Hanson brothers sought to recruit some respectable talent by initiating benchmark standards for prospective athletes (times that still guide the program today, save for the 2:20 marathon mark). The time standards coming in were sub-14 for 5k and sub-29 for 10k.

At the time, these performances were more competitive as the late 1990s yielded a relatively small number of such quality distance runners. Initially even Clint wasn't fast enough to be fully accepted into the program…he had to prove himself first:

> "I was going to be a second-tier guy and had to pay a little rent to live in the house. I got really fit training with those guys and jumped in the Chicago Marathon in the sub-elite corral and ran 2:19 for the Olympic Trials 'A' standard."

He was attending grad school at the time.

* * *

The program's humble beginnings had its ups and downs, with Keith and Kevin strictly enforcing new policies and procedures. It was a learning process for both the athletes and the coaches. Some stuff was trial and error as this was a revolutionary program that had a lot of question marks. Could they pull this off? How much money should they invest? Are these guys really going to run fast? Is it going to be worth it?

Clint talks about those early days, when things were more strict, and when the program was just getting off the ground:

> "We'd have these team meetings…almost weekly…if things weren't going right, Kevin or Keith would say something like: 'If you agree that 99% of the stuff we do is great, then you can just leave!'"

"Back then we did a tempo run every Thursday night in Royal Oak (suburb of Detroit where one of the running stores is located)…we had guys cranking under 40 for 8 miles…it was like an 8 mile race every Thursday…we put our flats on and everything… it was kind of dangerous, cutting diagonally across [busy] roads through 6 lanes of traffic…but it was fun! You would cut the tangents, and race people. Brian had run like 37 something there…as part of the community group run."

Clint pauses, his eyes staring back into a different time, a different era: "It was a do or die attitude on the team…It was more cut-throat."

On Tuesday nights they would do real speed workouts at Dodge Park, which is close to another one of the Hansons Running Shops. Workouts like repeat miles, 800s, and 1000s were typical "speed."

On Friday they would do a supplemental long run of 14, 15, or 16 miles. Sunday was another long run with the community. Despite the relatively high intensity and high volume weeks, the main focus of the initial runners in the program was half-marathon and shorter distances. Clint explains:

"Marathon was not on their radar screens…it wasn't something that they thought that they would even be training people for…they were thinking 5k/10k and cross country." Some of the guys got too competitive, and at times Keith and Kevin pushed them too hard, their expectations always high.

"A lot of stuff we do now we learned the hard way," says Clint.

* * *

Still, the early years of the group showed promise,

and the fact that the program had a home base and now an identity fused with the Hanson name eventually led to further success and growth. In Clint's mind, Rochester was a better place to train than Ypsilanti, or even Ann Arbor. The problem was there weren't any other elite runners to train with in the area, that is, until the program started.

After several years the program started shifting more towards the marathon as Hansons runners found success early at the distance. By 2000 Clint was 11th at the Olympic Trials Marathon, the second youngest finisher at the age of 24 [beating the slightly younger, media-attention magnet Josh Cox quite handily]. Things were looking up, the start of a professional running career became something doable all of a sudden.

"It was a defining moment in my running career…I went from not thinking I could do anything in my post-collegiate career to getting a Olympic Trials 'A' standard," Clint recalls.

Clint was one of the most experienced runners at the 2008 Olympic Marathon Trials

Jim Jurchevich and Kyle Baker ran in the track trials in 2000. Baker was very talented, but left after his first year in the program. He later battled with Dan Browne at the 2002 New Haven 20k National Championship where he ran 59:21 for 2nd place.

"Natural skills as a runner...Kyle Baker was up there," Clint recalls. "Jim was a grind-it-out type of guy...he would take whatever Keith and Kevin told him to do and add like 25% to it. Those 3 were the first wave." It was just Jim and Clint in the Bloomer house after Kyle left.

The next wave of runners included Chad Johnson and Richie Brinker. Brian Sell came into the program in 2001. According to Clint, "That first wave of guys were some of the most talented athletes ever in the program."

Another runner, Mark Menefee from Kansas, joined as a 5k specialist who eventually placed 5th in the 2004 Olympic Trials 5000m for Hansons. He also was featured in the documentary film "Five Thousand Meters." Chad won the 2002 25k national road title in Grand Rapids, MI while wearing the Hansons Singlet.

In 2001, Jeff Campbell and Joe Gibson also entered the program. Campbell had made the senior USATF national cross country team when he was in college. He got 8th in the 2000 Olympic Trials Marathon, having trained with legendary coach Joe Vigil in Alamosa, CO before he came out to Hansons, where he would finish his career.

* * *

Why would brothers from Michigan start such a program? What was a rather novel and unpredictable idea at the time turned out to have a sustainable return on investment.

"Keith and Kevin spend a lot of their time and energy [on the program] because they like running." Clint reasons.

"I think they like to root for the underdog...perhaps it's because they look at themselves as not the most talented athletes..." Clint pauses, and I recognize how the Hanson brothers have lived vicariously through the success of the runners in their program; they have experienced the elite treatment at major marathons and bumped heads with other coaches at the very highest level in the sport.

Such success was self-initiated; the two brothers reached this level of influence through good old-fashioned Midwestern hard work. "They did their time, putting themselves to the grinding wheel," Clint states, showing his appreciation for the effort that created the program in the first place.

When Brooks Sports, Inc. came along as a major sponsor in 2003, the Hansons-Brooks Distance Project was the real deal. The women's side of the program could be started with an additional house purchased. The athletes suddenly had a plethora of matching running gear to sport, including running shoes, and the group became easily recognizable in their off-the-wall colorful jerseys. Thanks to the addition of Brooks' sponsorship, the project would grow, increase in popularity, and allow sponsored athletes to pursue their Olympic dreams.

The Early Years: Kevin and Keith Hanson on the left;
a young Brian Sell 6th in from the left.

Rizzo is Fit
September 12, 2009

My first couple months in the program involved adjusting to a regimented routine containing many tiresome miles. I pushed my body harder than I ever did in college, but mentally it was easier because I could focus more on every run. I started viewing running as a job, but a job that I loved.

The daily grind. I had extra trouble getting out of bed this morning. Just another 14 mile morning, plus 5 mile afternoon run easy day to finish off another 120 mile week. Pat Rizzo (who claimed I had run "about 12 or 13 miles" after 88:00 at what felt surely to be 6:15 pace or faster on yesterday's morning run) had been putting in 140 mile weeks. Last weekend he rolled off a workout of 5 by 2 miles all around 9:50 on the rolling bike path at Stony Creek Metro Park. The park, which is our main workout venue, contains a 6 mile paved bike path that loops around a lake. The path is marked every quarter mile, and it contains some turns and little hills that are significant enough to make some mile splits much harder than others.

Today Rizzo looked like a machine. Those skinny legs were rapidly shuffling along, his calves were firing like narrow pistons, and his neck was cranked forward with a high, restricted arm carriage. At Chicago he is either going to have a breakout performance and smash his 2:17:05 PR set at Boston this year or he is going to blow up trying. Rizzo is fit!

The team morning easy runs are usually done at around 6:00 to 6:30 mile pace depending on who is leading. Rizzo loves to lead and loves to talk. You get in an argument with him and the pace will get uncomfortable real fast. Mike Morgan also likes to hammer every day. He's a little guy, maybe just shy of 5'8" and 112 lbs soaking wet. He swings his arms in full flight much like the Nintendo character Mario, with fist-pumping motions as his feet smack the ground and then bound high into the air. It looks like he is sprinting even at 6:30 pace. But his mechanics look almost exactly the same at 5:00 mile pace, which is very close to his marathon race pace. The guy has made two world teams: one in the half and one in the full, the latter in which he was 23rd in the world at the IAAF Championships in Japan on a humid, 90 degree day.

Anyway, back to Rizzo. Rizzo is Sicilian, and he is known to make some pretty damn delicious pasta sauce. Last weekend I dug into some of his homemade, family recipe sauce at the Bloomer house with Sell and Chad. It was delicious, and I ate a lot of it despite the fact that I'm a vegetarian and the sauce was full of meat. Whatever. Rizzo was jokingly flirting with the married and taken women on the team. This is typical of Rizzo, who has been a bachelor for quite some time now. As we all sit and devour our food around the humble, wooden table near the front bay windows of the Bloomer house, Rizzo directs the conversation on his experiences of being drug-tested. He exclaims how hard it is to pee with someone staring closely at your dick, waiting for those precious drops of yellow to squeeze out. Supposedly he was so dehydrated one time that this process took hours. The story provides a good laugh.

However, taking a long time to complete a drug test is the least of Rizzo's worries compared to what he's experienced as a young adult. As a happy-go-lucky guy, he has managd to roll with the blows he has been dealt. He has handicap status because he is technically deaf in his left ear, due to a freak allergic reaction that occurred when he got braces for his teeth in high school. Not to mention that a couple years ago when he was training for the Boston Marathon he got nailed by a car while out on a run with the team. He suffered head injuries and bleeding around his skull.

The conversation escalates to stories of runners

having to shit and piss as I devour my hot pasta. Sell has been tested like 50 times. "Wow," I think to myself. Maybe I don't belong here. I am surely a minority in this regard. I become self-conscious and a little ashamed that I have not been considered elite enough to have any drug-testing experiences to share with the rest of the group. Everyone here has lots of stories, and I have none.

Rizzo isn't the only really fit guy on the team right now. My housemate Nick Arciniaga has been gearing up for New York. He's been putting in 14/6-mile doubles nearly every day and doing tons of workouts right at 5:04 mile pace. He said the other day that he plans to hold this volume until he tapers, about 2 weeks before the race. Christ, that's 140 miles a week for over 2 months straight! It's not like we are lollygagging on our morning 14 milers either. Sub-6:00 pace is very common near the end of runs most days for Nick.

I guess adjusting to this training is either going to hurt my body or my fitness for a while. I figure that eventually when my body learns to super-compensate from such stress, I'll perhaps (hopefully!) hit a new plateau of strength. Already, that dull, dead ache in my quads is going away, but now I worry about my Achilles, and all my other lower leg tendons that are constantly being tested. I try to limit my coffee consumption to not become too reliant on caffeine to motivate me to get out the door. I try to eat a balanced, healthy diet with fruits and vegetables, however Taco Bell keeps beckoning me back. Committing to this stotan lifestyle is easier said than done.

The 2000 Trials to the 2008 Trials

In the first 8 years of the program (1999 to 2007) the Hansons progressed a lot. Many runners came and went, but "old man" Clint Verran stuck it out the entire time. Runners like Brian Sell demonstrated growth and contributed to the nationwide recognition of the program as a force to be reckoned with. Ultimately, the success of Brian Sell qualifying for the 2008 Olympic team in the marathon was a high point for the Project. Such a feat was a milestone for the Project because it served as an example to all the runners at Hansons that making the Olympics could very much be a reality; if one was willing to pay the price.

However, in all the years leading up to that victory, that defining moment, there were indicators that the Hansons runners were making an impact on the national scene and truly revitalizing the life of American marathon running one race at a time. Clint recalls the start of The Millennium and how performances had picked up between the last couple Olympic Trials that he participated in: "2000 was an all-time low for US distance running. 2:15 won the Olympic Trials, and I ran 2:20 and got 11th."

Clint's prowess on the roads earned him a spot to represent the US at the World Half Marathon in Veracruz, Mexico the same year. It was hot and humid in Veracruz, but Clint had a career-changing performance nonetheless. Going into the race he trained hard and was confident that he could do some damage:

> "I trained my face off...I remember running 10 weeks of 140 miles a week or more...I was running 5:40 pace on my easy days. I went to Worlds in sick shape. I was ridiculously fit so I just took off and moved up the whole race and ran 1:05 and got 17th. At the time it was the highest finish a US man

had had in the World Half.   I got interviews from
Runners World. After the race I was standing in the
street just dripping in sweat feeling like a rock star.
That was the first time the Hansons had had a World
Championship team runner."

The next year Clint started seeing more financial
benefits of being a sponsored, Hansons athlete. This was
something that he could make a living at. It was the real deal.
Those dreams of one day running in the Olympics really
weren't that far off! Says Clint:

> "In 2001 I ran the US marathon champs in NYC…I
> finished 2nd in the US Championships and had a big
> payday. The down payment on my [current] house
> was part of that 12 grand in winnings that day. Scott
> Larson got 1st. I got all my track PRs that year…I
> came off a 160 mile week and hit the indoor track at
> Michigan…we added to what the Hansons told us to
> do…if it said '6-mile easy afternoon double,' we'd do
> 12."

As Clint and the rest of the Hansons crew continued
to train harder and add more miles, things became more
optimistic for the group. Things were clicking, the program
was generating a lot of success, the workouts were becoming
legendary:

> "Going into Chicago in 2002 we ran 2 by 6 miles
> finishing at 4:50 pace [28:50 for 6 miles]…I remember
> thinking if things go right for me I could run the
> American record."

By 2004 Clint had established himself as one of the
top US Marathon runners, and leading into the Birmingham,
Alabama Olympic Trials that winter he had a legitimate

chance to make the team going to Athens:

> "I wasn't a favorite to make the team, but I made the short list. One of the top 10 guys in the country who had a chance to make the team…there was a lot of pressure. It came at a rough time of the year for us (training in the winter). You'll wake up and there will be a foot of snow on the ground and you think to yourself 'Where am I going to run?' I was freaking out a little bit."

The race played out like a strategic chess match with Clint's Hansons teammates Trent Briney and a young Brian Sell up in the lead pack. Eventually Brian took the lead and tried to run away with the race. Clint recalls:

> "It was like 20-something degrees at the start of the race…the pace was lethargic…5:25s for the first couple miles. Brian wanted an honest pace. We had talked about what we wanted, and it was a 2:12 pace. Brian basically panicked and he took off. I thought he was going to win the race…but he faded a lot."

As Brian slowly got caught by the chase pack, Clint was shocked to see his other teammate Trent Briney running ahead: "It was a huge surprise to have Trent up there. I moved up into 5th, following in a chase pack with Meb, Browne, Culpepper, and Shay.

Eventually, the finish of the 2004 US Olympic Marathon Trials saw the top two Hansons runners just missing an Olympic berth:

> "Trent was 4th, I was 5th [at the finish]. We thought there was a good chance that one or both of us might get to run on the Olympic team (if one of the top

three chose to focus on the just a track event in the Olympics instead)."

However, the top three in the trials that year, (Meb Keflezighi, Alan Culpepper, and Dan Browne) all decided to run the marathon in Athens. Says Clint:

> "They flew Trent and I out to Sacramento to get fitted for our Olympic uniforms and we got our papers processed." Keith and Kevin trained Trent with a marathon segment in case he was called upon to run the Olympics...but he wasn't."

The next year, however, Chad, Brian, and Clint all represented the US in the 2005 World Marathon Championships in Helsinki. Trent had actually qualified, but wasn't able to run due to a back injury. Clint notes: "We finished 4th as a team in the world, and most of the team consisted of Hansons guys."

The depth of the program was phenomenal, as the marathon results from that era speak for themselves:

Marathon Results:

Boston 2006:

Brian Sell 4th, 2:10:55, outkicked Culpepper and less than 1:00 behind Meb

Clint Verran 10th, 2:14:12

Luke Humphrey 11th, 2:15:23

Chad Johnson 15th, 2:19:29

Kyle O'Brien 18th, 2:19:57

Trent Briney 19th, 2:20:10

Marty Rosendahl 22nd, 2:21:12

Chicago 2006:

Brian Sell 6th, 2:10:47

Clint Verran 12th, 2:14:23

Chad Johnson 14th, 2:15:03

Mike Morgan 15th, 2:15:11

Kyle O'Brien 16th, 2:15:13

Luke Humphrey 18th, 2:15:22

Marty Rosendahl 23nd, 2:17:05

Dave Ernsberger 28th, 2:18:56

Pat Rizzo 35th, 2:20:12

2008 US Olympic Trials:

Brian Sell 3rd, 2:11:40

Mike Morgan 12th, 2:16:28

Nick Arciniaga 17th, 2:17:08

Clint Verran 18th, 2:17:10

Chad Johnson 20th, 2:17:58

Patrick Rizzo 26th, 2:18:30

Patrick Moulton 28th, 2:18:35

Michael Reneau 32nd, 2:18:51

Luke Humphrey 43rd, 2:20:34

Todd Snyder 47th, 2:21:30

The 2008 US Men's Marathon Trials were a culmination and exemplary testament to the strength of Hansons-Brooks runners. Competing on hilly courses, in adverse conditions…it didn't matter. A Hansons runner is a tough runner, an underdog, a runner that simultaneously supports his/her teammates while trying to kill them. No other running club in the country has had as much depth in the marathon as Hansons. And for the program to generate its first Olympian, it became evident that such hard work pays off! However, such results didn't happen overnight.

Back in 2006 the team was primarily lead by Clint and Brian. Clint looks back on his years of toil and suffering:

> "It was kind of the Brian and Clint show. Brian was half a step better than anyone here…so it was more me trying to keep up with him. We ran hard all the time - that was kind of the hallmark of what we would do. It was more instinctive training…easy runs would turn into kinds of individual battles."

At the peak of his running career with the Hansons, Clint ran 4 marathons in the 2:14 range, as well as a 2:15 at the 2002 Boston Marathon (which sadly earned him zero dollars as he was the 2nd American to the great Keith Dowling). Near the same time, a young Brian Sell started making his name in the program, pushing Clint and the rest of the Hansons with his competitive drive. Clint explains his training with Brian:

> "We had some epic battles, man. He could recover really fast and train really, really hard and not get hurt. He had a little plantar fasciitis here and there, but he just ran through it."

Hansons runners are known to be durable, tough, and competitive; however, Clint says that Brian's personality was what really fed his drive:

> "He [Brian] is a more visceral, emotional kind of runner...he creates these rivalries in his mind, he always needs an opponent, someone he was trying to beat...that's how Brian gets it out of himself."

Clint explains their training together as more of a love-hate relationship, a fierce competition that created tension:

> "I love that guy like he's my brother...but there were days when I was fit and he wanted to strangle me...I could tell when I was getting fit, because Brian would stop being my friend temporarily and want to beat me in every run...we were in great shape...I was trying to rip his throat out!"

The most epic struggles between the two stars of Hansons occurred on long runs, when pace wasn't regulated and it was a free-for-all to determine who would win that day. Long runs evolved into blood baths that tested each runner's will to cover 20 miles as fast as possible (something that simulates the drawn out agony of racing a marathon). Such hard workouts were prized as being negative split efforts, where the fastest miles occurred at the end when fatigue and pain reached a climax. Clint remembers:

> "I had talked to Khalid Khannouchi [2:04 marathoner and former world record holder] and his wife/coach Sandra about training and I remember Khannouchi ran the last 2 miles of his long run on the track. So then we started doing it; Kevin and Keith got the idea to make the last 3 miles hard, but not on the track. I started running faster and faster for those [final] miles. After a while I just started thinking that 3 miles wasn't long enough, so I started talking Brian into doing 5 miles hard. I remember coming down the Paint Creek trail running 4:45s, 20 miles deep into a 22-miler, where the miles before that were in the 5:20s."

Brian Sell recalls those long runs with Clint circa 2006:

> "The long runs were just ridiculous...I mean, we were probably running a 2:20 marathon [pace] for every 20 to 22 miler we were doing. Clint would try to destroy me right from the gun...I remember so many times we would meet at the pond at 7 AM and he would take off into the darkness. The only way I knew [where to go] was because we had a pre-determined course. I would start out at around 6-flat and then just keep notching it down. I was probably running 5-flat to 5:20 by 8 miles in. I would catch Clint 15 to 16 miles in (they had 3 fast miles scheduled) and by then

we were running down the trail at sub 5-pace…they were the best workouts I've ever had!"

Usually Brian caught Clint during these outings, however there was one memorable long run in Florida that the team did a week before the Boston Marathon, which Clint remembers fondly:

> "The first day there, in 90 degree heat in some orange groves…a week before Boston. We are out hammering [a 20 mile long run] and we are both fit. I was thinking anytime, I'm going to die…it was like swimming out into the ocean…I don't know if I'm going to make it back. He breaks before I do. I couldn't believe it…that rarely happens. I beat Brian in that run that day by like 5 minutes. He wanted to kill me; we wouldn't talk to each other for awhile."

A young Luke "Grizzly Bear" Humphrey struggled through that run in the heat. He ended up suffering from severe dehydration, partially soiling himself and walking it in half an hour later. Such extreme efforts merely a week out from a marathon was surely not without a physical cost. Clint may have won the long run workout that day, but Brian beat him soundly in the race by running a 2:10 and placing 4th! Clint still ended up 11th in 2:15.

The last marathon that Brian raced before the '08 trials was the 2006 Chicago Marathon where he ran a PR of 2:10:47. Brian Sell recalls the year leading up to the 2008 Olympic Marathon Trials:

> "The thing that cemented in my mind that I was a contender [to make the Olympic team] was the fact that I had run, basically, 3 really good marathons. It wasn't just a fluke thing…it was good because I was still hungry because [Ryan] Hall was out there running

2:06s, and Abdi [Abdirahman] had run a 2:08 and spanked me pretty bad in Chicago. It wasn't good enough to say I was going to make it…but there was also enough confidence in the back of my mind."

Brian remembers running better than ever before in training runs, bettering all his teammates, and hitting splits that allowed him to force a 2:10 marathon pace over a hilly course:

"It was kind of rough because I was kind of on my own in training…Clint was running 2:13 to 2:14 [marathon pace workouts], but would hammer long runs. I was doing workouts better than ever before, and my long runs were harder."

Brian ran similar times for the same workouts as he did pre-Boston, but he ran them on tougher, hillier courses. This conditioned him for the ups and downs in Central Park. He ran under 29 minutes for the last repetition of the fabled 2 by 6 mile workout:

"It was just another level of training…I don't know how I got there. Those three years in there were awesome. I just kept running faster and faster in workouts…the long runs just felt amazing. It wasn't just surviving a 20-miler. Every single run was an A or B in terms of quality."

When the Olympic Marathon Trials came to New York on a cold morning in November, Brian was ready to fulfill his dream. He was stronger than ever, more experienced, and ready to create an upset: "I had 3 weeks at 165 miles. I peaked out at that. Then I came down to 140 and 120 the last two weeks before the trials."

The odds were slightly against him, as the field assembled was arguably the best in US marathoning history:

> "It was going to take a little bit of luck. If everybody had their best day, I wouldn't make the team. I was confident in my ability to run my best race...I was content to let the chips fall where they may...I was 100 percent focused on my watch...I was just trying to run 5-flats."

He was a little worried about the first two miles because they were so slow. When Hall and that group took off several miles later he just stayed glued to his watch, intentionally letting them go.

> "There wasn't really anything I could do [about Browne, Ritz, Hall, and Meb taking off at 4:45s]...I knew that was not my best game plan. I just stuck to what I knew I was capable of."

As the drama unfolded, the race reached its later stages, and Brian made up ground: "I passed Dan [Browne], and I felt decent." Brian notes that he consciously tried to improve his form to make it appear to Dan that he was still fresh. However, once he got far enough ahead he went back to his real form: "My grittin' face and hobblin' along...my usual way of running."

From that moment on, Brian ran with fear:

> "Running scared...from 4 miles to go. I knew Khalid was behind me and could close fast. Who knows who else? It was the longest 20-25 minutes of my life. I knew my spot could be taken away at any moment."

When Brian crossed the finish line and finally sealed

his ticket to the Beijing Olympic Games he was "just happy." In typical Sell fashion, he was still the same blue-collar runner. Kevin Hanson noted his face displayed more of a sense of relief than elation or celebration when he crossed the line. Brian remained humble:

> "It was a long grueling race…[but] you have to keep a level head on your shoulders. You know, it was the greatest race of my life, but I certainly wasn't going to come high stepping across the finish line, because Hall had just laid the smack-down on me by 2:40 and Ritz was another 40 seconds up on me, so…you've got to realize your place in the cosmos. Ritz can be injured 8 or 9 months out of the year and still go out and kick my butt in the 10k."

A major difference between runners like Ritz and Meb, when compared to Brian is revealed in the day to day life and training of each: "I was working 20-25 hours a week at Home Depot through Boston and before the Trials. I'm pretty sure guys like Ritz aren't doing that."

When he looks back on his career, Sell remembers the price he had to pay for such improvement:

> "It was 8 years of getting out the door on some days when I really didn't want to…or going after the guy that took off the front of the pack [of Hansons teammates] when I really felt like just taking it easy that day."

But he relishes the time spent with peers, like-minded teammates that he could suffer in misery with:

> "My teammates along the way have been 100 percent who I owe everything to…from high school

teammate and rival Steve Moyer to Clint Verran. I had some caring coaches in high school and college. For me personally…the little things [really mattered the most]."

As an unselfish athlete, who prides himself on helping out others, Brian has been known to volunteer his time and give away gear to help others in need. This is shown not only with his family, friends, and teammates, but also with the local community and the running community. Brian donates many of his medals to the charity "Medals for Mettle," an organization that uses race medals to put a smile on the faces of children in hospitals. Such generosity and openness is typical of Brian once you get to know him.

First Workout
September 19th, 2009

So I've been here three weeks now. A couple days ago I got an email from Kevin detailing my training schedule for the next month. It was a surprisingly simple email with every easy day labeled as "14-4," which means an easy 14 miler in the morning, followed by an afternoon 4 mile run. Every 3rd day or so I had a workout, and one of those workout days I had a longer, single day of 16 miles all at once. Much to my dismay though, my very first workout as a Hansons-Brooks runner was 8 by 1000m on the track. It just said "8 x1k, track" for that slot, so the pace and recovery were unknown. In the last couple of days I had become a little worried about this Saturday morning track session. I mean, my weight had skyrocketed nearly to 160 lbs in the past month, and I was coming off of my third consecutive 120 mile week (relatively high volume for me). Also on my list of excuses: allergies had inflamed the mucus membranes in my nose, which has been especially irritating to my respiratory system. Not to mention, I knew that my two workout buddies for this particular track workout would be my housemate Nick Arciniaga (who was the top American finisher in the Boston marathon a couple years earlier) and of course Olympian Brian Sell. Both were preparing for the NYC marathon in a couple of months.

Despite my worries and complaints, I must note that Nick was coming into this workout at the end of a 145-mile week (and the week before he ran 140 miles). Given the relatively high intensity of most of those miles you can get an idea of the skeletal and muscular fatigue that has accumulated due to such heavy marathon training. Nick and Brian also were scheduled to do 10 by 1000m compared to my measly 8 repeats. Also, Brian had lately been struggling with some hip problems. He seemed to mask the pain on our easy days, but earlier in the week we had dropped him going up a hill. It was tough to pass him when he was in a state like this. It was just 4 years ago that I was looking at articles on the old MensRacing website about Brian and the Hansons program, idolizing their blue-collar work ethic and their underdog, toughness mentality.

I skipped drinking my usual single bottle of beer at dinner the previous night. This was a bad habit that I had formed during my senior year of college, and breaking it took significantly more self-discipline to break it than say, running a 20 miler at 6:00 pace. I can't physically afford anything that might give me gas or weigh me down the morning of a workout. I also can't financially afford such spoils, but that is a different story altogether.

So anyway, since it was Saturday morning and work at the running stores starts earlier than the normal weekday schedule, Nick and I pulled out of the Driftwood driveway at 6:45 AM in my paint-chipped, Burgundy-colored '98 Chevy Prism (which was making extra weird vibrating noises under the hood). We drove through downtown Rochester toward the track, playing some music on the radio to wake ourselves up.

It was dark and cold for a mid-September morning. After a 10-minute drive we pulled into a large empty parking lot at Stony Creek High School, one of the three high schools in Rochester. Nick wore gloves on our 3-mile warm-up and both of us were in long sleeves and pants. Midway through the warm-up Nick had to stop and peel off for a shit in the nearby woods as there were no porta-potties or open restroom facilities near the track.

We met Brian back at the 100m start line of the track at 7:20. I changed into my brand-new Brooks T6 racing flats. They felt good. Nick changed into the Brooks Launch, which was more like a lightweight trainer. Kevin came down the stairs that were built into the side of the hill that carved out a bowl-like pit surrounding the track. It made the track somewhat sheltered, but there was still some wind swirling about. I was almost warm enough to take off my long sleeve shirt now. After a couple of sloppy and awkward feeling strides, Kevin took me aside and told me to sit out the first couple of reps. I impatiently watched Nick gap Brian on the first kilometer, only running 3:00, or 72 seconds a lap. Ha, 72s! That's slower than my 10k pace. Heck, I did workouts faster than this in high school. But today I knew that 3-min kilometers weren't going to be a walk in the park. I was heavy, and my legs felt like lead pipes full of concrete. Shit, why couldn't my first workout at least be a tempo run or something I could work into more slowly?

Brian pulled out into lane 2 on the recovery 400m jog (done in less than 2 minutes) and signaled for me to start in front of him for the next rep. Reluctantly I tucked in behind Nick, and in front of my most respected idol in distance running. Now that is a weird feeling! Leading an Olympian in a workout? I definitely didn't belong here. We approached the 200m mark on the track where Kevin and assistant coach/store general manager Don Jackson were standing with stop watches. As we hit the line Nick accelerated into the turn and Kevin said, "Bang." I split my watch and we took off. It felt fast like I knew it would. It felt like a 68 or 66 second 400m pace. I could sense that Brian was dropping off behind me after only 200m. We came by for the first lap and I heard Kevin reading splits: "71, 72, 73...73 high." Fuck! I was already breathing hard and mechanically my legs felt stiff and slow like they couldn't turn over any faster. Nick picked up the pace over the next 200m and I think at that point Brian jogged off the track and stopped. I'm sure his hip pain was killing him. We ran the next lap in 70.0, and that kind of acceleration is something I am extremely sensitive to. I felt a trickle of lactic acid seep into my leg muscles, generating sensations of fatigue pumping through my blood. I knew at that point that if I made it through this workout, it wasn't going to be without tasting the bitter flavor of copper on my tongue…the taste of death!

The remaining kilometers were all covered in 2:57 to 3:00, with most lap splits going 73-70. On the 4th rep I was instructed to lead and I managed to split 72.1 and 71.8, which delighted Kevin. He exclaimed something along the lines of: "Hey, Nick maybe when you've been here as long as Sage has, you'll be better at hitting pace."

The tone of sarcasm made his voice extra gruff and hoarse. After my 4th rep (and Nick's 6th rep) we took an 800m jog in 4:00. This marked the half-way point. I realized later that we never stopped moving throughout the entire workout. As soon as we ran through the line we went straight into a recovery lap.

The last two reps challenged me as my quads seemed to fail and my biceps ached. I don't think this was the effect of lactic acid as much as the fact that my slow twitch and fast twitch muscles fibers had all been thoroughly exhausted. Sweat dripped into my eyes from my unsightly spike of hair, the result of a faux-hawk that I had attempted to cut into my head a month ago before I left home in Oregon. The temperature was probably in the 50s now and the sun had finally peeked its glare over the hill that sheltered the track on the backstretch. A noticeable wind had swirled around the grass bowl, encompassing the track. I glanced up and saw the American flag flapping around. I was glad when I finished my last rep in 2:57. Nick had told me to go 71-71, which is what I pretty much nailed after flailing my arms a bit as the effort of just holding pace had increased.

On our cool-down we intersected some of the women's team out on their daily run. Rizzo, Morgan, and Chad were also rolling at about 6:00 pace and about to pass them. Nick and I turned to run with them, but after a couple of minutes we decided to drop off the group. I really didn't feel like doing my cool-down at 6:00 pace anyway.

After downing some Endurox RX4 and Gatorade, we drove back to the smelly Driftwood house, where I promptly consumed my typical breakfast of 2 scrambled eggs and a large bowl of quick-cook oatmeal. I usually pour in about a quarter of a cup of pure maple syrup, a couple tablespoons of peanut butter (which I was unfortunately out of this morning so I used regular butter instead), and a couple tablespoons of brown sugar. I was so glad I didn't have to work on this day. I then showered and passed out for a 2.5 hour nap. Such is the life of a "starving artist"(the term Mike Kilburg had used on his Facebook profile to describe his job as a Hansons runner)…so am I a professional runner now?

The Area

Disclaimer: The following section consists of information that contains both opinions and facts. Many of the perceptions and statements noted are merely one man's observations of how things appear to be (which may or may not be exactly what they are to others). I fully admit to stating generalizations and making stereotypes; the following should be taken with a grain of salt.

As an outsider from the west coast who went to college on the east coast, I came to find the state of Michigan (and perhaps other parts of the Midwest?) to be quite different. Running at Cornell in upstate New York hardened me to the elements of winter weather and sub-freezing temperatures common in both areas. However, it wasn't the harsh weather that initially presented any challenges of adaptation for me. Rather it was the culture and socioeconomics of the locals that generated the most shock. The heavy Metro Detroit traffic and the demographics of Michigan were radical changes from the small, liberal college towns in rural areas along the coasts that I had grown accustomed to.

I quickly learned that the typical Michigander around the Detroit area is very loquacious, upfront, and in-your-face personal. Customers at the store routinely violate what I perceive as my own personal space bubble by getting within three feet of my face when I am talking to them. In college I read that there are different distances of social intimacy that range from touching to keeping a formal, "stranger" distance. These measurements vary by culture and familiarity of individuals communicating with each other. Apparently my perception of a "safe and reasonable" social distance between a stranger and myself is far greater than the typical Michigander's perception of that distance. Part of the lingo used in the Detroit area involves the word "boss." I don't know if it is derived from the factory culture or what, but customers (and Kevin and Keith) love to say "Thanks, Boss!" or "What's up, Boss!" The locals speak with (what sounds to me as) a dry, flat accent. Some even pick up on the fact that I am not from the area based on my "other" vocal inflections. Sometimes they'll ask if I'm from Canada because I sound different.

Aside from being verbose and openly social, Michiganders love their cars. This is not a surprise as everyone living in the area is closely connected to the auto industry. If they don't work in it, they either used to or know someone close who does. The bigger the vehicle the better, and it also better be American-made. Foreign cars are still frowned upon in many circles. Every household seems to own at least four cars, and they seem to all drive them frequently. This is probably due to the fact that there is no reliable form of public transportation in the Detroit metro area. Just as I am writing this page I've seen our neighbor Jeff and/or some member of his family drive back and forth in front of our house multiple times in several different vehicles. Having a large Ford truck, a jeep, or an SUV is a must to fit in, although the percentage of Audis and BMWs in the ritzy Rochester Hills area is relatively higher than one would expect. Kevin owns a Hummer, which he can maneuver around quite aggressively in traffic while getting about 9 miles to the gallon. Keith's main vehicle is a Suburban that he uses mainly to commute to workouts and for the 35 min drive from his house in Rochester to the main store in Royal Oak. It seems like fuel efficient, electric hybrid cars are not very common or popular.

Michiganders also love to talk about the UP, or Michigan's upper peninsula, which is simply referred to as "up north." Talk of going up north is especially frequent in the summertime when it is hot and humid around Detroit. Some say that the dream used to be that autoworkers could make enough financially to buy a cottage or cabin in the northern part of the state for weekend retreats, hunting, fishing, and lake expeditions on holidays. Unfortunately I have yet to make the drive up to this pristine area, but according to nearly every local I've talked to it's "the most beautiful country I'll ever see!" (At least in the summer when it is not totally covered in snow and below zero). Being from the Oregon wilderness I am a bit skeptical that I'll be impressed. However, Keith claims that the UP is better, cleaner, and more scenic than Canada and Alaska. Did I mention that Michiganders are also extremely proud of their state?

There also seems to be a strong, blue-collar type of Midwestern work ethic that grips the state. This is a good thing, since the unemployment rate right now is hovering above the national average at about 10%. Individuals often employ themselves in the fields of auto repair and home improvement and advertise by printing logos on all of their cars. People seem to get up earlier (the crack of dawn) than what I am used to on the more laid-back west coast. Customers complain about our store hours, and often show up early and wait outside the front door on Saturday morning, patiently waiting for our "late" 10 AM opening. We are, however, open until 8 PM on weekdays (and we're open 359 days a year), so I hope that makes up for it.

One of the part-time workers at the store is a local, middle-aged runner named John who has had a passion for the sport for over three decades. As a runner he has cracked 3 hours in the marathon and run at Boston. As a person he is a true Michigander, someone who worked in an auto factory doing die-casting and sanding of large auto part molds. He told me stories about how he used to wake up everyday at 4:30 and go to work in this outdoor shed of a factory that had leaky roofs. It was a dirty and noisy environment. He'd stand there for a full shift, wearing a heavy jacket in the freezing winters and help guide tons of steel that floated around overhead. One of his co-workers got crushed to death on the job from an accident involving such heavy, moving machinery. It was a dangerous and physically demanding job with long, hard hours. But the pay was good! Thanks to the power of unions, the workers could obtain wages ranging from $25 per hour or more plus benefits. John told me that on holidays like Christmas or Thanksgiving the factory would be open and you could work for triple pay. That's some damn good money right out of high school! Working the factories, working long hours, and working with cars has been a driving force in shaping the culture of the area. Such a blue-collar work ethic has been reflected in guys like John who worked the floors and got up on cold winter mornings to work a 10 hour shift on their feet and then go for a run. I couldn't possibly relate to working manual labor in those conditions. However, I have a ton of respect for individuals who sacrifice their bodies, sleep, and health to accomplish such demanding work.

* * *

Geographically our base in Rochester Hills is about 30 miles north of downtown Detroit. Roads running east and west are numbered by mile markers as approximate distances from the city, so we are out well beyond 23 Mile Road. Get down to about 8 Mile and, depending on how far east or west you are, you might find yourself in a pretty sketchy area. Of course "8 Mile" was where Eminem launched his career and established his street cred.

Rochester Hills is relatively small compared to other cities surrounding the Detroit Metro area with a population of just under 70,000. It has a quaint little downtown stretch about a mile long with upscale shops, a couple fancy restaurants, a post office, and a public library. It has the feel of a well-to-do suburb area, with some houses on the outskirts costing several million apiece. Celebrities Tim Allen, Madonna, and Eminem all have had (or still have) houses in the area - as well as the guy who invented the UPC code (his house is a mansion that contains a 20+ car garage!). However, despite the average household income of Rochester being around 80k, there are still many locals having difficulty scraping by in a tough economy. My theory is that there is a large (and growing) discrepancy between the very rich and the less fortunate (something that statistically makes that average income distorted and misleading).

If you drive about 25 minutes northwest of Rochester you hit the small town of Lake Orion, MI. Lake Orion is where one of the Hansons Running Shops is located, so we go there quite often to work and sometimes run. It was formerly considered a "bedroom community" where the wealthy would live and sleep between bouts of work in downtown Detroit. In the olden days lumberjacks would bunk in the village on their way to bringing lumber by railroad to the big city. Lake Orion's proximity as a halfway point between the factories in Flint (farther north) and Detroit made it a convenient place to take a load off. Off to the southwest is the Palace of Auburn Hills (the sports facility where the Pistons play basketball) and a little farther south of that is Pontiac. With a population of just over 2,000, Lake Orion is very small. It is located near the top of Oakland County (same county as Rochester Hills), and it has a short downtown stretch that contains one of our favorite Mexican food venues: The Sagebrush Cantina. There have been a couple of late Friday nights of drinking and karaoke singing there already and it's a place I always look forward to eating at and enjoying a good time.

Heading about 30 minutes south of our base in Rochester Hills will lead you into Royal Oak, which is the location of the Hansons Running Shop headquarters store. Royal Oak is also a part of Oakland County (which is the 4th wealthiest county in the United States amongst counties with more than 1 million people). Nestled roughly between Nine Mile and Twelve Mile, Royal Oak is a lot closer to downtown Detroit. However, as a town Royal Oak has a vibrant nightlife and it attracts a younger, more liberal crowd. With a population of just over 60,000 it has a healthy reputation for working professionals and new business developments. Highlights of the area include Mark Ridley's Comedy Castle, where Tim Allen made a start. Also, the show *Home Improvement* is based in Royal Oak. More recently the film *Youth in Revolt* had bits filmed in the town. Given it's proximity to Detroit, it has a surprisingly safe vibe, and the bars and restaurants on its main stretch have a rather upscale, modern atmosphere. If you want to clubbing on a Friday or Saturday night, Royal Oak is the place to go. I recommend the BlackFinn or Luna.

A little south and about 15 minutes east of Rochester leads you into Utica, MI. This is another Hansons Running Shop store location and this year it has even surpassed Royal Oak in sales at times. Utica is in Macomb County, which has a large population of over 788,000 and includes the Sterling Heights area and Clinton Township. The household median income in this county is 38 grand, and Sterling Heights is the 4th largest city in Michigan. Musicians Eminem and Bob Seger both lived in Sterling Heights. When Keith and Kevin opened their first running store it was in a building in Sterling Heights, before they moved to the Utica location farther west. The Utica store here brings in a totally different market of customers, many who are headed out mall shopping along the strip of highway M-59 and Interstate 94 leading northeast into Canada. In contrast to the wealthy customers that pop into the Royal Oak, Lake Orion, and Grosse Pointe stores, it seems like most of the customers at the Utica stores are generally more working class. Many are first-time runners, or contract/construction workers looking for a comfortable shoe to work in. The whole area has a more traditional, blue-collar vibe to it and many customers place an extra emphasis on your ability to provide superior customer service. Our no-refund, exchange-only return policy seems to tick off the most people at this store.

The farthest store away from our base in Rochester Hills is the Grosse Pointe shop. On a good day with no traffic it takes 45 minutes to drive there, and the commute is something that makes working in that store a drag. Grosse Pointe is located slightly east of downtown Detroit, close to the Canadian border and as far south at the infamous 8 Mile. However, despite its proximity to metro crime and other sketchy areas, Grosse Pointe is a wealthy suburb, home to many lakefront mansions and big names in the auto industry. It was the original commuter suburb into the city, and now the median household income is a healthy 81,000 dollars. The small Grosse Pointe area is technically only 1 square mile (more if you count Grosse Pointe Farms) and the population is still under 6,000. Aside from the long commute, this is a favorite store to work at because the customers are usually long-time, loyal Hansons fans and they even know about the distance project. The store is also considerably less busy than the Utica and Royal Oak stores.

Overall, it appears that the whole Detroit metro area is a continuous stretch of old industrial complexes, residences, and heavily traveled roads that are always under construction. The apparent socioeconomic discrepancies between neighboring areas and the city have contributed to the crimes, ill-will, and racial tensions that people identify with when they think of the Detroit area. Politically, the heart of the city is liberal with many diverse viewpoints. Further up towards Oakland County, the populace becomes more homogenous and heavily leans to the right.

Fortunately the pride and work ethic of native Detroiters is still strong, as it seems many are determined to persevere despite the challenges of crime, a tough economy, and the biting cold of winter. Being a soft touch from the mild climates (and more liberal yuppie towns) in the Pacific Northwest and New York, I'm not sure if I am cut out to really thrive here.

Hardest Training Week of My Life
So Far
September 25th, 2009

I ran 125 miles in the last 7 days, including three significant workout days: the 8 by 1000m workout, a grueling session of 4 by 4k, and a tough 10 mile cut-down (negative split) run which was done in around 54 minutes on a hilly course. It has been the hardest training week of my life to date. I guess I'm kind of on the New York Marathon training schedule that Nick and Brian are on. Nick is fit! The 10 mile cut down that I did was only part of his 12 mile cut-down which we did on the rolling, golf course road loop route that the Hansons used to prepare the team for the 2007 US Olympic Marathon Trials in the hilly Central Park. The loop is really a 1.5 mile stretch of road that goes up from the clubhouse parking lot in Stony Creek Metropark to a U-turn at the top of a hill. The elevation change makes it rough on the quads. Hitting pace requires extremely uneven efforts.

As we warmed up around the wooded trails at Stony Creek Metropark, Nick commented on my slow, loopy stride. "You're a heel-striker!" he states in disbelief. At this level in running you'd think we would all run on our forefeet like the Kenyans. Being a slow heel striker and running for Hansons is rare. I suddenly become ashamed and sensitive of my over-extended, beginner-like striding tendencies, the result of hard-wired bad form (perhaps also due to my lack of fast-twitch muscle fibers). Everyone else on the team has a speedy cadence of 180 steps per minute or faster, and most glide effortlessly across the ground, hitting with their forefoot and pawing back forcefully. Brian, Chad, and Nick definitely have the most pop in their strides. Their legs spring off the ground and snap back quickly. Such attributes are indicative of speed. We see Mike and Brian pull up in a car together. It isn't a particularly hot morning, but we are definitely going shirtless during the workout. I prepare for the sweat bath that I always seem to generate on such hard efforts in the sun.

Kevin instructs us on the pace for the cut-down: "First 3 miles at 6:00 pace, next 3 miles at 5:40 pace, next 3 at 5:20, last 3 at 5:00 pace!" Luckily, I only have to do one at 5:00 pace since I am ending after 10 miles. I feel sorry for Nick and Brian, as a sub-15 last 3 miles on this course looks impossible! We start off rather comfortably, as cut-downs always seem to feel.

"Wait until you have to run up this hill at 4:50 pace," Brian says, foreshadowing the difficulty of grinding up such an incline at race pace velocity. We head up around the U-turn 1.5 miles into the workout, and I'm still feeling good. Time for the downhill! Holding back, I watch as Mike takes off, arms swinging and legs springing. He runs like he has a rocket up his ass. Zipping around a corner we come up to the 3-mile point: "5:27…5:28." I can hear Kevin calling out Mike's mile split. Brian, Nick, and I are about 5 seconds back. Damn! This is too fast. We are supposed to be hitting 5:40. I am only agitated because I know that for every second I am fast early on, I will pay for with progressively higher concentrations of lactic acid in my legs later into the workout. My breathing crosses a threshold halfway in; time to do work!

Coming down the hill in our last 5:20-pace set of miles (which ended up being more like 5:12 to 5:15), I am suddenly getting dropped. We pull a quick U-turn at the bottom of the hill where Kevin is stationed with fluid bottles. I follow Nick as he snags his bottle, full of 12 ounces of purple Gatorade Rain. He also had a Tri-Berry flavored Gu gel packet is his hand.

"Okay guys, 5-flat pace now!" Kevin barks as we accelerate into the formidable uphill. I am sweating bullets and breathing uncontrollably, totally beyond my lactate threshold. This last mile is going to be a 100% Vo2max, all-out aerobic capacity effort for me. Nick pulls ahead, surging while simultaneously chugging all 12 ounces of his Gatorade and inhaling his Gu in one smooth motion. I will never forget that image. Nick's legs were just popping off the ground; his torso was straight, his arms in relaxed swinging arcs against his sides. He just looked so smooth, flying up the hill.

"2:28...2:29," Kevin calls out our uphill half mile split...thank God! I just have to hold this pace. I barely do it. It takes a kick and a lot of mental gusto to make it through this one. By now Brian and Nick have pulled away and are chasing Mike. I heard they ran a 4:55 for that 10th mile up the hill! After finishing I am gasping for air and drenched in sweat that stings my eyes and nostrils. I feel fat and out-of-shape compared to those guys. Kevin and Don shake my hand and say good job. I start cooling down back down the hill so I can catch Nick and Brian finish.

Brian is back! We see him charging down the hill, 50m ahead of Nick. His face is gritty; his T6 racing flats are flying under his legs as he charges to finish his 12th mile. "4:52...4:53," Kevin reads the split times. Brian bursts across the line and turns around to see where Nick finishes up. He ran around 14:47 for the last 3 miles. Tough! It seems like Brian is finally coming around in his fitness. Later I learn that before the trials Brian ran a 14:17 once on this 3-mile stretch...at the end of a 12-mile cut-down. I suddenly feel like this "hardest training week of my life" isn't so bad. It is going to be interesting to see what kind of monster this amount of volume and intensity can generate!

The Hanson Brothers

If Kevin and Keith Hanson were cartoon characters they could respectively be like Mario and Luigi. Contrasting, yet complimentary in their personalities, the brothers balance each other out much like a system of checks and balances. They make an effective management team because of this equilibrium. One brother may be understanding of you at times; while the other may be upset. Keith focuses a lot of his attention on the stores; while Kevin pretty much sticks to the running and coaching aspects of the program. Clint Verran recalls: "They are completely different people."

I think that any two close brothers growing up can relate to the teamwork that such a relationship provides. The older brother picks on the younger one; but then the younger one ends up growing taller. You could tell from the onset that the whole Distance Project, and the family business of the Hansons Running Shops, were the brainchild of brotherly love. The competitive streaks of running between the two brothers may have been laced with the occasional sarcastic joke, but over time it has been solidified with blood loyalty, trust, and compassion. Even though the brothers look as though they could be twins, they are two very different individuals, shaped by different environments of parenting and separated by 4 years.

Kevin, the go-to, more upfront and direct of the two, has the street smarts and direct approach of orchestrating a lot of the details within the program. He writes the workouts, yells more forcefully during workouts, and schedules meeting times to which you can never be late. He is very methodical and his interpersonal intelligence is very high. Clint describes him as being "calculating" and says that "everything he says he's thought through." A more stressed, obsessive, type-A personality differentiates him from his brother along with his dry sense of humor and ability to recall details from stories and countless interactions with all of his runners. He undoubtedly influenced his younger brother in their early running years as he let Keith tag along on his longer training runs (Kevin was in college while Keith was still a young teen). Kevin graduated from local Oakland University, where he posted some solid times in the 5k.

Keith has garnered more of the book smarts on paper. He earned an MBA from Indiana State University after graduating with a BA from Michigan State. He scored at the Big Ten Conference as an undergrad, and was a captain of the cross country team. Tall and more lanky, he appears more laid-back and casual during race weekends, but has a very sensitive and defensive streak when complications occur. Clint describes him: "Keith is the more emotional guy, he reacts."

Keith delights in eating at BBQ pits whenever we visit Florida, and the team is occasionally invited over for functions at his house in Rochester Hills, like having doughnuts after a long run, or pizza dinners with his family (that includes two youngsters currently aged 7 and 5). Both brothers place a high value on family, and of course, running.

The environment in which the brothers were raised had a large influence on how they evolved as people, and how their attitudes were shaped. One major difference in the brother's early life development was the influence of their father.

Now, I am not going to delve very deep into the personal matters of Keith and Kevin's family history, as there are many facts and incidences that I am not aware of. I feel it is not my place to pry into family secrets or disclose any information that is unnecessary for the scope and theme of this book. I deliberately chose not to personally interview Keith and Kevin because of this reasoning, and what I have gathered has been from what each has disclosed to me of the various car rides, meetings about running, and general questions about their past that have occurred in open discussion. I do however, feel that this information is essential because it gives one some perspective on where the founders of the Hansons Distance Project are coming from, and where the forces that drive such individuals to make such decisions originate.

"My dad was a card-carrying Mensa," says Kevin, whose memory of his father is drastically different from his younger brother Keith's, who spent considerably less time with their dad.

"He would get bored with every new job he got; he would just quit," Kevin explains, indicating how the family's early financial situation created some tension. There were painful times involving a divorce, and eventually a long, drawn-out fight with cancer. The death of his father in this manner is one of the reasons why Kevin hasn't touched a drop of alcohol for years; he has thoughtfully made that lifestyle choice with conviction.

On the other hand Keith hasn't mentioned as much about his father since I've been around. Unlike Kevin, who was around their dad a lot more, Keith's memory is a lot different; he didn't spend as much time with his dad. What Keith did have as a young adolescent was an escape into running, and running a lot! When he was 13 years old Keith decided to take on the first ever Detroit Free Press Marathon in 1978, where he debuted in 3:20:01 after training all summer in the same pair of shoes. A year later he came back and ran a 2:59:29 in the Baltimore Marathon. He was running 100 miles a week in training at times. Their mom, Walda, really had no idea that what her son was doing was out of the ordinary, that that kind of volume for a young adolescent was somewhat absurd. Now, much later in life Walda is a jolly character who enjoys working in her son's stores, and sharing stories about the old times. Keith seems to identify a lot more with his mom. At one point, when the family was torn apart and struggling financially, Keith and Walda were living in a trailer while Kevin had to pull out of Central

Michigan and transfer to nearby Oakland University. Such changes tend to generate stress on a young adult's upbringing. However, through that whole time at least Keith and Kevin had something constant, some variable that they could control and excel at; they had running.

* * *

In the years following college there was a period of time when the Hanson brothers dominated the local road racing circuit. Winning a race didn't just provide satisfaction and recognition; it was about advertising and branding a name. "Kevin and I ran local races as marketing for the stores...we'd alternate who'd run every weekend," Keith recalls.

Across Michigan, the brothers garnered some attention as both runners and businessmen. Kevin ran just under 51:00 at the Crim 10 miler in Flint, while Keith was slightly over 51. Kevin also traveled to the Boson Marathon and ran a 2:32. Business in running just got better and better. "Keith and Kevin are self-made people...they are first generation rich guys," Clint states, summing up the career choices made by the brothers.

Initially Keith worked in purchasing for Pfizer Pharmaceuticals for a couple years before he and Kevin went into business together. Many articles like to use the term "shoe-string budget" in describing the financial investment that the brothers made in early days of their operations. However, after the first year of opening, sales in the shoe store took off and there has never been a year where the business hasn't grown.

Start slow and finish well! The success of the business grew from struggling to fill the shelves to a stronghold monopoly of the Detroit metro area. Of course the Distance Project's success and media attention were an extra boost in garnering credibility, an experienced sales team, and a unique rags-to-riches story about two local boys who grew up with running on the auto-factory-worker side of Detroit.

"We didn't have enough product to fill the shelves, so we asked vendors to send us empty shoe boxes," Keith explains, remembering the early years in the store. The empty shoeboxes were stacked on the shelves in order for the store to appear well-stocked and successful. Of course then the trick was being able to sell a customer a shoe size that you actually had! Their reputation grew, and Michiganders spread the word that Hansons is the best place in Detroit to go to buy running shoes. Word of mouth marketing is very powerful when you build such a reputation.

As the profit margin grew, the brothers were able to strategically purchase stores in Grosse Pointe, Auburn Hills, and Royal Oak areas. The Hanson Brothers had also developed a reputation for coaching runners in the metro Detroit area. Keith had stints as a coach early on, and Kevin coached at the community college and high school levels (he is still currently the Stevenson High School girls cross country and track coach). One athlete, Don Jackson, who went on to run a 1:51.8 800m, was coached by Kevin at Macomb Community College. Don was a local athlete, and he eventually joined the Hansons Running Shops as a manager. In the beginning, Don lived at the Royal Oak store, on the upstairs level.

Now Don Jackson is the general manager of the Hansons Running Shops, and the assistant coach of the Distance Project. When Keith and Kevin are out of town or away at a race it is Don who shows up and times splits for workouts, hands out water bottles, and drives around to support the athletes. Don also is a force when it comes to the success and ultimate bottom line of the stores, but that is for another chapter. The stores quickly grew, and as athletes came to Michigan to run, people's heads started to turn. There was some extremely positive publicity generated about what two brothers from Michigan had done.

All small businesses may dream about the day that they make it big and appear on the cover of *The Wall Street Journal*. Kevin and Keith Hanson did just that on the June 10th, 2003 issue. But it wasn't the successes of the actual running store that garnished such attention. Rather, it was the idea behind the Distance Project, the dream of investing on a project that at the time may have seemed absurd to even pull off financially. A decade later the project is flourishing, and it would be safe to say that the Hansons return on investment was great. Thanks to the support of Brooks, Inc. the program rose in success due to its ability to produce national class marathoners seemingly out of nowhere. A key marketing tool, of course, was the progression of Brian Sell, whose gritty character inspired less talented, developing runners to dream big and continue training.

Keith (left) and Kevin Hanson oversee a workout with Desiree Davila on the country roads by Lake Orion, Michigan.

Fall
October 1st, 2009

September came and went. Yesterday I rolled out of
Driftwood by myself at 6:45 AM for a scheduled 18 miler.
It was dark, wet, and cold. Lights from a school bus flashed
over me. I had almost forgotten that from 6th to 12th grade I
woke up at 5:30 every weekday to commute 45:00 to an out
of district school that my dad taught in. Back in those days, a
morning run was out of the question for me. I had thought
about it, but the idea of starting out with a flashlight at 4:30
is a bit extreme in the backwoods of Oregon. I was only
running about 50 miles at week tops during the school year
anyway, so doubling wasn't really necessary. Furthermore, my
ability to learn was drastically affected by the 7 hours of sleep
a night I averaged as a teen. I had to save all the extra energy
I could for plowing through tests and homework. Burning
the midnight oil, waking up early, and hard work all seemed
to go together back then...they still do now. At Hansons
you can get plenty of sleep, but you can't sleep in. Kevin
is a person who effectively budgets his time and he always
emphasizes the importance of the morning routine in both
training and consistency of performances.

"Don't tell me you're going to fucking 'try,' just
go out and do it!" Kevin pauses after shouting this out,
perhaps realizing that he has just uttered a part of a rival
shoe company's slogan. We are having one of our monthly
team meetings in a large room above the store at Royal
Oak. Amidst a table full of greasy Jet's deep dish, square
pepperoni pizza and mixed greens, the team sits and listens.
Most of us have our heads down, with our eyes focused low
on the table. It is nine at night and we are tired from a day
of running and working in the stores selling countless shoes.
Giant, larger than life cut-out images of past and current

Hansons team members hang high on the walls of the room, towering over our meeting table. They serve as a formidable reminder of the '07 trials, when fans held cut-out faces of Brian and passed out Hansons-Brooks t-shirts to the crowds of spectators. I was a little jealous that I didn't have my own cut-out figure and trading card like a lot of the other guys. I haven't done my time yet though. I haven't done shit.

Kevin's statement is in regards to what our racing mindset should be: you don't say you're going to 'try' to get a top 10 finish in a major marathon, or 'try' to run a 2:15… you just 'do.' The guys running fall marathons are getting fired up. Chicago is less than 2 weeks away, New York is in about a month, and Chad is running the local Detroit Free Press Marathon this weekend. They are about to see if the fruits of their labor are going to pay off this marathon-racing season. I impatiently stir in my seat, thinking about when it will be my turn to run the marathon wearing the Hansons singlet. Boston in April is just too far away to get worked up about now!

Brian's Shenanigans
October 10th, 2009

My initial impressions of Sell have changed. If he was the character in a fictional story he would serve the role of the jokester; a trickster. The more time you spend around Brian, the more you witness this upbeat side to him that provides a lot of comic relief. Almost every morning run with him becomes a feature presentation full of entertainment from his various antics. When he gets this mischievous look in his eye and drops back from lead the pack you know something is going to happen. Today, he did this when we passed a dead squirrel in the road, its head recently smashed open by a tire. Brian's eyes light up at the sight. He suddenly acts like he's going to stop and pick it up.

"Don't you dare!" Morgan warns, with a sense of urgent caution in his voice. I remember hearing a story about how Brian has been known to throw dead squirrels on the run…I can now probably confirm that Morgan is referencing that time. Anything that Sell does or may do, you have to believe is possible, no matter how ridiculous.

"I used to collect squirrel tails as a kid…I put them out on my back porch…it was pretty cool until all the hairs fell out…then there were just a bunch of nasty tail bones lying around!" Sell reminisces out-loud about his childhood on a farm.

We continue on at 6:00 pace down a gravel road. When Sell wants to get my attention he refers to me as "Ivy League" or "Sagnasty." His fitness seems to finally be rounding into shape. He could go without running for a couple months and still be more fit than I am right now - although his intensity just hasn't been nearly the same since the Olympics and the years before that. He recently did 3 by 3 miles out at the boat launch bike path and averaged around 15:00 flat for each one, on a windy day. That was like my all-time PR for a single 3-mile race in high school. Put that in the context of a 140 mile week. Sell's personality may appear to have a tough and formidable exterior shell; however, inside that shell there is a witty comedian full of jokes.

Sell

To understand what compels a man you have to run in his shoes for a while. By the time I joined Hansons, Brian was nearing retirement. His best competitive days were already behind him, at least in his mind. And who could blame him? He did what he wanted to ultimately do in running. He made the Olympics as an underdog. In terms of running, that's where the buck ended for him. Now it was time to focus on his future, his career, his brand new baby boy Levi, his daughter Lily, and his wife Sara.

During my initial visit to Michigan I had heard that Brian Sell was like a cranky old man. When I first saw him on my recruiting trip, I had this pre-conceived notion in my mind. I was wrong. After working and running with Brian you get to know him as a genuinely friendly, loyal, well educated individual with a sense of humor. He has been one of the nicest and most welcoming guys on the team…even to the slow and fat new guy (me). He also respects all of his teammates and his sense of humility is uncommon amongst Olympians. Longtime teammate and friend Mike Morgan sums it up: "He's a good guy to be around…he's always on time…he's always hard-working at the store…he's a good dad and husband to his family."

To me, Brian Sell is (and will always be) a badass. As cliché as that sounds, it is probably the most accurate description that comes to mind. Sometimes he sports a handlebar mustache and would convincingly fit into a crowd at a NASCAR rally. But upon closer inspection, one may start to notice that this is not just a man who likes planes and motorcycles, but one of those rare individuals who possesses a drive beyond what most people will ever experience in their lifetime. Maybe it was an innate force; maybe it was transfused into him as blue-collar blood. Whatever the case, Sell decided what he wanted and went for it. Few of us have the tenacity to experience life full-throttle and put everything on the line. We worry about our reputations, securing our future, and hurting ourselves (physically, financially, or emotionally). Brian was willing to take those risks and fully commit to them.

One of the first memories of Brian bursting out to fame on the running scene was when he took the lead in the 2004 US Men's Olympic Trials Marathon in Birmingham, AL. It was a gutsy move in the cold wind against favorites like Meb Keflezighi, Abdi Abdirahman, Dan Browne, and Alan Culpepper, to name a few. Of course he was passed later by all the previously mentioned runners, and also his teammates Trent Briney and Clint Verran, who ran slightly more conservative races. Some runners might throw in the towel after such a disappointment, some might continue training and hope to improve. Brian went back the drawing board, put his head down, and cranked 160-mile weeks with a sole focus of making the Olympic Team for 2008. He poured himself into that goal and put immense pressure on himself to accomplish it.

* * *

The path to Olympic stardom for Brian Sell started long before that though. Perhaps it was not so much his physical, innate ability or talent as a runner, but more a function of his personality that led him to pursue such a feat. The values instilled in youth, the character shapers, and tests of mental fortitude are ultimately prime motivators. His passion, his drive, and his dedication allowed him to make the necessary sacrifices to slowly and surely accomplish what he wanted to do in running. This was a process, and before the Hansons even started, it was obvious that Brian wasn't just any scrappy, working-class runner. He was an individual that earned a reputation as a dependable workhorse, the underdog achiever that bested prediction charts through solid determination. The long-term pursuit of such endeavors is most revealing of his character. To examine the foundation that built such an individual, one must examine his origins, and the forces that tested and matured him as a person.

As an only child growing up in the outskirts of rural Woodbury, Pennsylvania (a small town of a couple hundred in population about 2 hours east of Pittsburgh), Sell developed a thirst for hard work and athleticism. He grew up on an old dairy farm that no longer had cows. Instead, Sell immersed himself in nurturing and growing pigs to several hundred pounds:

"I raised a half dozen pigs for 4-H and the county fair," Sell sheepishly recalls of his childhood on the farm. The work involved some responsibility and planning as well as fueling his initial attitude towards self-discipline, goal setting, and plain old hard work.

Said Sell, "[Raising pigs] instilled a work ethic for me because you had to get up in the morning before school to feed the pigs and clean the pens." On Saturday mornings, Sell would be out mowing their 2-acre lawn. If he didn't finish before his soccer games that afternoon, he would come back and make sure it got done. Waking up at dawn to do work obviously was a habit that Sell continued through early morning runs throughout his 20s.

Although Sell was active in farm work and installing swimming pools in his adolescence, he hadn't committed to any particular sport, but was more a jack-of-all-trades. His high school didn't even have a cross country team so he did what most Pennsylvania high school kids did: played football every fall. He also was on the wrestling team starting in middle school, and then decided to go out for track in the 9th grade because, "track was pretty much something to do in the spring...[and plus] I got beamed 20 or 30 times in baseball in little league..."

As a sophomore in high school Sell realized that winning was fun, and a glimpse of his natural ability as a distance runner was slowly revealed when he won the district title with a 4:48 1600m. "It wasn't blazing, but to win was enough to definitely motivate me to keep going with it," Sell recalls fondly, with an emphasis on the fact that winning was more important than the time.

Articles and message boards blow up with the fact that Sell ended his high school career with a very modest 10:06 personal best in the 2-mile. His progression from that defining figure to 2:10 marathoner and Olympian has received a lot of press because it is evidence that there are sometimes diamonds in the rough that might get lost in the mix. While he was perhaps considerably undertrained in high school compared to the Footlocker finalists and 9:00 2-milers, Sell possessed a winning attitude and had the strong desire to better himself.

"I was probably running 30 miles a week...but I thought I was doing a ton of work," Sell recalls. Perhaps his ignorance (and the lack of widespread internet results about his faster peers) ended up being a blessing because he wasn't discouraged. He enjoyed running; it wasn't an obsession.

Sell admits: "The longest run I did in high school was 5 or 6 miles." Little did he know at the time that in another decade he would be running 160 miles a week and solidifying himself as one of the top 3 marathon runners in the country. Arthur Lydiard always said, "There are champions everywhere." Well, it soon became obvious that the little town of Woodbury, PA had produced one.

Upon graduating from high school, Sell wasn't interested in considering running anymore. He didn't think he was good enough to be on a college team. Who had time for a sport in college anyway? College was where you focused on academics, right? Sell was initially concerned with balancing academics with his other activities and free time. He enrolled in the small college of Messiah, where he "wanted to focus on studies right out of the gate." He didn't go out for the cross country team his first year, and was content not running anymore until he saw the opportunity to improve himself and perhaps gain some recognition through competition. Sell explains:

> "I sat behind the captain of the cross country team in biology lab, and he was this big stud. He knew all these pretty girls in class and I thought that was pretty cool, so I asked him what his PR in the mile was, and it was like 4:52. I thought to myself, well I've run faster than that."

So Sell went out for the track team at Messiah, and he started winning. His times weren't all that fast, but he didn't know enough about the sport to become discouraged. Plus, he was doing fine adjusting to college academics: "Grades were okay. I had like a 3.8 first semester. I ran 32:30 in the 10k and like 15:17 in the 5k. I won some small- time meets."

More importantly though, he was finding a balance and channeling his energy into improving himself through hard work:

> "I remember going down to an indoor square track with a tape player [listening to Milli Vanilli and Blink 182] with my big headphones on and running around for an hour…I was getting pretty fired up about running!"

Although his training volume at Messiah was only a modest 60 to 70 miles a week, Sell's dedication to pushing his limits and testing his fitness had begun in earnest. He remembers starting to go down to the gym every evening after class and putting in extra second runs, hammering them at around 5:30 per mile pace.

His drive and intensity became a cornerstone to his personality. I began to wonder if that fiery look in his eyes had developed from this period in his life and heated up a decade later in 2007. He was just beginning his large volume of tens of thousands of miles of training; he was just starting to have fun.

Sell transferred to St. Francis University kind of on a whim. He was getting more serious about running, and the fact that his Messiah teammates liked to skip morning runs and practices kind of bothered him. Furthermore, Sell was driving home a lot from Messiah…a 1.5 hour drive each way. St. Francis was just right up the road from his house, plus the coach there offered him a small scholarship (this was a D-I athletic program by the way)! At St. Francis things changed. Most notably he had teammates that now pushed him to the next level. He was able to more accurately gauge times that he thought were fast and become more knowledgeable about the sport: "I had no idea who Pre was at the time…at that point I had no idea what a good 5k was. I thought I was doing really well with a 15:17."

On the pre-med track, Sell took challenging classes and held a solid GPA. He lost some transfer credits and was able to compete at St. Francis for an extra year - so he did. His running really started to blossom. He got to go to the big distance meets in California: Stanford and Mt. Sac. He busted a 28:58 in the 10k, and ran 13:59 in the 5k.

More notably than his times, Sell credits his teammates for motivating him and helping him run fast. Much like in his later years in the Hansons program, Sell emphasizes the importance of team chemistry and the enjoyment of the camaraderie:

> "I really liked the team…we had a close-knit team… missed NCAAs by one spot. Conference was like our national meet. We wanted to win, and we took things personally."

Sell remembers the time fondly, hinting that the label of blue-collar becoming attributed to his character was no coincidence: "We were like these low-class guys." Other more preppy teams in the conference made fun of them for not having matching uniforms, "…then we went out and beat them."

* * *

In retrospect, Brian is really what put the Hansons program on the map…leading the rest of the group figuratively and literally by his performances from the 2004 trials through the 2008 trials. I mean, here were these guys, not even college superstars and they were placing in the top 15 at the Boston and Chicago Marathons as a large pack. They had 5 guys in the same race run 2:15:30 or faster. In 2006 those were some of the top times in the country. Wearing these flashy, bright orange, yellow, and red singlets, you couldn't miss them. Brian ran with guts.

He inspired the term "blue-collar runner" because of his work ethic, his strength, his will. An All-American farm boy from Pennsylvania who regularly ate McDonald's and would say things like: "I'm shaving my ass to save money on toilet paper." Fans saw that in him and admired him. He logged the mileage, still worked 25 to 30 hours a week on his feet, and supported his family. Like many impressionable high school runners searching the Internet for information on training and distance running news, I aspired to be like him. Websites like LetsRun, Mensracing, and Dyestat back in those days were very influential. To me Brian was an idol, a hero. And he still is, to me and to many others. Badass or not, you decide.

Day After Chicago
October 12th, 2009

The first major fall marathon for the team occurred in Chicago. Boston, and the other major spring marathons, still seem like a world away for me. However, I can now at least take comfort in the success from the team's most recent race results.

All three of the Hansons runners participating in the 2009 Bank of America Chicago Marathon set PRs. In her debut marathon, Liberty University standout Carol Jefferson (who is actually leaving the program next week to start working full-time) ran 2:41:15. Melissa White finished 8th overall and was the 2nd American (behind Deena Kastor who ran 2:28:50) with a 5-minute PR in 2:32:55. Finally, in the cold conditions that gripped the windy city, Patrick Rizzo finished 10th overall in the men's race with a PR in 2:15:48. He was later quoted as saying, "My fluids froze to my teeth!" in regards to the temperatures in the 30s. He ended up being the 2nd American in the race. 2008 Olympic Champion Sammy Wanjiru won the race in a course record of 2:05:41. He was making an attempt at world record pace early on, but faded over the final 10k.

Damn! I wish I could have run Chicago. A sub 2:19 finish would not only qualify you for the 2012 Olympic Trials, but you would also get $2500 from the race as a time bonus. That is just sweet. The amount of support that that marathon offers developing elite Americans is phenomenal. I am so eager to run a marathon…but now is the time to be patient.

Today sucked; it's getting cold in Detroit now. My left quad is stiff and feels like shit. Brian and I worked together at the Royal Oak Store. He met me at the Driftwood house at 10:15, and we carpooled in my '98 Chevy Prizm for the 30 minutes. It's not every day that you get to drive around an Olympian!

I had to get gas and grab coffee at Dunkin' Donuts to gear myself up for work all day selling shoes. Brian chowed down on his McDonald's breakfast that he brought with him in the passenger seat. We ended up being 5 minutes late to the Royal Oak store because of the traffic and construction work that unpredictably slowed the whole commute. I thought Providence, Boston, Chicago, and New York drivers were bad...then I came here! You have a lot of people driving oversized vehicles that are just not practical or fuel-efficient. It seems like rush hour all the time. Maybe being a country boy who grew up driving a stick shift pickup truck on the isolated dirt roads in Oregon has influenced my perception of the fast, crowded city life. I'm not used to all the exhaust.

Anyway, it was a busy day at the store. In a rare moment when the store is not full of customers, Brian takes a couple minutes to rest his sinewy legs. He is excited as he digs into his brown paper lunch bag and finds that his wife has included a whole deli pickle to go along with his ham and cheese sandwich.

"One regret that I have here is that I didn't run smarter in Birmingham (2004 Olympic Trials Marathon) and make the Olympic team there. If I did that, I'd be through dental school now," he mentions between gulps of his lunch, a look of regret on his face.

Blood and guts: Brian led most of the '04 Olympic Trials
Marathon into a cold wind.

Brian sighs and changes the radio station to a country channel. Very soon we are back to helping customers, answering close to 50 phone calls for the day and restocking countless boxes of shoes.

Later in the evening, Mike meets us and we roll out of Driftwood for a brisk 6-mile run out on the leaf-covered dirt trails encompassing Bloomer Park and the Yates Cider Mill in Rochester. Young couples and families with little kids flock to the cider mills for fresh pressed apple cider and greasy doughnuts. The sweet, sugary fat smells like heaven as we fly by at sub-6 pace. I was anxious to get the run over with because it still isn't a walk in the park for me to run at this "easy" pace everyday. Plus, I wanted to rest up for my early morning workout the very next day, which would be followed by a solo evening shift at the Royal Oak store.

Tragedy
October 23rd, 2009

I've spent the last 55 out of 56 hours in my little room at Driftwood. A strange, flu-like illness got hold of me a couple days ago. It started off like a bad cold so I ran through it and still went to work, but that night I felt like I had a fever so I went to bed early at 8:30. I knew I had a workout of 4 by (1600m, 800m) scheduled the very next morning…tough! Well, I woke up at 6:30 and felt like death with a fever, sore throat, mucus-oozing nose, killer headache, and a high level of fatigue. Running or working was out of the question. In retrospect I think maybe I got the swine flu, although at the time I didn't think it had hit Michigan that hard yet. Hopefully I'll recover soon enough; I just hope I don't get pneumonia or a lung-infection. Most importantly I am worried about infecting my teammates/housemates, especially Nick. I would feel horrible if he got sick now, a week out from the New York City Marathon that he has targeted and trained for for over a year. He's put in such a hard training segment the last three months, and it could be the biggest race of his life! My other housemate Christian Wagner has a track 10k coming up in a week also, something that he has been training for since he came here. It would be devastating now if he got my disease at this point as well. I'd feel so guilty. I've always thought of myself as having a strong immune system. However, I guess since I have asthma and have been exposed to a lot of people at the store, I am more susceptible to illness (or maybe I've just had bad luck recently?). Whatever, swine flu sucks.

Last weekend was the Detroit Free Press Marathon and we had to go downtown a couple times for that. The day before the race I worked at the expo where I signed a total of four autographs on posters and gave-out Hansons "elite athlete trading cards" (unfortunately I don't have one though). The expo made bank and luckily I got paid in cash for my time. There was a lot of talking about the upcoming race, and some questions about the program. People came flocking in for gear and Gu and shoes the whole time. The store made like $1000 just off of selling running gloves alone!

Early the very next morning we came back downtown to run and watch our very own Chad "Nails" Johnson battle it out for the title. I woke up at 5. It was cold and I was bloated from the 2 tall beers and greasy swiss mushroom burger I downed at Hooters late the previous night heading back from the expo with Luke, Rizzo, and Paul...good times. Anyway, a caravan of cars led by infamous driver Rizzo headed out of Rochester Hills in the dark. The ice that coated my windshield reminded me that I still need to purchase an ice scraper in order to survive much longer.

Anyway, we rolled out of Rochester Hills around 6:15, a string cars with Rizzo in his Mercury Sable leading. I followed him closely, and two cars of girls from the Tienken house followed me. We didn't know the best way to drive downtown. Following Rizzo's notoriously bad driving, we ran several yellow/red traffic lights and cruised along in excess of 80 mph on the interstate into downtown Detroit (very stupid because there were surely ice patches in such cold, dark weather!). I pray for my safely every time I step into a car around here (if I make it though a year without crashing then I'm going to come out as a damn good driver).

After a brisk 10-miler on the streets of the marathon course, Luke and I dipped into a Tim Hortons for coffee and doughnuts. It was still freezing cold outside and standing around was uncomfortable. We waited at mile 19 for Chad to come by, anxiously eyeing the time and calculating what his 5:15 to 5:20 mile pace will put him there in. When we finally see Chad, he is dueling with another local elite, Nick Stanko. Todd told us a week earlier that he had heard Stanko talk about his marathon build-up. "I didn't want to tell Chad, but

Stanko was doing faster workouts and had a better marathon segment," Todd informed us.

It then appeared that Stanko and Chad were trading the lead after each mile, and they were on about 2:20 marathon pace when they passed us and went across a bridge to Belle Isle, which is like a little appendix loop on the course. The marathon itself goes into Canada and then comes back, which makes it an interesting, international experience for the runners! I had to drive off to work so at that point I attempted to maneuver my car out of Detroit. However I miscalculated the course of the marathon and got stuck for 45 minutes behind a wall of marathon runners that seemed to never end. I didn't hear who won the race or that a horrific tragedy had struck during the race until much later in the day.

"3 Runners Die During Detroit Half-Marathon," a headline read. What? I've known from first-hand experience that individuals die during marathons. I thought back to the 2007 Olympic Trials, where I vividly remember seeing the late Ryan Shay on the ground in the middle of the Central Park course. During that race we had know idea what had happened. When a runner in a crowd goes down you first assume that they just got tripped and took a tumble, and you keep running because you are sure they'll get back up and continue. Heart failure, heat stroke, and over-hydration become lethal dangers quickly when you are stressing your body out on the pavement. But 3 people in one race? And in the half marathon too? One was a seemingly young and otherwise healthy adult. Others were experienced marathoners. This kind of news was devastating to the nation and especially the city of Detroit. The race was a large event with lots of runners participating, but to have 3 people die was just uncanny. It was a sad day. Such events make you appreciate the gift of life and running, and recognize the inherent danger that is attached to our sport.

New York City Marathon
November 1st, 2009

The Big Apple. The splendor and excitement of fans yelling in all 5 boroughs makes it the most exciting marathon in the world. This year the New York City Marathon not only boasted its typical, world class international field, but it also brought out some of the best American distance runners because it was a USATF National Championship. In any case, it was a great day for American marathoning, one for the history books. An American won the race for the first time since 1982 when Alberto Salazar grinded his way to the finish. Despite the loaded field of talent, including former Olympians and past NYC and Boston Marathon champions, American Meb Keflezighi came out on top decisively with a 2:09:15 pulling away from Kenya's Robert Cheruiyot in the 22nd mile to win by 41 seconds.

The Hansons program had another great success story: Nick "Snick" Arciniaga dropped an incredible race, running a perfectly executed 2:13:46 to place 8th overall and 4th for Americans! Only Meb, Ryan Hall (4th), and Jorge Torres (7th) beat him. Despite the wind and the 1:05 half-way split of the lead pack, Nick went out in 1:06:40 with Brian. He was able to mow down the likes of Olympian Abdi Abdirahman and 2:12 marathoner Jason Lehmkuhle to name a few. Not to mention the numerous quality runners that ended up not finishing or totally blowing up on the unforgiving course.

For those of you who have run New York, you know that it is a difficult course. In fact, when I ran the marathon there the previous year I slowed to a walk (and pair of ten-minute miles) after an aggressive early pace that was outdoing myself at the time (1:09 first half). Every bridge you cross is a giant hill, and the course has little ups and downs much like Boston…except it isn't a net downhill. A bad day turns into a really bad day on such a challenging course, where the screaming crowds of spectators might excite you into running 10-15 seconds too fast for each mile early on. I remember thinking I would pass out and get my second concussion on the street before Central Park because I was so dizzy and delusional from my drop in blood sugar. The only saving grace was that the NYRR threw a sick party for us elites after the race and I chatted with Kara Goucher (see picture) after her impressive debut. She beat me. I also got my ass thoroughly handed to me by the great Paula Radcliffe.

Me and Kara Goucher after the 2009 NYC Marathon. The NYRR after party was amazing!

Anyway, back to the success of the Hansons this year:

> Rizzo and I had to work in the shoe store during the race and every 5 minutes we had Luke call and give us split updates as he tracked runners on his computer at home. The phone updates went like this:

> > "Josh Moen just ran 5:40/mile pace for the last 2k leading up to his 25k split...he's done!"
> > "Nick and Brian through the half together..."
> > "Brian 5 seconds back..."
> > "Meb surging to the lead..."
> > "...he's got 20m....80m..."
> > "...Meb's going to win!"

> Brian Sell, despite his late streak of faster-paced workouts during his final marathon segment, finished in a gritty 2:24. Unlike other elites who were "not feeling it" or "hitting the wall," Brian was determined not to DNF. There is no way Brian would DNF in such a race. He could have broken his femur, lost a shoe, and been sick, and he still would have finished. It was a true test of his character. He's been getting some flack lately for his planned retirement, and now for running a "slow" time. What people don't understand is his life situation now, and the fact that running means different things to different people at various stages in their lives. He's got 2 kids to care for now...his hips hurt... he burned the candle hot for years and got the most out of himself...he already accomplished his ultimate goal in running and succeeded. How could you not respect that? Today, he certainly helped Nick stay on pace for the first half of the race. You could always depend on Brian to help a teammate out like that.

> Nick is going to come out with a substantial payday. Let's just say it is more than what he makes working 30 hours a week at the running store for the whole year! Not

to mention that his nearly 3 minute PR put him on the map big time for LetsRun.com message board fodder. People are like, "Who is this guy? And where did he come from?" Also now, more importantly, the name Nick Arciniaga can be recognized as someone who will be in serious contention for making the 2012 US Olympic Marathon team. I'm proud to be housemates with him.

Nick "Snick" Arciniaga doing his NYC Marathon "Simulator Workout" via a 1:06 half marathon tune-up race in Rochester Hills a month before his 2:13.

C'mon You Wuss-Cake!
November 7th, 2009

"C'mon you puss-cake!" Mike Morgan taunts me, as
we roll down the leaf-covered trails of the Sheldon Estates
Forrest Preserve near the edge of Stony Creek Metropark. It
is a gorgeous, cool fall morning, and as usual my quads are
screaming. This was the same situation I was in last week;
I can now tell this is how it's going to be most days though.
There are lots of guys on a break from running right now.
Morgan isn't though! He's piling on another 140 mile week,
and next week he said he'll hit 145. The guy never backs off!
Every single day is push, push, push! 6-minute miles or faster
all the time. This is a part of the Hansons way...the Brian
Sell mentality. It is reflected within the drive of high school
teams, college teams, and older, adult club running teams. Get
some competitive, fit, and tough distance runners together
for an easy run and it can turn into an ego-boosting workout
or team time trial any day. It goes against what I learned
from reading training books, from learning to run relaxed by
feel, and from what was preached to me in college. Yes, I had
success running 7:30 pace on my easy days...those really were
easy for me! Now, being a 2:20 + marathoner with a bunch
of 2:15 guys, I am just holding on to the back of the pack
looking at my watch and wishing the run were over!

But to be a tough, gnarly, and strong marathoner
you have to gamble sometimes, you have to push your limits
to see what you are made of...push your body to the brink
of injury and illness and back off just in time so that you
can reach a new performance peak. That's what it takes to
become elite in anything, always pushing the envelope and
not compromising for mediocrity. At Hansons you beat
yourself up day in and day out; you go into workouts tired,
and hope you can recover fast...or you don't make it...you

get injured. You may burn out mentally or drop out of the program altogether (or get cut). I ponder over thoughts like this all the time now...

Recently I took a low mileage week of only 90 miles because I still felt like I had swine flu symptoms from the previous week. Now on my run with Morgan through the woods I state that I'm not sure I want to take the long loop with him, and he quickly counters by calling out my weakness. I'm going to take it as a test of my masculinity. It is a reflection of his somewhat brash attitude and outgoing personality. It was something Sell-like in terms of adding mileage.

Paul and Chad drop off on the short-loop...I hesitate, feeling like that is exactly what I should be doing. However, I was quite insulted from being called a puss-cake so I stick with Morgan as we roll through the wooded trails at over 11 mph. Every step is a struggle, and my breathing isn't easy.

Over the weekend I had a long run with Mike, who is about a month away from his marathon at Cal International. He had 20 miles on his schedule and I only had 18. Brian came out wearing shorts (it was 30 degrees and windy!) and road his bike with us for most of the run. Keith met us along the hilly route to hand out fluids every 3 miles or so. I didn't bring anything, but Mike was stuffing down 10 ounces of Gatorade Endurance Formula every checkpoint. Luckily, Brian had some fruit punch Gatorade in a little, dirty New Balance squirt bottle attached to his bike that he let me sip out of.

"Don't let Keith see the logo," Brian mentions as we grind up an incline at about 5:45 pace. Mike had 3 miles near the end of the run scheduled as "hard and fast." Luckily, I did not have those fast 3 miles because I was already struggling to hold on to the pace.

"I'm getting nice and tired for these fast ones," Mike exclaims as we roll down a hill at sub 5:30 pace and turn

onto the Paint Creek Trail. This trail is awesome. It is like
a little gravel road for bikers and runners, and it runs from
Rochester to Lake Orion. It's flat, there are mile markers, and
it's where we do nearly half of all our training. Mike goes on
to split 4:44, 4:52, and 4:53 for his next 3 consecutive miles…
tough! I just pound splits of 5:33, 5:33, 5:32 and 5:28 for
my last 4 miles back on the trail. I feel my right quad really
stiffen up as I run at that pace. It was my second long run in
3 days as I had an easier 20 miler with Paul two days before
this effort. Fortunately, despite my rather large and clumsy
frame for an elite distance runner (and besides the fact my
teammates call me 'Fatboy') I have sturdy bones. Unlike Paul
and Morgan (who have had about 17 stress fractures between
them) I have been very fortunate to have never required time
off from training due to injury. Knock on wood!

Poker Night
November 15th, 2009

Last night most of the guys on the team and a couple of the women all had dinner together at Antoniou's, which is our favorite local place to hang out and get pizza. We all sat at a large table and enjoyed some greasy deep-dish, beer, and homemade desserts (a highlight of the meal for me). It was my 24th birthday, and I was just glad that I wasn't home alone watching TV with a frozen pizza on my lap. Sometimes you have to change up the monotony of cooking in and go out to eat, even if that means spending dough that you don't have.

Pizza at Antoniou's on my birthday. Left to right: Nick
Arciniaga, Emily Mortensen, Luke Humphrey, Mike Morgan,
(Brian is hiding behind them out of sight), Lily Sell, Sarah
Sell, Melissa White, Kelly Morgan, Pat Rizzo, and Me.

Tonight we had another fun event, something to help with team bonding and give you something to look forward to: poker night at Brian Sell's house. I had never been to Brian's house before. He lives in a rather quaint (but not fancy) neighborhood several miles from the duck pond near downtown Rochester Hills. When Nick and I pulled up around 6:30 Brian was standing out by the garage manning the grill and drinking a beer (it was either a Miller Lite or PBR). Smells from the aroma of sizzling hamburger, sausage, and hot dogs even made my vegetarian mouth water. Upon our entrance into the house, I discovered a cozy modern looking kitchen and living room on the lower floor. Melissa White was carrying around baby Levi, while Sarah Sell was busy in the kitchen prepping food while watching daughter Lily run around at full speed...Lily later yelled proudly how she was able to "potty" independently now for the first time.

I gravitated towards the Sells' friendly, cuddly, and affectionate golden retriever, Toby. Toby was Brian's first "baby," and he was trained very well. Toby could "speak" at various volumes, shake with both paws, and balance food on his nose. Brian proudly demonstrated these tricks with his favorite pet. Toby still smelled like the skunk that he had interacted with several weeks earlier. He drooled while watching Brian dig into some of the barbecued meat from the grill. Brian tore off some sausage chunks from a plate nearby and fed them to the happy canine who was waiting under the table.

We sat at the large dining room table, which had stacks of poker chips laid out already. A couple of fold-out chairs and additional tables were pushed together against the main table to accommodate all eleven of us. Texas hold'em was the game, and my $10 buy-in was due. I don't think I'd be playing this game if it were much more than that. I am not the best poker player, and my ability to win a game rests largely on the element of good luck rather than any skill or strategy. However, an early hand of pocket jacks got me excited enough to put a considerable amount into the pot. Unfortunately, to my surprise, Chad called on me and sheepishly revealed his hand of pocket kings. More beers, burgers, and chips were passed around the table. I was down early in the game and Chad had started to amass a small fortune. After about two hours I was out, but not until after 7 other guys ended up empty handed. The riches Chad had built up dwindled away, and eventually only the old guys (Brian and Clint) were left playing, each with huge piles of chips. It came down to one monster bluff and bet, but Brian came out on top. We joked that he probably won *almost* enough money to cover the costs of inviting us all over to consume his food and beer. It was a fun night.

Living The Dream

It's sad that in this day and age a US Olympic athlete has to worry about finances. I used to think that if you made it to the Olympics, you would become like a celebrity with money pouring in. Your sport would be your only career, your full-time profession and your savings for retirement. Money wouldn't be a problem because you'd be a sponsored Olympian for the rest of your days, right? Well, I guess that's not really true, at least in competitive distance running.

The obvious thing is running just doesn't have a whole lot of entertainment value. As a society we value entertainment and more exciting "real sports" like golf, NASCAR, poker, and bowling. We pump millions of dollars into these activities and the top athletes like Tiger Woods and Danica Patrick make major bank. But do they work that much more (or harder) than a guy like Brian Sell?

You don't do this for the money or the glory or fame. It's just not one of those things. While about 467,000 Americans are out finishing a marathon each year (in 2009), running is still not a fan-based sport that is exciting for most of the public to watch. However, to me, running is more than a sport; it's a lifestyle and I guess that's why we keep "wasting" our time at it.

What am I doing here? Delaying my career, delaying any further education, hopelessly attached and clinging to a fruitless dream? What am I becoming? I hear voices judging: "You have an Ivy League degree and you work in a shoe store for $10 an hour?" C'mon now, we are young…but we aren't just poor college kids anymore. Somewhere between the ages of 21 and 25 you need to learn how to really grow up and become financially independent!

I mean, I know the economy is bad now, but that's embarrassing. We're near the poverty line here. If my rent weren't covered I'd basically be broke. I'm very thankful for the housing situation, the Brooks running gear and shoes, the plane flights, fancy dinners, and hotels...but when you're getting a $300-400 paycheck every two weeks it's hard to scrape by. There aren't enough racing opportunities that you can engage yourself in since the schedule is set up mainly for training. I want to race just to make more money. I love the excitement, the exposure, the opportunity to meet like-minded runners from all over the country and around the world! I mean, paying about $350 a month in student loans, $100 for house utilities, Internet, and hot water, $85 a month for car insurance, and $75 in gasoline for commuting to work adds up quickly. The rest of my paycheck is left for food, and I'm trying to eat healthy so that doesn't mean buying the cheapest shit in the world. Not to mention, since I'm knocking back 18 mile days regularly, I probably eat twice as much as a normal, frugal person. So you can run out of cash real fast if you aren't careful. The good thing is at least I can be selfish and only care for myself. This is the best time in my life, and just like in college, I really only have to worry about covering my own ass. I am not totally naïve, and I feel fortunate to embrace this level of support. I realize that my few responsibilities and financial woes pale in comparison to most others struggling to get by in the real world.

The opportunity cost of spending time focusing on running can essentially be compared to working an additional 15-20 hours at a higher paying, full-time job. Financially that would be great. I see tremendous value in gaining additional work experience, meeting other college graduates, and going to happy hour. However, the energy cost of working that much and running 120 to 140 miles a week seems unbearable. I know there are few out there that can pull it off, but I don't see that as being enjoyable or practical for me at this stage in life. I feel like if you are truly dedicated to something you should pursue it whole-heartedly, and I think the sacrifice of working and running as both full-time endeavors would be short changing one over the other. Balance is key though, and one day perhaps I can actually work full-time and still run a more modest amount of 70-80 miles per week. Will that result in more happiness and fulfillment? Maybe. But of course there are several other powerful influences besides financial stability that can help you achieve success, happiness, and satisfaction. Here I'm talking about close relationships, more specifically the importance of having a significant other.

There is an unwritten aspect of the newest Hansons contract that was never formally presented to me by the coaching staff. It regarded relations between members of the men's and women's teams. Like some businesses, intra-team (or intra-office) dating is frowned upon by the administration. This may be a problem for me.

Traditionally, I have only dated running girls. Now perhaps I shouldn't judge, and maybe I shouldn't be so shallow. However, something is sparked inside of me when a fit, athletic female is competing fiercely in something that I am so passionate about. Much like the phenomenon of beer goggles, I admit to having speed goggles influence my perception of the ideal mate. So yes, that means the faster a girl runs, the more likely I am going to overlook other attributes that might not be so desirable to me. Much like women who have a height standard or income bracket preference in men they date, I have some preconceived time standards. For example, in college a sub-10:00 3k or a sub-17:00 5k earned major bonus points. Of course these standards aren't set in stone because other things such as, oh, personality also played a role in whether or not she would be compatible.

As some may be astounded by this admission, let me first clarify that I believe it is perfectly natural to be attracted to a member of the opposite sex that has demonstrated exceptional ability in an outlet that instinctively may have been essential to survival and the production of healthy offspring. Faster runners are usually equipped with strong hearts, efficient respiratory systems, well-toned muscles, low cholesterol, and generally more symmetrical bodies. How can you argue against that?

Perhaps my own insecurities of not being the smartest or best-looking kid in the class are now finally being reflected on how I judge which types of female I like to pursue? I guess I've become trapped into believing that my self-worth is attached to my running performances. In this cruel, quantitative world (and especially the competitive world of distance running), one measure of your value as an athlete to your team or coaches is directly attached to the minutes and seconds that it takes you to run a certain number of miles or kilometers. The clock never lies. You can be compared directly; you can be cut from the team or carried on their shoulders as a hero.

Shortly after the formation of the Hansons women's team, there was an incident that resulted in the dismissal of two athletes from the program. These two athletes, Nick Cordes and Leigh Daniels, were both very attractive (and fast) runners who happened to fall in love during their time together in Michigan. Dating between the two teams was forbidden, and the consequences were well known; however, the heart (and also perhaps some hormones) tend to be irrational. Clint recalls the guy's initial reactions to the Brooks sponsored women's team:

> "The day they told us they were going to start the women's team…all the single, 24 year old guys on the team were excited. However, Keith then mentioned that there would be no inter-squad dating, you had to sign a form saying you understood the policy and that it was grounds for dismissal."

The policy was strict, and the consequences were going to be enforced. Clint outlined some of the rules:

> "You are not to be at the same social engagement if

a coach isn't present…you are not to share rides to
the airport without a coach present…there can't be
a member of the women's and men's team together
without a coach present."

Keith and Kevin sensed there might be some inter-
mingling. Finally, it was observed that Nick and Leigh
had crossed the line, and they were told to leave. Former
teammates recall how it all went down:

> "Leigh showed up to run one day, instead she was
> questioned about where she had gone over the
> weekend…and she just admitted that she had gone
> with Nick to his parent's house."

Despite Leigh being a multiple NCAA champion
talent, and despite the fact that Nick had qualified for the
Olympic Trials and run a 1:05 half marathon while in the
program, both athletes were promptly told to leave. Kevin
and Keith stuck to their policy. Clint looks back on the whole
saga and mentions that the drama of the incident "…almost
tore the team apart."

Fortunately, the relationship withstood the test of
leaving the program, as Leigh and Nick were happily married
in 2009. In fact, the couple won an appearance on the *Today
Show*, as a featured wedding. The two currently reside in Ohio
where they work as coaches.

As the days go by and I remain single, isolated out in
Rochester, MI, I reminisce about my college days and how
the whole college lifestyle was set up so perfectly to meet
girls (if you are in college now, appreciate it!). I knew in my
fifth year how good I had it. I really didn't want to leave
Cornell. There were intelligent, athletic, interesting females
around my age everywhere. Go to the Starbucks in college
town and it was almost all preppy students; go to a Starbucks
here and there are a bunch of people two decades older than

me who don't know the difference between a grande and a venti (not that there is anything wrong with that as I am a total "wannabe yuppie" for even going to Starbucks and writing about such things). Furthermore, the general political spectrum has shifted considerably and I feel that many of the females in the Rochester area don't carry similar enough ideals as I when it comes to religion, diet, and politics.

On my recruiting trip out to Hansons (and in several published articles about the Project), the lifestyle out here is described as "like college, but without the homework!" That's not really true at all! The only thing that I find similar out here to my college running experience is that I still train with a team and I still live in a dilapidated, old house with a bunch of smelly running gear. That's about where the comparisons end for me.

Unlike the rest of the world, I feel like we are isolated to a solitary lifestyle of boring predictability and extreme physical fatigue. All the days blur together in a confusing continuum so that I often lose track of what day of the week it is. There is so much consistency it is mind-numbing. Nick Arciniaga summed up the routine well by saying, "Time goes by faster here." You are dispersed from reality and sheltered from the real world living this kind of lifestyle.

At Cornell we didn't have to run in the morning at all (this is probably different from most college teams). If I doubled, I did it on my own time at say, 11 AM between classes. We had a mandatory afternoon practice on weekdays, and at least one weekend day was on your own. Here at Hansons, the majority of the miles are put in before 9 AM, and often weekend days require earlier start-times of 7. That totally kills any opportunity of social life fun and going out on Friday and Saturday nights (not that we'd even do that more than once a month)! Perhaps the biggest nuisance of being in the program for me: not having a single day during the 7-day week to sleep in past 7:30 and rest up. I still have a lot of trouble going to bed early at 10 PM to try to get enough sleep. I'm still hardwired like a teen who wants to stay up well past midnight and sleep in until 10.

However, despite the early morning runs on the weekends, we still manage to go out once in a while. I'd feel horrible if I spent all of my early twenties never going to the bar! Sometimes you just have to get out just to remember what it was like to be a normal person. Just to dance and flirt with some young, attractive women while intoxicated. For some it's going to be the only thing that keeps you sane. It isn't natural to be cooped up in a box totally consumed with running and recovery every minute of the day. It is essential in the development of the psyche to sometimes break routine and experience something new and exciting.

Being here is like being rich, but (at times) unhappy and unsatisfied. The freedoms and liberties that you sacrifice for the whole of the program are conflicting. I am torn between the opportunity cost of securing a career in life, making a steady income, dating more girls, and enjoying other things too. I love running, I like my life to be about running, but when I see how my other teammates have different, more obsessive perceptions with running I feel unsatisfied. What I want to accomplish in life outside of running before I am 30 requires different priorities. Why can't I be the 2:15 marathoner who also works a real job full-time. How am I ever going to be able to financially support kids at this rate?

In retrospect I wish the program were based out of Ann Arbor (or somewhere warm like California!). There would be a lot more interesting college girls to meet. I don't mean to vent and complain too much, but being single in the program is tough. It's like I've regressed and become retarded in social development, and everything that went down in college has gone out the door…everything except for the running…

Perks of the Program

For a 2:20 marathoner or 29:30 10k runner coming out of college, there are limited funds and opportunities available to run post-collegiately. Shoe sponsors won't fully pick you up with an individual contract. Fortunately for us at Hansons-Brooks, there is substantial financial support in terms of paid rent, gear, and Brooks time bonuses.

Coming from college I paid $400 to $500 month to share a dilapidated house with seven teammates at the old track house. Rent was overpriced (for such poor housing) in the college town of Ithaca because demand was so high. Such is the financial drain of college. Here in Michigan, living at the Bloomer house or Driftwood house is comparable, but I'm not paying that amount of money each month. This a huge advantage to being in the program and something that I can really appreciate.

Thanks to Brooks, our gear sponsorship includes enough product for me to get two pairs of shoes a month if I so desired. I mostly decide to get training shoes like the Brooks Adrenaline, Defyance, or Ghost. The rest of my shoe money goes towards racing shoes. I'll indulge in 3 to 4 pairs of the lightweight Brooks Green Silence, which I have used in most of my workouts and half marathon to marathon races. I've also received some T7 Racers from Brooks as an early gift, and used the Brooks Wire distance track spike to race cross country and do workouts on the grass. Bi-annually Brooks also gives us a kit – one for the fall and one for the spring. In these kits we usually receive a long-sleeve Equilibrium shirt, a pair or two of shorts (or long running pants like the Spartan II pant in the fall), a new racing singlet with shorts, an Infiniti half-zip warm-up top, and a nice jacket (such as the Utopia Shell or the LSD Lite Jacket). Kevin and Keith have the Hansons-Brooks ODP logo printed on them for us. Sometimes we get several Brooks t-shirts as well, which have some pretty unique graphics on them. I now have enough gear and Brooks clothing to wear that I can go two weeks without doing laundry and still have something clean. If we go out to the movies on a weekend or go to a restaurant for dinner we always support our sponsorship brand by wearing Brooks gear. I'm proud to represent a company that makes high quality running shoes and apparel, especially because they have been a leader in sustainability and green design.

When it comes time to really make some dough on the roads, Brooks and the Hansons offer some extra incentives. Keith and Kevin treat you to some nice meals before most races, especially if the race doesn't give out food stipends. Obviously the faster you run the better, as Brooks has offered us a time bonus structure with cash incentives that usually pay more than what you'd get just from placing well in a race. For example, a sub-1:05:30 half marathon earns you a $2000 check at the end of the calendar year; a sub-1:04:30 moves the earnings up to $3000, and a sub-2:15 marathon gets you $4000. There are some higher bonuses the faster you run, culminating with the 6-figure guarantee bonus with a sub-28:00 10k or sub-2:11 marathon. Furthermore, in some races (such as the Disney Half Marathon) Brooks pays you just for placing in the top 5 overall. This was a great deal for me as a race like Disney doesn't have any open prize money. The support from these time and place bonuses from Brooks is a huge benefit to being in the program as is the support from Keith and Kevin. Not only am I motivated to race well to earn that money, but I also want to help expose the Hansons Distance Project and the Brooks brand because they have put faith in me and allowed me to develop as a runner through their sponsorship.

It sounds cliché, but being a professional runner really is a dream come true for me. I feel very fortunate to actually make enough money and receive such generosity and support to actually make a living running. I never thought that that would be financially possible. It is a simple life that involves some sacrifices, but without Brooks and Kevin and Keith Hanson, I probably would've given up on the dream a long time ago.

We Don't Need Any Heroes Today
November 17th, 2009

"Last one, fast one!" This is the motto that the guys like to throw around here when you are starting the last repeat of a workout. It is a motto that Keith and Kevin aren't fond of.

"We don't need any heroes today," Kevin instructs Paul and I as we accelerate into our 5th and final 1600m repeat at the Stoney Creek High School track. Our pace was supposed to be 4:50 per 1600m for this workout, but as typical with the Hansons athlete mentality that translates to the slowest pace that you want to hit. We made sure all our 1600s were actually under 4:50. So 4:49 to 4:45. However, going too fast and kicking it in on the last one (or any repeats for that matter) is frowned upon by the coaching staff. The pace is the pace you are supposed to run; faster or slower is wrong. In college and high school I loved to rip the last rep and finish like it was the last lap of a race. My teammates and I would itch to demonstrate to each other who had the most left in the tank, who was to be feared on race day. On some teams it is a measuring stick or a way for older, more experienced runners to put the younger, cocky teammates in their place. However, on this cold and windy Tuesday morning I was glad that Paul was leading us through an even string of 71-second to 72-second lap splits. On the first 4 reps of the workout we had hit 4:45, 4:49, 4:48, 4:46. Put that in the context of a 120-mile week and an easy run that got down to 5:40 pace, and I was feeling pretty decent about my fitness. The 800m jog between each rep gave us a good 3:30 to 4:00 minutes between each hard effort...plenty of time for my breathing to return to normal.

As usual my legs were stiff and there was the burn of lactic acid. I cleared my throat and gulped in some fresh oxygen as we rounded the 2nd turn and confronted the inevitable backstretch headwind. The workout was manageable enough, no need to brace myself for real race effort pain yet. Luckily there was no ice on the track, as we were wearing the Brooks T6 racing flats instead of spikes. I figured that since I am training for road races in the T6 I might as well break them in on these faster, track workouts. The wind chill was under 30 degrees and I decided to put a second layer long-sleeve Brooks Equilibrium running shirt back on as the workout progressed. Despite the chill, we ran the workout in shorts.

In college, during my best 5 by 1600m workout I averaged 4:42. Today, I am slower, but I am not worried. Running faster for the sake of beating my college times was not the goal of the day's workout. Unlike in college and high school, I haven't been doing any 400s or any other traditional speed work. Grinding out 12-14 mile morning runs at near 6:00 mile pace has taken its toll on my exhausted muscle fibers, but I'm thinking that each steady mile is like money in the bank for the marathon. I want to be strong as hell!

It Happens: Rock 'n' Roll Las Vegas Half Marathon
December 6th, 2009

My first significant test as a Hansons-Brooks athlete occurred in a city that never sleeps. I viewed this event as an indicator that would tell me whether or not I was going to be worthy of having elite status at Boston in the spring. I also wanted to see if I was deserving enough to wear the Hansons elite racing singlet and proudly represent Brooks. Finally, I wanted to make sure that I was adapting well to this whole post-collegiate running thing. I failed miserably on all accounts...

"It happens!" Fernando Cabada says, looking at me intensely.

"It happens, bro," he exclaims. It is about 11 hours after the Las Vegas Rock 'n' Roll Half Marathon and we are ready for a night out in Sin City. I had chugged some soda, a grande Starbucks coffee, and some chocolate covered coffee beans to appear more awake and alert. Fail. I pour some Visine into my blood shot eyes…there, looking much better now.

Fernando is tall, dark, and slender. He still holds the American 25k US road record, and was the US Champion in that event the previous year, as well as the US marathon champion in 2008. He ran his debut marathon in 2:12 in Fukuoka, Japan, and ever since those successes he has been plagued with sub-par performances. It happens. Distance running is a fickle sport, and one season you may be at the top of your game, only to find yourself struggling or hurt the very next year. Fernando was in a bit of a slump, but his brashness and openness on the LetsRun.com message boards, as well as the Internet training videos he posted, made him more respected in my book. I knew who he was because he had such a web presence, was open and honest with his opinions, and of course because of his speed.

At dinner that night in the elite athlete suite he was nice enough to introduce himself to me. I don't feel like I belong in the same room as such fast company - especially after today's disastrous performance in the half marathon.

In a field with several notable Kenyans and Ethiopians (but also containing some Americans whose names I didn't even recognize), I placed a dismal 15th. Even worse was my embarrassingly slow (for Hansons standards) finishing time of 1:07:51. Wearing the bright orange/red/yellow Hansons-Brooks singlet and running such a lethargic pace is an insult to what the program stands for and all previous runners who proudly have displayed their speed and guts with more respectable, much faster times. What the fuck am I doing? I'm supposed to be an elite American distance runner and I can't even hold the marathon winner's pace for the half?

Fernando finished a competitive 5th place overall, and was the top American in 1:04:56. It was the last place to earn any prize money (which is a feat that has still eluded me). I was told by Keith and Kevin to run my pace and go out at 5-flat per mile, which would've landed me a respectable 1:05:33. Well, I did go out right at 5 flat, and it never felt so fast! Looking back at the race, maybe I am losing it mentally? Maybe my iron shot down over the last couple of weeks? Maybe weighing 155 lbs instead of my usual 152 is killing my times? Maybe the mold and dust in the Driftwood house has aggravated my asthma? Too many questions. Too many variables. Whatever. I'm upset. It happens.

In the very same race, Desiree Davila, our Hansons female phenom, runs a 1:12 for 2nd (1st American) about 1:30 behind World Cross Country medalist Werknesh Kidane. Contrast with my performance: I seriously was dying so bad during the race that I glanced back behind to see if she was gunning me down. I just wanted to forget this race, take a break, regroup, and come back for vengeance later. First, it was time for some post-race fun though!

* * *

"You got your pimpin' clothes on?" Cabada eyes me as I walk into his hotel room wearing some cheap, faded jeans, a wrinkled dress shirt, and some Sperry Top-Siders. I felt a little under-dressed for the high rolling-styles of Vegas. Cabada had some shiny black dress shoes on and a matching sport coat as part of his ensemble. I suddenly wished I had pulled a suit from the dry cleaners.

Earlier in the evening we had walked over to a local CVS and purchased a 15-pack of Coronas to split with a guy from Team Indiana Elite. We planned our assault on the strip: we were going to the hot clubs, and we were going to get crunk!

Now, later in the night we decided a pregame in the hotel was a good choice to get the night rolling. So in Cabada's room the three of us regrouped. A 2:13 marathoner and ex-Hansons runner Justin Young and his wife soon came out to hang with all of us, ready to grab a couple drinks before our journey through the strip. We headed down to the Hard Rock Hotel lobby, where we met at the bar for more drinks on the house (i.e., Competitor.com), courtesy of our elite athlete status. Soon a small group of us elites, including some Russian women, some other Americans and their respective agents, were gathered around waiting for our adventure to begin!

Our hospitality group conveniently set us up with a van and driver that promptly pulled up outside the hotel. We piled in to full capacity (like how those vans usually are filled), our destination none other than the Coyote Ugly bar that attempted to fulfill its reputation from the namesake movie.

At the Ugly we found more free drinks, some scantily clad women, and water and beer spraying in the air; what more could a man want, really? Well, apparently more:

Cabada wasn't satisfied. Come to think of it, I really wasn't either! I was actually looking for a new scene, so we decided that we'd up and go for some more craziness on the strip. We abandoned the rest of the group and tore out of the club on a mission.

"Shit, man, I really gotta piss!" Cabada says while looking over his shoulder, and then walks over to a tree lining the sidewalk. It is surprisingly chilly out on the street, and my "beer blanket" isn't keeping me warm. After the pit stop we start running for some reason (drunk runners tend to do that!), and the heat generated from such effort made me feel better. We were caught up in the excitement and the bright lights, with all the other drunken idiots looking for "hot" clubs.

Totally lost, we stumbled upon the shooting fountains of the Bellagio Hotel, which was quite the sight. Cabada was intrigued, so we wandered in looking for a fresh scene. Upon entering the Bellagio we were directed to a "hot" club called The Bank. A line of fashionably dressed, mid-30s types were waiting outside the door.

"This place has a $40 cover! Fuck!" Cabada shouts. He reasons that we can pay it anyway. I think twice about opening up my wallet. I'm definitely under-dressed here; people are wearing tuxes. In a last effort of desperation, we get to the front of the line and display the stamps on our arms from Coyote Ugly. The gate opens for us! We are in for free. Score! This definitely is not supposed to be a cheap place to get into…but we pulled it off.

Feeling rich from saving dough on the cover, we unload our wads of green promptly for some $8 bottles of beer. We walk around The Bank, eyeing the floor for hot girls dancing, like most guys creepily do. The scene is definitely different, but not really in a good way for me. I feel like I'm the youngest person there! Lights outline the edges of the dance floor and sparkle against hand railings, table edges, and steps. The Team Indiana guy gets out on the dance floor and is promptly shut down by a group of rather attractive women.

We drink more and take in the scene. "Aren't you going to try and dance, bro?" Cabada asks, eyeing me suspiciously. I mean, we got into this fancy club and I'm just feeling tired and out of place.

"Um, yeah." I get out and bust a couple moves on the floor briefly. I have to be quite drunk to "dance." The women around me appear to be in their 30s, almost cougars but not quite. We decide to leave and try to find the rest of our group of elites back at Coyote Ugly.

Eventually the night ends at another bar with the whole gang of us dancing and singing in a very crowded, hot, stinky group. Cabada disappears into the crowd, and I don't see him for the rest of the night. We are picked up by our special shuttle and transported back to the hotel. One of the elites throws up in the parking lot. An elite Russian woman comments on how she thinks that us American runners are crazy and can't hold their liquor. I retire to my hotel room not feeling so good myself, but I am content enough with my first experience seeing some of the Vegas nightlife.

Mike at Cal International Marathon
December 2009

"I was probably a little too aggressive. It kind of blew up in my face the last couple of miles…I wouldn't do it any other way."

That quote from Mike Morgan made the front page Quote of the Day on LetsRun.com. It accurately summarized how the California International Marathon played out for Mike. After leading a blistering 2:12 pace through the half, Mike found himself all alone, breaking the cold wind at the front of the race. For 23 miles he ran solo, skipping his water bottles that were on fluid stations positioned on the outside of curves so he could run the tangents. Eventually the lack of drinking, the early leading, the cold weather, and the ambitious pace caught up to him. A pack, consisting of an Ethiopian, a Kenyan, and the American 50k record holder Josh Cox, caught and passed him. Cox went on to run a PR of 2:13:51, after several years of struggling with the marathon distance. Cox is well known for being on *The Bachelorette* television show, being a running model on the cover of *Runner's World*, starring in old PowerBar ads, and recently setting the American record at 50k on the roads. He ran a better race then Mike did today, and his time demonstrated that he is still a force to be reckoned with for the next Olympic Trials. Tesfaye Bekele of Ethiopia won the race in 2:13:42.

Keith, who was with us in Las Vegas, got updates via cell phone during the race from Kevin who was out on the course in California. When he heard that Mike had been caught and passed, he threw his phone down on the floor of our rental car. Desi and I sat quietly in the back; we were still recovering from the Las Vegas Rock 'n' Roll Half Marathon. I think everyone was a little frustrated that Mike failed to set a marathon PR. He had had such a strong training segment leading up to the race that everyone was thinking he could pop a 2:13 or so…it just wasn't in the cards.

Pushing the Envelope

Witnessing my teammates set high standards for themselves, and then going about doggedly pursuing them, is motivating. We all have pie-in-the-sky goals at times, and in reality we inevitably set ourselves up for failure in this regard. But isn't pushing the envelope and seeking to attain that seemingly impossible dream the reason why we work so hard in life?

Going into Boston in the spring, I am cautious in making bold statements about how fast I think I can run. Like most obsessive runners, I tend to be critical of myself; I expect my teammates to be openly critical of me:

The other day I came back from a slam of Mike's by admitting to my large, fat-ass size, but also pointing out my strength…(and his weakness): "I have big-bones, I'm strong, and so at least I don't get stress fractures…I've never been hurt."

Mike came back with a statement that made me think, made me feel like a sissy again: "Well, that means you haven't been training hard enough yet!" I thought back to something that Snick mentioned about the "myth" of overtraining. It is really only overtraining if you are doing more than your body is prepared to handle at the time. For Snick maybe that was three months instead of two months of 140 mile weeks; for Brian that was more than 160 miles a week…most of my college teammates would be overtrained running the volume and intensity that I am now, but in the spectrum of the Hansons program I've done (and have been doing) diddly squat.

But why? Why are we doing this shit? Putting our bodies through the wringer, risking overuse injuries and stress fractures? When most guys want to get big and buff lifting weights in the gym we intentionally try to stay lightweight, skinny, and sickly looking. When I go home and my mom comments how my cheekbones are sunken in I take it as a compliment!

I think that for most of us we do this simply because we have a passion for running, and we are fortunate enough to be given an opportunity to pursue it. We may be a little obsessed and crazy about running; we may have a compulsive attachment to it where it has become fused into our identity. Like a drug addict looking for his next fix, perhaps we are simply addicted to the high it all brings. I know personally that running has brought me so much satisfaction in life that I like to think that I am capitalizing on what my body was built to do. I may or may not have been given a unique gift, but for some reason running long distances has proven to be something I can do relatively well…something quantifiable that allowed me to travel to international destinations, and garner attention that I couldn't attract in any other aspect of my life. Sage "the Runner" is what I am known as to relatives, family friends, and old classmates. No other label. It has become an essential part of who I am.

Am I training for the Olympics? Yes and no. I think as children competing in sports we all have dreams of making it big, playing on the professional level and representing our country in the Olympic Games. Making an Olympic team could be the ultimate goal and dream of many of the guys in the program. That's how it was for Brian, and that's why he did this shit. But what about all of us that fall short of that goal? Are we failures? The Hansons-Brooks "ODP" stands for Olympic Development Project, and the ultimate focus was to not only revitalize American distance running, but to have runners (Americans!) compete on a world stage. We've had many team members make US national squads, and we've had an Olympian (and potential for more!).

When I entered the program, I told Keith and Kevin that my ultimate goal in running would be to at least run under 2:15 for the marathon. I didn't say by how much because I didn't want to limit myself, however I tried to be realistic with myself and I'm not sure if I can crack 2:15 by much (if at all). To them it was good enough, I guess, as they let me join. They didn't say I couldn't make an Olympic team, but in the back of my mind I know the chances of that happening are slim to none at this point. I can't say that is true for most of the guys currently on the team now. I think for most guys the point of being here, of busting your ass and running 140 miles a week, is to actually make the Olympic team. But if not, then at least giving it a run for all your worth. Of course I want to maximize my potential, to suck every second out of my body and pound the life out of my legs. I want to wear that US jersey in at least something (it may be the 50k trail run for all I know). I love the marathon, I want to be at least top 20 in the country at the event - however, to be top 3 is going to require perhaps more talent than I possess. At least that's what I believe. Maybe I'm limiting myself too much? Perhaps I am afraid of failure, of falling short? Whatever. I'm all for dreaming about the impossible, rooting for the underdog, and believing that hard work can conquer many deficits. It's just at this point in my life, in my running career I'm going to be protecting myself with back-up plans, things to fall back on in case running doesn't work out as well as imagined. It is the conservative way to live and train. Some would say it's the more cowardly way to live, train, and race. But such attitudes (however negative at times) are my convictions, my perception of what reality is, and how I want to live my life.

For teammates like Mike, Luke, Chad, Drew, and Desi, making an Olympic team is definitely more realistic. One would say that for Desi it is something very, very attainable, whereas the other guys would still be a long-shot, but not out of the question. Mike was 12th at the last Olympic Trials. Going into Houston in 2012 if he is in sub-2:12 shape he could sneak into the top 3 quite realistically. Chad made his runs at the Olympic teams back on the track in 2000 and 2004 where he was in the mix with the lead pack; a mere 400m separating him from a berth to the games…he was 8th.

So back to the question: Why? Well, why would you try hard at anything in life? Why would you play the guitar if you weren't ever going to be a rockstar millionaire? The simple answer is you do it because you love it. You have a passion for it, you find meaning in it, and you are curious as to what you can accomplish in it. Yeah, maybe there are some financial motives, some satisfaction of bragging rights to friends and family, but when push comes to shove the real motivation to pursue anything whole-heartedly has to come from within. It is the internal drive inside that beckons you out the door everyday, to push one mile, one step, further. Faster and faster. You need to see and feel that progression and change in your life; you have an instinctual desire to improve your "skills" in something that may help you survive. But in this day and age, if you have a choice with what you do in your free time and what you do for work, how would you make a living? Wouldn't you choose to do something you love for as long as you can if you were able to scrape by financially? That's what I feel like I'm doing here.

Team Morale is down in the Winter
Start of Winter 2009

"Don't enter the program in the winter. Team morale is down in the winter…you'll probably become an alcoholic within 3 months of being there," an ex-Hansons runner once warned me of the challenges that occur with changing of the seasons and the resulting effects that pressure the lifestyle of a runner in Michigan during the cold months. The weather and external stresses have a way of altering one's mood and perception. Perhaps seasonal affective disorder is more potent here? I find myself still wondering about my place in the world, as a new graduate who is adjusting to something not quite like the real world, but still a post-collegiate life nonetheless.

A depressing difference between being in school and running versus being in the Hansons as a young bachelor is the fact that now I feel as though I have no other outlet in my life but running. In college our coach used to explain to us that we had three main aspects of our life to focus on: academics, athletics, and a social life. Social life would be something like having a girlfriend and going out and partying with friends outside the team. Out of those three, you could really only excel at two simultaneously. He'd say, "And you know which two to really focus on…" I've found that this balancing law of averages was usually quite consistent during my college years. At times I was occasionally batting three out of three, and during brief slumps I was zero for three… however, within a short period of time things tipped back so that I was excelling in one or two of those major aspects of college life.

Here at Hansons I feel like I don't have that. As a single guy I have no significant other wishing me luck or consoling me when I feel like shit (now) on cold winter nights. This is my bland social life: I mean, come on, now! When you are in bed by 10 every night and work most weekends while running in excess of 120 miles per week, there's not a whole lot of partying, networking, or variation in life to meet new, exciting, and interesting people. Not much travel, aside from races that we do very infrequently. I'm always stuck in the same running niche, the same routine, the same numbing mindset. So no social life outside of teammates. In college there were a lot more things going on, a weekend party to look forward to at least. Classes that stimulated your mind and your perceptions on life and what the bright future holds. There used to be intelligent discussions with fellow classmates about careers and philosophy. There were always the bars every weekend (and some weeknights) packed with young co-eds who'd show up hung-over to class on Monday. Not that I went out and partied a whole lot in college, but there was the once in a month occasion where we'd really go to the well and drink hard. I remember having that extra spring in my step, heading out the door for a date with a new college girl. It is a lot different now.

In college academics and academic success largely determined one's outlook on life. An A on a recent test or paper provided marginal satisfaction and stimulated positive learning experiences that made up for events like a sub-par race or a time-consuming, impossible problem set in another class. In Michigan now, I flew back from the wild lights of Vegas upset with my half-marathon performance. I arrived back at the stinky Driftwood house where I was instantly surrounded by an over-powering, love-hate relationship with running and everything that revolves around it. I will rise tomorrow (barring death or some severe injury/illness) at 6:45 and run off into the cold, dark snow with my housemates to meet at the duck pond. Then I will be working a solo shift in the running store, surrounded by hundreds of running shoes and running apparel. Repeat day in and day out. If running is my life here, and if running is not going well, then it feels like nothing in my life is going well.

Wow! That sounds really bad. I chose to come out here to see how good of a runner I could be. I've made some sacrifices, some leaps of faith. It was once a dream; now it's true in a slightly twisted version:

I have actually have regressed in distance running…

The Store

Disclaimer: The following section contains my opinions and perceptions (however biased) of what one may find in a specialty running store. The following is not meant to be presented as fact, and the inevitable generalizations and possible exaggerations of my viewpoints should be viewed lightly with a sense of humor.

Before I left for Hansons, my Dad (the optimist) told me that working in a running shoe store would be perfect because the majority of my customers would be young, hot, female runners. He was wrong.

Now, I had worked at a specialty shoe running store before, when I had a summer gig at the Finger Lakes Running Company, a local shop in the small college town of Ithaca, NY. There were serious runners and college-aged customers that came into the store, as well as people that were generally active. Such was the liberal-minded, outdoor culture of Ithaca.

In the metro Detroit area the customer base is a lot larger, and the demographics are quite different. The customer's expectations are high, as the locals pride themselves on an ideal of "American business" that goes above and beyond making a simple sale on a product. As mentioned in the earlier section titled "The Area," Michiganders generally love to talk and they seem to love the idea that a shoe salesman should be as savvy as a car salesman. I hate feeling like a sleazy, used car salesman, but working in the store makes me feel like that. Customers prod for mileage figures, ask for model numbers, manufacturing information, and then weigh in on their decision to purchase a pair of shoes or not. They come in to "just browse" and to "start the research process," long and arduous as it is for some. They expect to bring a shoe back that they have scuffed on pavement for a full refund (something against store policy).

Like many proud, patriotic Americans in a tough economy they are sometimes disgusted at any foreign sounding brand names like Mizuno. They demand something made in America, by Americans. However, to their dismay they unfortunately hear from me that in fact all the shoes in the store (save for some parts of New Balance) are totally assembled in some Asian country such as China! Furthermore, they often seem to confuse a brand name as being synonymous with a specific model (i.e., thinking there is only one shoe called Asics). They often mispronounce such brand names as well. For example, a common pronunciation of the iconic brand Nike is as if it rhymes with "bike." I'm from Niketown, Oregon, and I have never heard such a pronunciation. Usually Asics is referred to as "Basics" or "the Oasis" or "Oasics." Okay, that's understandable. Most of the customers around here aren't what LetsRun.com message boarders would refer to as "hobby joggers." Rather, they are a mix of blue-collar, out-of-shape individuals striving to improve themselves through exercise. I applaud them for that effort of self-improvement, as long as they aren't racist or rude or short with me when I assist them in picking out a shoe. One of the most fulfilling aspects of being a shoes salesman is remembering that you're helping people improve their health, fitness, and well-being by enabling them to exercise in quality running shoes. Few customers know about the Hansons-Brooks Distance Project, and many ask if I am also a runner? They then often ask what local high school I go to (I do look young for my age, so you can't argue with that!).

To stereotype, there are essentially five main categories of people that make up the bulk of Hansons Running Shop customers. I'm sure that a lot of running stores across the country are similar in this regard, although the degrees to which personalities of customers (and their temperaments) vary is probably specific to the region of the country. Michigan may be considered part of the Midwest region geographically, but I have come to speculate that real Michiganders are a unique breed of their own. While it may not be fair to stereotype and categorize customers into the following five types, I've found that identifying and defining specific market segments is an effective strategy in retail sales. For example, it seems that as a salesman is it best to cater to the desires and needs of each customer type accordingly, realizing that each individual sale is a transaction not of mere monetary gains, but also a transaction of trust, loyalty, and satisfaction, aided by appealing to the customer's respective differences in personality and life experiences. People have different expectations, and some seem to be seeking confirmation and assurance when making a purchase with their hard-earned money. I would be too - especially if I was spending over a hundred bucks on an unfamiliar product.

The first main type of customer is the middle-aged woman who is looking to lose a few pounds. She has had a couple of kids, and she sometimes will bring them into the store with her during the early afternoon. The kids run around the store and knock over shoes. Babies cry as Mom takes her time trying on multiple pairs of shoes. This type of customer is usually already a runner, and perhaps they are training for their first marathon or half marathon. They generally are very picky about the color of the shoes they are trying on, and find that there are little irritating bumps or some nuances that feel weird on their foot no matter which shoe or brand they have on. Usually they insist that they wear a size 7, when in fact they need a size 9 or 10 extra wide. One of the Brooks Adrenaline series easily fits the bill for this customer, as it is a shoe that we carry in a wide variety of widths. Furthermore, the stability of the Adrenaline is usually essential in supporting this type of customer (who more than likely over-pronates).

The second main type of customer in Hansons Running Shop is a senior citizen who has bunions, plantar fasciitis, heel spurs, and/or hammer toes and needs a shoe for walking. They are usually very cranky when they come in the store because they are in pain and seeing all the brightly colored running shoes out on display is often upsetting to them. Usually the Brooks Addiction Walker is a perfect type of shoe for this customer, especially if they insist on a plain-colored walking shoe with a full-leather upper. As long as we have them stocked in their size and extra wide widths, these customers are usually easy to satisfy (even if they grumble about the $100 price).

The third main type of customer at Hansons is what I like to call a "Stroke." The Stroke is usually a middle-aged man who is somewhat financially well-off and also fairly active. He often comes in wearing sunglasses with his chest thrust forward and high. Often, he is both a runner and a triathlete, and he lets you know that right away. He is usually obsessed with the latest running trends like minimalist running shoes and Vibram Five Fingers, and he usually will start telling you about the book *Born to Run* and a guy named Dean Karnazes. He is slightly self-absorbed, sometimes a little arrogant, and assumes that he knows more about running than you do. The Stroke usually likes to look at all the newest and best Garmins and models of racing shoes. He usually spends a prolonged amount of time in the store because he loves to brag about his racing exploits. The Stroke can be a great customer because he is often a frequent shopper and is loyal to the identity of the store.

One time I had one of these Strokes proudly tell me how he illegally cut ahead of his slower starting corral so he could "sprint out with the elites" at the very front line. It happened to be a race that I participated in. I thought to myself, "So these are the kinds of people that you see getting in your way the first 100m, crowding you out for a good position at the start so they can be ahead in their moment of glory for 20 seconds and then fade to their much slower average mile pace…" Kip Litton would qualify as a Stroke, as would anyone who finagles his or her way into the Boston Marathon! Strokes will usually at least purchase some Gu, but not until they tell you that the marathon is too easy for them, so they moved up to the Ironman. They might test your prowess in running by asking you whether or not you have qualified for Boston, and if so, how many times. Brian was particularly annoyed with the Strokes, especially since they would give him advice on how to run the Boston marathon, and tell him "what it took" to be competitive in such a race (these people had no idea that they were talking to a 2:10 marathoner that got 4th at Boston). Brian would put up with them though, and he would never put them in their place by mentioning that he was actually an Olympian!

The fourth main type of customer is the first-time, working class runner. Usually these people start shopping for shoes just after New Years or in the early spring. They are often not at their desired weight and realize that it is time to get serious about exercising. The first-time, working class runner often hasn't purchased a pair of athletic shoes that cost over $100, and the shock value of finding out the price tag sometimes scares them away. I take these individuals through the entire fitting process by looking at their feet, watching them walk, and learning about their aches and pains. They usually respond well to such attention and customized fitting recommendations. Good for them.

The last main type of Hansons Running Shop customers is the student-athlete. These are usually local high school students that need spikes or trainers for cross country and track. They are easy to work with, and asking them about their season reminds me of when I started running in those nostalgic glory days of dual meets and state championships. Usually the student-athlete has a parent along with them who is clueless about running and just makes things complicated. The parent sometimes argues about the price, demands the kids wear a certain size, or gets picky about which shoes bring out school colors. Collegiate student athletes are the best to work with because they usually don't have a parent with them and they know what they want.

Of course, there are those few customers that don't exactly fit into these customer types and some that may overlap into several of the general categories. These people are usually the easiest people to talk with: people who are well-mannered (like yourself), or regulars that always wear the same shoe. There are even those few, other serious runners that have perhaps worked in a shoe store as well! I am grateful when people like you walk in.

While most of the Hansons athletes work in the stores part-time, assistant coach Don Jackson is the full-time store general manager. Don is the muscle power literally and figuratively of the store. He deals with the nitty-gritty aspects of the business and ensures that things run smoothly. From providing customer service and re-organizing inventory to training new hires, Don handles a lot of different responsibilities. He tirelessly works to improve the stores' bottom line while making sure everyone is doing their job properly. Ever since 1996 he has been an essential key to why the stores have been so successful in profitability and growth, and why they are open about 359 days a year.

Where'd My Brain Go?

As runners, we are generally seen as academic-minded, skilled with balancing athletics with school and other intellectual endeavors. Often it is the cross country team that wins the highest average GPA of any sport in the school. The dedication and determination derived from distance running goes a long way towards the ultimate, peak performance come championship race (or test) time. We challenge our self-control, gauge our bodies' capacities, and mentally discipline ourselves to push above and beyond preconceived thresholds. It is no surprise that when we are suddenly put into an environment where there is a lack of intellectual stimulus, our minds start to settle for mediocrity. We lose our sharpness, our focus, and start to wander aimlessly. This has happened to me since I moved away from a college campus, and became immersed in "the simple life" of running, selling running shoes, eating, running, and sleeping.

Now don't get me wrong, I love simplicity in life. In one of my favorite literary works, *Walden*, Henry David Thoreau writes: "Simplify, simplify, simplify!" We can live a meaningful, fulfilling life with few material possessions. There are less variables to stress about, and it is easy to focus on one or two specific tasks (the goal for me now is to run a fast marathon). I'm just trying to say that it was an initial shock that I didn't even consider when coming out of formal schooling after all these years. Now my peers who've graduated and were lucky enough to snag a job (or continue to graduate school) are still intellectually stimulated to a high degree. Being out in Michigan, out of my element, I have felt initially displaced. I find myself longing to visit the University in Ann Arbor to rekindle that spark generated from hundreds of sharp young minds working arduously in the library. Perhaps, ultimately that desire, that pinnacle on Maslow's pyramid consisting of self-actualization, was what initially compelled me to start writing this book. And it wouldn't hurt to read more.

Other athletes in the program are at a different stage in their lives. They are older, and it is hard for us youngins to relate. For example, Brian lives with his family; he has kids and multiple obligations as a father. There wasn't much time for him to take naps (and in the later days, to even run). He lived several miles away from the team, and even grew up listening to 90s music in college. Dot McMahan is also married with children, and she lives her own separate life away from the team, full of family adventures and household chores. Luke and Mike are both around 30 years old. A 5-6 year gap is significant when you are fresh out of college. As a worker in health care at a hospital, Luke lives a more independent life, away from the hoopla generated from working in the running stores.

Sometimes it just gets mind-numbing, thinking about running all the time. Then I just remind myself that running is my passion, it is something that I daydreamed about constantly growing up. Of the many hobbies that I could have chosen to explore as a young adult, running came out on top. Intellectually, running may not be the most stimulating outlet to be pursuing, although I feel as though the mind-body connection that it addresses is an essential component of one's well-being. The mind does a curious thing when it adapts and decides to challenge itself to learn more through the stimulus of new activities. I feel like I haven't been getting enough of that stimulus lately. The mind-numbing myopia of being a stubborn, hard-core distance runner (and shoe salesman!) has molded me into a boring, thoughtless individual. It's like being a machine on an assembly line… programmed for the mundane, repetitive tasks and rewarded for working without break, distraction, or respite. But will this machine last without breaking down before the Boston Marathon?

2010
January 4th, 2010

New Years came and went. The program has been around for about a decade now. I had a brief, week-long vacation home in Oregon for the holidays. It was nice running outside in shorts in the balmy 45-degree rain on New Years Day. I found that at home 10-milers felt long, and the motivation to run any real distance in the morning had totally diminished. I wasn't used to running alone so much again.

Michigan winter officially arrived with the New Year. Yesterday was our coldest morning of running yet. We met at the Boat Launch in Stony Creek Metropark in 5-degree weather for an 8 AM Sunday morning community group run. I was still jet-lagged and sluggish from the long plane flight back. There was a 10 MPH wind coming off the lake as we blasted off the first mile near 6:00 flat pace. The air temperature may have been 5 degrees, but with the wind chill it felt like -15. Clint wisely had a facemask on.

"I need to get one of those!" Christian exclaimed. Luckily, I had worn my wind-boxer running briefs that had an insulated, cup-like pouch around the whole crotch area. You have to go to drastic measures here to keep your junk warm! I remember painfully getting cold in that area and suffering for a good 30 minutes in a warm shower trying to de-thaw. I had learned my lesson since then and would never again forget to wear protection in the winter. In college we used to stuff a third sock over that region when we did long runs on cold Sunday mornings on a mountainous run we nicknamed "Stonecar." The wind-boxer briefs were less restrictive, and helped deflect the knife-like wind. I also wore knee-high Oxysoc compression socks to keep my shins from turning to ice and splintering. However, my face went numb as a stinging pain spread across my cheek bones and made my eyes water. Eventually one of my eyelids almost completely froze shut! When you get the sensation that the eyelash is sticking, you must forcefully blink to prevent this from happening.

We stopped halfway into the run for a quick pee break. "You have to make sure to shake off all the drops… uh…" Chad sheepishly comments as we start off again. No one wants a "pee-sicle." Chad and Clint reminisce about how they've had frostbite before.

"It's just like a burn," Clint states matter-of-factly, his tone informative. "Your skin turns all white and then red and it starts to peel." Clint recalls that he had frostbite on his nose, while Chad says he got "the burn" on his ankles.

Most of the run is close to 6:00 pace, even on the snowy gravel roads. I kept thinking how "old man" Clint got 5th in the 2004 Olympic Marathon Trials. Just another 2:14 marathoner, which was really something back then…it still is impressive to me now, but on the national scene it just doesn't rank you as high as it used to. Chad and Clint think out loud about running a decade ago, way back in the year 2000, when they were younger and more competitive at the national level. I think to myself, I was just graduating from 8th grade at the turn of The Millennium. These guys have been doing this shit for a long time! Respect.

Bloomer

[See corresponding video "Bloomer House Tour" at
www.Vo2maxProductions.com for the complete experience]

When I moved from the Driftwood house to the Bloomer house at the start of 2010 I was excited because I would get an upstairs room in what I thought was a clearly superior living environment. After living in Bloomer for several months, and after Driftwood underwent some renovations, I am inclined to believe now that it is a toss-up between which residence is the better place to spend my days in.

The Bloomer house is located on a plateau about three-quarters of a mile Northwest of Driftwood. It has a decent sized backyard, which includes a fire pit. Bloomer was the very first house to be purchased by the Hansons for the athletes and all the old-school guys like Brian, Clint, Luke, and Chad had resided within its hallowed walls. Upon entering the front door there is a large, smelly shoe rack that contains shelves of shoes and a display case of various road race trophies and awards accumulated from Hansons runners over the years. There are awards from the Emerald Nuts Run, Club Cross Country Nationals, Peachtree, Crim, the Disney Half Marathon, and the Detroit Turkey Trot to name a few. There's also an old, outdated issue of *Michigan Runner* from the year 2000 with Clint on the cover leading the Crim 10 Mile road race through the streets of Flint. Further down the entrance hall there is a framed Brooks poster that has images of Clint, Chad, Melissa, Brian, and Luke displayed on it, outlined by the phrase "Banded by the Run." The two downstairs bedrooms, which have been vacant for some time, include the infamous panic room, which is entirely bullet proof. One of my teammates originally thought the panic room would be a good place to live, but after I reminded him that the window doesn't open from the inside, and that the ambient temperature is always about 10 degrees colder (in the winter), we decided it wouldn't be so great after all.

Iron-filled, mineral-rich (and unpleasant to drink) well water from the tap is a highlight of Bloomer's kitchen amenities. The shower, sink, and toilet bowls are a tinted orange yellow rust color from the residue. Any laundry that I've done that used to be a white has become tinted a light yellow, including my treasured Ralph Lauren and American Eagle polos that I so proudly wore in college. [Editor's note: at the time of printing, the Bloomer House has finally been hooked up to cleaner, city water.]

Upstairs reveals 4 bedrooms and a full bathroom. When Drew and I moved into Bloomer we quickly joined Luke and Christian in filling all the upstairs bedrooms. I've learned from my college days in the infamous track house that being upstairs has its advantages. It's usually warmer upstairs, there are less bugs and rodents, and noise from the living room TV downstairs or from your roommates doesn't smother you as much.

Every room in the Bloomer house upstairs has concave ceilings where the angle of the roof curves inward, creating spaces where it is easy to hit your head if you aren't careful. I don't mind. The windows in most of the upstairs bedrooms provide a rather pleasant view of the nearby trees in the Bloomer house yard, and the nearest neighbor's house is at least 75 feet away. There is a little more privacy and space to what I was used to in college, where our houses were practically on top of each other.

Outside the front kitchen and dining table area there is a small stoop where we have a grill and a little fold-out table with a couple of chairs. In good weather this is a prime spot for me to sit and read, while watching our neighbor's multiple cars driving back and forth on our shared driveway. Black squirrels, all sorts of little birds, and a woodchuck (who we named Oscar) prowl around in the yard and are spotted frequently. It is rejuvenating and refreshing to see such natural beauty. It makes me miss my parents' house in the backwoods of Oregon, and the forest trails of upstate New York that we ran in college.

A New Era
January 20th, 2010

A lot has happened in the last couple of weeks. I went down to Florida with teammates Chad Johnson, Emily Mortensen, and Erin Richard to compete in the world's largest marathon/half marathon weekend to date. The Walt Disney World race weekend, which accommodates over 55,000 runners! It was unusually cold in Orlando, and we were welcomed with below-freezing temperatures, some sleet, rain, and a cold wind. Not what you'd usually expect when you go to Florida, even in the winter. Keith and Kevin were joking that it was colder down there than it was back in Michigan. It might have been close actually. Anyway, we weren't going to let the cold spoil our fun. We all ran the half marathon, which was appropriately called the "Donald Duck Half." Some runners were doing The Goofy Challenge, which involved running the half marathon one day and then running the full marathon the next day. I was more excited about reliving my childhood and getting to go on the new rides and amusements that the parks had to offer. It had been a good 15 years since I had last been to this magical place.

Chad ended up winning our race in 1:07:02, and I finished 18 seconds back in a new PR. I am still not proud of my half marathon PR, because I feel that to be treated as an elite I should be running closer to 1:05 or faster. However, given the conditions and the multiple turns and bumps on the course, this performance was one of my most solid efforts to date.

The starting gun went off at 5:40 AM, and we ran in the dark for the first half of the race. The venue scenically meandered through parts of the Disney park, like the Magic Kingdom and Epcot. I was too focused on racing and not slipping on the icy turns to notice much of the scenery. However, I'm sure for the thousands of other runners participating, the park views were positive distractions from the pain. Chad and I started off conservatively, as told by Kevin, and ran the opening 5 miles or so all at 5:10 to 5:15 pace. We alternated who led each mile. There was a little headwind and the pace didn't feel as easy as it should have been. A couple of US Olympic Triathletes were hanging with us through halfway, drafting off of us and chatting it up. They were also pretending the pace was something they could handle. The tri-guys were Jarrod Shoemaker and three-time Olympian Hunter Kemper, who trained in the area. The duo started a conversation with each other in a futile attempt to psyche us out. Chad said that they do this every year to pretend that they are barely breathing above their aerobic threshold because they can talk.

"Hey man, how's your training going?" Tri guy one enthusiastically exclaims.

"Great! Ah, real great, man! I'm in awesome shape… I'm really ready to bust one today!" Tri guy two answers.

"Niiicee! You know, I've just got so many fans and sponsors out here today…it's really great to show how fit I am!"

I admit, it started to piss me off. I asked Chad out loud if it felt like the pace was about right. After that we were pretty much silent though. Last year Paul only ran a 1:09 (he only had 2 weeks of training under his belt) and one of these tri guys beat him. I knew Jarrod Shoemaker ran for Dartmouth back in the day and had a 5k PR of around 14-flat on the track, so it's not like these guys were slow. In fact they were arguably the best runners on the US Olympic Distance Triathlon team. Despite that, there was no way in hell I was going to let myself lose to someone wearing a full-body suit! At 6 miles I thought, "Fuck it!" and surged decisively. After a series of mile splits in the 4:58 to 5:00 range, I had shut 'em up. Actually, I opened up a gap of about 10 seconds on Chad and the rest of the group. Chad then recalls that one of the tri guys said to him, "What pace are you going to run now?"

Chad replied: "5 flat."

"Perfect! That's what I'll do, and then I'll speed it up from there!"

Well, that definitely didn't happen, because after that Chad took off to chase me down, and the tri-guys ended up positive splitting and finishing several minutes behind us (in 1:09 and 1:11). I was running for the win now! I didn't look back, but at mile 10 (reached in 51:20 or so) I heard a fast pitter-patter of footsteps closing in on me. No way! Couldn't be a tri-guy? I was running 5 min pace and whoever it was behind me must be dropping a 4:50. I was over my threshold and really starting to hurt. Out of the corner of my eyes I saw a flash of our red/yellow singlet fly past me. It was Chad. I was warned that he likes to sit and kick!

I guess they don't call him Chad "Nails" Johnson for no reason. It was a tough move he made, a race closer. When you are 10 miles into a hard half marathon, just maintaining pace is a demanding endeavor that involves dialing into the dark depths of pain and digging hard into your final reserves. And here comes Chad, running close to my college 10k PR pace. At this point Chad was decisively taking control of the lead and dropping me like a fat turtle. Discouraged, I knew I couldn't outkick him. He had 4:00 mile speed. Over that last 5k Chad slowly opened up a little more space on me. I tried to get pulled along in that chasm of empty space...the space that was going to separate 1st and 2nd...the winner and the loser...the earnings of $1500 and $1000 respectively (due to Brooks bonuses for placing in such a race; the event itself had no actual prize money in the half marathon). As I rounded a sharp turn into the final 100m straightaway I glanced up and saw Chad break the finish line tape, hands in the air, victorious. A colorful shower of confetti blanketed him. As the defending champion (from 2 years prior) of this race he had finally regained his crown! I crossed the finish line and almost puked on the confetti pile that covered the asphalt.

Although our times were relatively slow, the negative split effort pleased Keith and Kevin as Chad and I placed 1st and 2nd in the men's half marathon, Emily won the women's half marathon in 1:20, and Erin was 4th (running a controlled, tempo effort). I was stoked, because due to Brooks bonuses, just placing in this race earned me enough cash to justify buying a MacBook. Furthermore, as always, Disney treated us like rock stars, putting us up in suites near the parks and giving us day passes for 4 full days of fun. In return for their generous hospitality, we spoke at the pre-race expo in front of several hundred people, answering questions about the Hansons program and assuring the masses that we feel the same pain and struggles as they experience from racing such distances [see video "Speaking Before Disney Half Marathon" at www.Vo2maxProductions.com]. The night before the race we were entertained along with other major sponsors, VIPs, and elite runners at a showing of Indiana Jones and the Last Crusade reenactments. The night was capped off with a catered Mediterranean dinner featuring magicians, belly dancers, and jugglers. It was a blast!

When we were in Florida, Kevin drove us around in the new team van. This slick vehicle, which I'd estimate cost at least 50 grand, came complete with a large satellite dish on top, a TV inside, and large seats that swiveled 360 degrees. A fold out card table was embedded in the floor in the back, not to mention iPod chargers and limo-style lights lining the interior. The tires had something like 20" rims, and the whole vehicle just had the presence of a massive transporter. Cruising around Disney or even going to a supermarket like Publix always turned heads.

In our last couple days at Disney, Kevin was like a crazy tour guide, pulling us around the parks and providing lengthy commentary on all the rides. He had been there so many times he knows all the ins and outs of every park, all the secrets and shortcuts to circumnavigate lines. It was exhausting to follow him from one attraction to the next. I relived many of my childhood memories on the Big Thunder rollercoaster, and finally learned why my brother liked the "scary" twists and turns in the dark of Space Mountain so much. It was like a rebirth after 18 years. I can tell that 2010 is going to be a better running year for me. It will be interesting to see how the team dynamic changes in the next 12 months…

The new Hansons-Brooks team van in Florida

The night before the Disney half marathon teammate Erin Richard and I met Goofy.

Drew "T. Rex" Polley

The start of 2010 brought a new face to the program, a runner from Washington State by the name of Drew Polley. "Drew...who?" I thought. Being from the Pacific Northwest I thought I knew pretty much all the good runners from the Oregon and Washington area. When I was in high school we ran in the Nike Oregon versus Washington Borderclash cross country meet, which pitted the best high school runners in each state against each other. But Drew hadn't run at that level in high school...he wasn't fast enough or good enough to place even in the top 20 at the state meet to qualify for such prestigious events. In college, he was just another no-name DI runner who only made NCAAs once in 2006 because his team barely qualified. Drew may have started from humble beginnings, but his determination and willingness to pay the price in order to improve may be his greatest asset. Despite his relatively modest high school and college times, Drew developed enough strength to run a 1:06 half-marathon in Seattle and a 2:20 full (in sweltering heat) in San Antonio the year after he graduated from Washington State. In the fall of 2009 he had started graduate school at WSU to earn a Masters in Engineering, but after visiting Hansons he decided to drop out and pursue his dream of running professionally with Hansons. Drew's high school running credentials were as follows:

Drew Polley
High school: South Kitsap, WA
1600m: 4:26
3200m: 9:36

The "T. Rex" nickname for Drew is because he has

unusually large feet for a distance runner (and for someone who barely stands 6 feet tall). Drew wears a size 14, so we had to special order certain models of Brooks shoes for him since the Hansons' Running Shops don't always stock that size. With such big clunkers on his feet, we initially made fun of his clumsy stride and the fact that his shoes are heavy and disproportionate. He first moved into the Bloomer house in a room adjacent to mine. Being from the same region, I was pleased to have a new teammate who shared a lot of similarities with me in terms of caring about environmental issues, political beliefs, and varied musical tastes. Drew plays the banjo; I play the guitar. We quickly learned the song "Wagon Wheel" made famous by Old Crow Medicine Show and played it together. Furthermore, Drew and I knew a lot of runners from the Pacific Northwest. Former high school teammates and rivals that went to places like the University of Portland, Washington, Montana State, Arizona State, and Cal.

"I don't think I could look at myself in the mirror in the morning if I knew I wasn't doing everything I could to be the best runner I could be." Drew makes statements like that from time to time when he senses other teammates (i.e., me) are being "lazy" and not going "the extra mile."

I admit, sometimes the other guys and I don't do core work or even drills every week like Drew does. I never saw Nick Arciniaga doing abs or stretching on the floor of the Driftwood house after our morning runs. Instead, he'd promptly jump in the shower and then whip up a breakfast burrito of beans and eggs in a tortilla. After that he'd either go straight to work at the store or, if we worked later, he'd sit on the couch and/or take a nap. Brian Sell never let on that he did much extra strength training, however I later found out that he had a core routine involving some basic variations of sit-ups and push-ups using a chair to add incline. Chad regularly goes to the gym and lifts upper body weights and works with his legs. My worthless days of maxing out on the bench, struggling to put up 175 lbs in the college track team weight room are over. The rest of us that don't lift or do drills anymore claim that we are too tired from all the mileage, or drained from work to do all that extra stuff. But then Drew points out that we are professional runners, and should live the lifestyle focused around training accordingly. He cuts through the bullshit and obsessively does all the extra little things that he came out here to do.

"I'm a little bit of a perfectionist and running is one of the areas where I really express that now." Those that know Drew, know that that is kind of an understatement. Drew knows that we are not all talented enough to compete with the other US elites, so we can't leave any stone unturned. Ritz, Hall, Meb…these guys have way more talent than us. They train at altitude, doing drills and exercises for hours each day, piling on workouts at 4:40 mile pace or faster. Rupp is running extra mileage on underwater and anti-gravity treadmills, and then fine-tuning his speed on the European track circuit, running quarters in 56 during workouts. I see videos on Flotrack of Anna Pierce and Maggie Vessey doing delicate drills and warm-up routines, their form ironed, toned and perfect. We should be more motivated than ever to be at the top of our game, to get that extra edge. In college I lifted a lot, I did 16-minute abs with 10 lb weights, I did hurdle drills. That stuff kind of went out the back door when I came here. Drew is surprised that a lot of us don't go to the gym or do drills in the park like he does. It makes me feel guilty, but it is motivating as hell. So sometimes I join Drew for drills, and we push each other to run 6- or 7-mile evening runs instead of the 4 miles we have scheduled. Working together, challenging each other and ultimately trying to improve as a team is a cornerstone of the whole Hansons program. It's a large part of the reason why runners like Drew and I came out here in the first place. It pushes you to run with other like-minded guys that are faster.

Drew comments, "I couldn't train at the level that I am now if I were by myself…it would be hard to get motivated to run such volume and intensity." It's safe to say that the majority of us, if not all of us, agree.

Drew started off as a soccer player, and it wasn't until later in high school that he became more serious about running cross country and track. Just to continue running in college was something that he didn't take for granted:

> "I was a walk-on [in college]. I was happy I was allowed even to walk on...I remember the day I got the email from my college coach that I had made the college team...I thought it was the highest I'd ever make it in the sport."

However, at WSU Drew blossomed as a DI walk-on. Staying for a 5th year to compete, he had some breakthrough PRs and races to cap off his collegiate career. As a 5th year senior in college his PR performances included:

> 5k: 14:18
> 10k: 29:26
> All west region in XC

Consistently running over 100 miles a week as a junior and senior, Drew was a high mileage runner. His 1500m PR is still above 4:00, his weakness being top-end speed. He states, "I always saw myself as someone who wasn't talented, who was an underdog, and I knew I had to outwork everybody...at least that's how I saw it." But the mileage started paying off.

"That cumulative fitness started to really help me," says Drew. By the time Drew started grad school at WSU, he was ready to jump up to the marathon with hopes of trying to qualify for the 2012 US Olympic Trials on his own. He became more immersed in the running scene on the roads.

"I'd start seeing their affiliation [the Hansons] in results as I became more and more of a running nerd," Drew recalls. Still, the jump from collegiate to post-collegiate running is a big one, the chasm between qualifying for the Olympic Trials and being a varsity DI runner required more miles, sacrifice, and a jump up to the new marathon racing distance. Drew recalls his initial impressions about joining a group like Hansons:

> "I never really considered it...I never thought I'd have an opportunity like that. It sounded awesome to me. When I started running better and better in college [my friends] would say I should look into post collegiate running options...I'd say I wouldn't be able to do that."

Despite Drew's initial lack of confidence in his running ability, he diligently trained on campus during the fall of 2009 while taking grad school classes and working in a lab. His mileage in the 120-140 mile per week range, he made his debut in brutal fashion at the San Antonio Rock 'n' Roll Marathon in November. It was hot and humid, and the sweltering temperatures caused many a good runner to slow down or drop out. Drew finished with a positive split (undoubtedly dehydrated), running an impressive 2:20:59 to be the top American in the field. Not a trials qualifier, but a promising sign nonetheless.

Afterwards, he sent Keith and Kevin an email and they (surprisingly) took interest. "I knew I'd regret it if I didn't jump on it and go for it," Drew remembers. After a quick recruiting trip out to Michigan in December 2009, Drew was accepted into the program. He promptly dropped out of grad school in Washington and drove his Saturn through blizzards in North Dakota to start his post-collegiate journey out in Michigan the first week of January 2010. Drew recalls his initial impressions of the program:

> "It was a little bit scary. I wondered if I had made the

right decision. It was kind of like coming to college. I saw myself as an underdog who had to work hard and do everything right. I took this big chance, I put grad school on hold and moved across the country…I had no excuse…there was no option but to work hard."

And work hard he did. Drew felt like he had to prove his worth to the team right away. After struggling with some injuries after his November marathon debut, Drew fell into the Hansons routine and mentality of banging out runs continuously. He recalls the first couple weeks of running:

"Everyday is more consistent, we run at the same time every morning. There are no 'garbage' easy days like in college. I was never questioning if I'd finish a run or cut a run short. I knew there was never really an option of 'not' doing."

With Chad "Nails" Johnson in tow, Drew and I started putting in the miles together with Boston in the back of our minds.

Houston
January 2010

Houston is going to be the site of the 2012 US
Olympic Marathon Trials for both the men and women.
The temperature there in January is usually around 50 to 60
degrees in the morning, which is a perfect climate for running
a fast marathon. Furthermore, the traditional Houston
Marathon course is a very flat race and the possibility of
running fast times at such a venue will be golden. (Editor's
note: the proposed course for the Trials will involve multiple
laps around a criterion loop, or loops, different from the
traditional course, and may involve a hill or two.)

This year, a full two years before the trials, the
Houston Marathon yielded some very fast times by
Americans. One of the most impressive performances
of the day was a debut marathon by Brett Gotcher of the
Adidas-sponsored McMillan Elite training group based out of
Flagstaff, AZ. Gotcher dropped a 2:10:36, and finished as the
top American in the race with 7th place overall. Suddenly here
is another young American who is in the mix of making an
Olympic Team. This guy is on fire. Gotcher, formerly from
Stanford, has been training with Greg McMillan and his post-
collegiate group based at altitude for several years, and really
demonstrated his fitness earlier in the fall by winning the
New Haven 20k US National Championship. The Flagstaff
group is smaller than Hansons, but the talent there is high,
with top female athletes Paige Higgins and Lindsay Allen to
name a few [editor's note: both Paige and Lindsay have now
left the program]. Post-collegiate groups such as McMillan
Elite and Zap Fitness, based in Blowing Rock, North
Carolina, have emerged after Hansons, and the comparisons
between training groups has created some competition. The
top, cream of the crop athletes of course go to groups like

the Nike Oregon Project, The Bay Area Track Club, and
Mammoth Lakes - but those are for the select few who
are able to obtain substantial, independent shoe company
contracts. If you aren't an NCAA champion, then you
usually need the support of a group such as McMillan, Zap,
or Hansons to provide financial bonuses, act as agents, coach
you, provide gear, and pay the rent. There are time standards
to get in, and some offer varying levels of support depending
on how fast and elite your times are. Just having a supply of
shoes, running gear, access to medical care, and a roof over
your head is huge. Being able to have time to take naps and
ice baths after workouts is also a luxury that gives you the
edge to compete at the elite level. With this kind of support
one should never lose a race to a runner who actually works a
9 to 5 job.

Much like when you apply to colleges and go through
an athletic recruiting process, these post-collegiate distance
programs usually require official visits to see if the program
is a good match for the prospective athlete. A lot of top
college runners may have a choice between several of the
programs, while others (perhaps the ones that weren't All-
American) get rejected by them all. A lot has to do with
personalities, interviews, references and attitude. Much like
a college recruiting trip, the prospective athlete is advised
to stay a couple nights or a weekend with members of the
team and experience the lifestyle firsthand. I wouldn't say
that spending a couple days immersed in a program is going
to give one a very rounded perspective of what it's like
to be on the team, but it's definitely a good start. On my
recruiting trip out to Hansons (which happened to coincide
with Christian Wagner's trip) we toured the Hansons Running
Shops, ate meals with Kevin and Keith, and drove around
the Rochester area to observe the training grounds. We also
visited with the guys and drank beer at Driftwood. I know
that when you are in high school and get recruited to college
programs there is occasionally some underage drinking and

partying going on to show the recruit a good time. That never happened for me when I was looking at colleges, but then again I only took official visits to Harvard, Cornell, and The University of Portland. Perhaps the student-athletes were too focused on their studies and reputation to take me out to parties (a huge violation of all sorts of rules and laws by-the-way) - or, perhaps, I just wasn't fast enough to warrant much attention.

When you are the cream of the crop it seems like you have more choices, more options. It's like buying a high-priced stock, where you are aggressively investing in your self-worth, your time and energy, and your future earnings potential. When runners look to go pro and sign that big contract to make such a commitment, they are aware that their value is attributed to performances and marketing appeal. For a blue-chip runner like Jenny Barringer [editor's note: now Jenny Simpson], coming out of NCAA success and signing with a major shoe brand was inevitable. We were actually happy that she didn't sign with Brooks because there is only so much money per shoe company to go around. Instead, Jenny B decided to sign a professional contract with New Balance (a surprise because it's not Nike). I think this distribution of contracts and talent is good for the sport. There is now a sense of checks and balances in sponsorship and brand representation for a variety of post-collegiate athletes. The Hansons have Brooks support, McMillian has mostly Adidas, and now Mizuno is jumping in more and sponsoring Team Strands [editor's note: that group is now defunct] as well as athletes in USA Team Minnesota like Antonio Vega, who just won the US National Half-Marathon Championship. Reebok gives Zap some support, and of course the old powerhouse Nike has the state of Oregon in its grip. Asics doesn't seem to be represented as prominently now, with their American star in Hall not running as fast as many projected he would to date.

It may actually be the start of the end of Olympian

Hall's total dominance of the US marathoning scene. Unlike in the 2008 Olympic Trials when he convincingly won by a record margin, Hall has shown that he is human after all. At the recent Rock 'n' Roll Arizona Half Marathon in Phoenix, Hall got handily destroyed by Canadian (and former Wisconsin star) Simon Bairu. Hall was broken after 9 miles, coming in with a 1:04 finishing time. Mike and Luke were also in the race and finished about 1:30 behind him.

The elite coordinating staff at these Rock 'n' Roll events are top notch, and being an invited athlete makes them fun and exciting events for us. With the merging of Brooks sponsorship and the Competitor Group making more and more of the country's best marathons Rock 'n' Roll events, there are plenty of opportunities for fast times, exposure and entertainment. For the masses these events provide a fun and exciting atmosphere, especially for first-time marathoners and music enthusiasts. For the elites like Hall and the occasional internationals that show up, there is usually prize money that pays the top 5 in each race [editor's note: now only the top 3 get paid]. I'd do these races every month if I could just for the fun! Drew and I are already looking forward to convincing Keith and Kevin to let us race the Rock 'n' Roll Seattle half marathon in June. I doubt Hall will show up there, but if he does, I'd look forward to perhaps only finishing 2 to 3 full minutes behind him.

Boston Training Segment
January 22nd, 2010

Kevin showed up with a clipboard and a two and a half foot long, laminated, cardboard-backed, over-sized map of the Boston Marathon route. The map contained all historic landmarks, including the infamous Heartbreak Hill. Also highlighted was the old fire station, the large Citco sign at mile 25, and the old starting line. Every mile mark on the course was also noted on this detailed visual display.

It was my first daytime meeting with Kevin outside of our monthly Thursday night full-team meetings. Along with the new guy, Drew Polley, we were going to outline the game plan for the Boston Marathon, which was a mere 12.5 weeks away. I have been absolutely pumped that the Hansons are letting us run this historic and prestigious event. When customers at the store ask me what I'm training for, I say "Boston" proudly. This impresses them greatly and such qualification seems to give me much more credibility. They then proceed to ask how I got my "BQ," or Boston qualifier. The fact that I qualified for the Olympic Trials isn't nearly as important and impressive to them for some reason. I guess Boston just has a certain ring to it because it is steeped in so much history and tradition.

The three of us walked a half block from the Lake Orion store over to the popular Sagebrush Cantina just across Main Street for a lunch meeting. The place is always hopping, and we had a 15-minute wait for a table. Whiffs of the Mexican food, including 10 inch high piles of nachos, enchiladas, and monster burritos filled the air and made me salivate like a starving dog. We took a seat by the front door entrance area to wait while Kevin quickly began to discuss the map he was holding. There was excitement in his voice, and he flapped the map around like it was on fire.

"The first half is downhill, but that doesn't mean you should run it faster," Kevin stated. The importance of holding back on the downhill start was heavily emphasized.

"We are going to play this one conservatively." The main objective here was to get the 2012 trials qualifier: "just" a sub-2:19:00. That was to be our training pace, which is what we will hold ourselves back to…a 5:17 per mile. The number is burned into my head.

We finally got a seat near the front windows. I perched up on one of the high chairs surrounding the small round table we gathered around. Kevin ordered his typical drink: a Diet Coke. We snacked on chips and salsa as we waited for our enormous entrees. Kevin's tone got more serious: "If you are having an off-day in a workout, you still NEED to make sure you stay faster than that pace."

Most of our strength workouts and longer workouts were to be done at 10 seconds per mile faster than the marathon goal race pace - so anywhere between 5:05 to 5:07 a mile. I realized that these paces happen to be very close to my lactate threshold pace and current half marathon race pace. The game plan of preparing for the course was fairly detailed.

We were to be traveling to Florida in a mere week and a half for a brief training stint of 5 days. After that we were going to fly directly from Florida to Boston for 3 days to run two workouts on the course. The first workout was going to be a 3 by 3 mile downhill segment run, repeating the first 3 miles of the course. We would drive up to the starting line between each 3-mile rep. That workout would be run right at marathon goal pace (5:17/mile). The next day there was a 20-mile long run scheduled from mile markers 6 to 26 on the route. Also, there were going to be several drive-overs of the course in the rental van during that weekend in Boston. Basically, we were going to cover the entire course on foot, on tired legs, and we were going to see the infamous Newton hills in full multiple times. Such intense preparation was totally foreign to me.

The Hansons mentioned that they like to take as many variables of uncertainty as possible out of the marathon. This included training to the course's terrain, drinking fluids on the run, and running a lot of miles around marathon goal pace (details that I will delve into more in the upcoming chapter "Training Philosophy"). Their approach isn't scientific per se: "I use the science of observation," Keith once admitted. They have consulted with many of the greats: Vigil, Rogers, Greg Meyer, and Shorter to name a few. They bump heads with Mahon and Salazar. Over nearly a decade of training and racing nearly 40 post collegiate athletes, you start to see some patterns in success, perhaps a set of logical reasons for improvement. Kevin was 100% confident in the program he outlined for us. It was very similar (minus the speed and some volume) to what got Brian Sell to place 4th in the 2006 Boston marathon. In fact, the long line of success that Hansons runners have had at Boston over the last 5 years was most inspiring to me. Kevin explained, "We always surprise people in the marathon…you will be the surprise at Boston."

Our platters arrived. I pride myself on cleaning my plate at every restaurant I go to as restaurant portions are usually way too small for me. Here at Sagebrush though, I struggled with my vegetable fajita as it came with a plate of rice and beans. Drew ordered a giant taco salad. Greasy and full of fat, the meal was delicious as usual.

"Brian learned to pace himself after the '04 trials," Kevin said, pounding home the importance of negative splitting. He mentioned that in the history of the US Olympic Marathon Trials [to date], every runner who ran the last 10 miles under 50 minutes had made an Olympic team. I thought about that last comment for a while, realizing I still have yet to crack 50 minutes for an open 10 miles. This was going to be a lot of work.

A day after our meeting, official training for the

marathon began. We received a simple email schedule that appeared as follows (a "12 4" day means run 12 miles in the morning, and then 4 miles in the afternoon):

BOSTON CREW

Jan 23: 12   7 am go time from Hart [a school]

Jan 24: 10 [and] 4

Jan 25: 12

Jan 26: 10   4

Jan 27: 12

Jan 28: 10   4

Jan 29: 12

Jan 30: 10   4

Jan 31: 16   HEAD TO FLORIDA

Feb 1:   12   4

Feb 2:   12   4

Feb 3:   5 x 2 mile

Feb 4:   12   4

Feb 5:   10   Last 10k [of Boston marathon course]

Feb 6:   *3 x 3 downhill*

Feb 7:   *20*

As you can see, our schedule was pretty barebone. The whole training plan was really just a skeleton of easy day mileage figures with no limits on pace or effort. However, this was just the start of the marathon segment as the bulk of the training was yet to come...

January 29th, 2010

For the first couple weeks of January newbie Drew has been working in the store wearing a large boot, his foot encased and supported to take the strain off of a near-injury. He has been nursing his foot back to health by cross training at the gym for the last couple of weeks, and running only 5 to 8 miles most days. He most recently took 2 full days off from running in an attempt to fully heal. Today he is back at it again as he joins Chad, Brian, and me on a slushy and muddy 91-minute run on the back roads of Rochester before heading off to work in Utica at the running shop.

The rest of the team did an indoor workout at a local indoor soccer complex lined with artificial grass out near Pontiac, Michigan. We are able to rent the facility for a couple hours on select mornings of each week. Often the local Oakland University track team is there training during the same time slot. With no indoor track to go to nearby, this is our only outlet for speedwork during the winter months. The team does a workout of 8 by 800m in around 2:20. I'm glad I'm not doing this speed segment that Luke, Mike, and Christian are doing. My legs are more stiff and slow than ever before, and the thought of indoor track brings up memories of being ruthlessly outkicked during the "sprint" that is required in an event like the indoor 3k. Pain train.

Luke "Pants" Humphrey and Christian recently raced this brutal 1.8-mile distance as a tune-up race at the nearby Grand Valley State University open meet. Christian easily won in 8:10, and Luke was not far back in 8:14. It is amazing they can race that fast as the workouts that they've been doing are never faster than 66-68 seconds/400m. In fact, the Hansons speed training would be a joke to most NCAA programs as the actual velocities we run at are quite low relative to our race pace. Most workouts are at a pace that any 30:00 10k or 14:30 5k runner could handle. The trick is balancing our overall high volume with the moderate intensities of these track workouts (and of course the 6-minute pace "recovery jogs" between reps, courtesy of Mike Morgan). History has shown that the moderate intensity of the workouts, coupled with consistently high mileage, eventually pays dividends.

Training Philosophy

Strength! Strength! Strength!

"All the great marathoners were great cross country runners," Kevin likes to reemphasize his reasoning as to why we do some fast workouts through parks on uneven trails through leaves and mud even though we are preparing for a half marathon road race. There is strength in high mileage and from consistent, moderate intensity.

Keith explains, "Since you have two easy days of recovery between hard workouts, you can run a faster pace on at least one of those days." Keith also supports the attitude behind going 6:00 per mile pace or faster nearly every single non-workout day.

The only acknowledgment of any speed training whatsoever is when an athlete is coming off of a marathon segment (training block of 12 weeks or so) and needs to work on racing shorter distances in the 5k to half-marathon range. At times like these, we are able to do a speed segment that involves less emphasis on mileage and long runs, and slightly more emphasis on running shorter, faster workouts. However, usually these faster workouts are very similar in structure to what the marathoners are doing, with the main deviation being a handful of workouts like repeat 800s on a cross-country course or repeat 1000s on the track (when it isn't covered in snow). In the winter, we don't get to do workouts on an indoor track, but rather run loops around the indoor soccer facility. I've never done 400s so far in the program or worked on my raw speed with all-out track accelerations and short hill sprints. There are no agility or supplemental drills that we have been told to do, and a lot of us just quit doing strides altogether. There was one month or so when we had build-ups or "blast-offs" as the guys call them, which were basically half a dozen fast accelerations of 80m in length that were listed on the schedule after some easy runs (these could be called strides I guess). In terms of auxiliary training, there is no structure either. I totally stopped lifting weights and my double 8-minute ab routine in college has been cut to a 2-minute, half-hearted session.

It's not that we don't have enough time for all these cross training components of training - it's more a matter of being totally exhausted from the act of running so many miles, at a relatively high intensity, day in and day out. There is no local "speed lab" gym or athletic campus like there is in Niketown, Oregon. No video analysis or altitude houses for testing and stressing our systems at varying levels. There are no underwater treadmills or hyperbolic suits to dissipate muscle soreness and promote recovery. Instead, Drew went to the local Home Depot and purchased a large, plastic garbage bin to fill with ice water. That is our ice bath. He puts it outside at night, and it chills.

Am I being a little lazy, not going the extra mile? Yes and no. Different team members have opposing views on all the extra stuff in distance running training; some (like Drew) continue to spend considerable time and energy doing drills, lifting, and stretching. Others (like me, Christian, and Nick) concentrate just on the running. With us, many runs end promptly with a walk straight into the shower. My opinion has changed over time, and I like to think back to the Bill Rodgers and Frank Shorter days when guys mainly just ran tons and tons of miles. Keith and Kevin seem to embrace that mentality, and they don't ask if we do core-work and drills. I honestly don't care that I can't touch my toes anymore - I'm not going to pull my hamstring stretching in an attempt to regain the lost flexibility of my youth. If I got injured it might be another story altogether, because I see value in cross training to circumnavigate repetitive strain problems and develop general fitness. I feel that individualized programs with specific injury-prevention exercises can make the difference for certain athletes seeking to achieve their potential in the sport (rather than just saying "add more training miles"). For me, at this moment in my career, I believe the magic is in the miles.

In our marathon program we have long runs top out at 20 miles, and the Hansons' "Marathon Program for the Masses" tops out at only 16 miles for the longest single run in the marathon segment. During our speed segments our longest single runs usually top out at only 16 miles. This was a surprise for me, because I had read most marathon training programs give you at least a 22 mile long run. Before I came out to Michigan I had entertained the idea of doing a 25-30 mile easy, ultra long run to really boost my strength, endurance, and fat-burning capabilities. Although I initially doubted a schedule that topped out with a 20-mile long run, I couldn't argue with the fact that over 20 guys in the program to date had cracked 2:20 in the marathon. When Kevin first started writing marathon-training schedules, even his own wife Nancy had doubts that she could run fast off of just a 20 miler and an "SOS" (something of substance) workout every 3 days. To prove her wrong, Kevin had her follow his schedule to a T, and she cracked 3 hours for the first time in her life. To put that accomplishment in perspective, Nancy wasn't a full-time, professional runner, and she now works full-time balancing business matters involving the stores, the distance project, and being a mom. The Hansons will be quick to explain that the effect of continual high mileage and moderate intensity makes it so the body is constantly adapting to cumulative fatigue. Therefore, the long run doesn't have to be longer to tire you out; you are already tired early on in the long run because of the steady, high mileage "easy" days preceding it.

* * *

Specific Marathon Preparations:

One of the key aspects of the Hansons' marathoning

program is methodically eliminating as many unknown variables as possible in the preparation for a marathon. Racing a marathon for the Hansons is a big event, and most athletes are only allowed to race 3 marathons for every 2 years in the program. To prepare one mentally and physically for such a demanding distance, the Hansons not only train their runners with a diet of steady, high mileage, but they also go to great lengths to ensure that their runners know the race course and practice consuming the fluids and carbohydrates that they plan to use on race day (AKA "payday"). "We try to control as many things as we can," Kevin would quip, in regards to such preparations.

About a month and a half before the date of your marathon, Kevin and Keith travel with you out for a weekend that involves running the entire 26.2 miles of the actual race course. In Boston this involved even doing a workout at race pace on the notorious downhills early in the race and then doing a 20-mile long run the very next day on the latter part of the course. We are given maps of the course to learn the street names, main landmarks, and the relative positioning of each mile marker. Then, when we are out running the course, Keith and Kevin drive alongside on the roads, yelling out mile markers and street names on the fly. After spending a solid weekend on the route, you get a feel for not only the course but also for the city that the event is run in. Such meticulous detail allows the athletes to mentally prepare for the task at hand come race day. Feeling the terrain and forming a mental image of the journey you must cover on race day is a key aspect in ensuring that performance is maximized. We arrive at the starting line fully prepared because we have done our homework.

Another essential component of ultimately preparing the body for race-specific demands is to practice drinking a fluid mixture that you will consume during the marathon. As elite athletes in most marathons, we are fortunate to be given the option of having our very own fluid bottles on special tables lined throughout the course. Often these tables are situated every 3 miles or so during a marathon, and when you run by you can conveniently grab your bottle from a designated place on each table. This is a huge advantage compared to the rest of the runners and general masses, who are usually stuck trying to grab paper cups from the hands of volunteers. Drinking out of a paper cup on the run is hard, and often half of the fluid spills all over your face. However, with your own personal fluid bottle, you have exact control of how much and what you are drinking. If you want watered-down Gatorade at different percentages of carbohydrate strength as the race progresses, you can do that. If you want flat Coke in your bottle at mile 20, you can do that too. Races usually organize cups of water and Gatorade (or the like) at the public fluid stations, and you can also grab those in case you miss your elite fluids. To ensure that our stomachs are up to the challenge of drinking 8 to 10 ounces of fluid at marathon race velocity, Keith and Kevin are stringent in having us bring race bottles to every marathon paced workout in the months leading up to the race. We religiously practice downing our exact fluid mixture while on the run, right in the middle of hard efforts to mimic race-day conditions. Desiree Davila, the star female of the program, was said to have vomited during such preparations as the stomach pain can become quite intense!

A Day in the Life
January 30th, 2010

A lot of people ask me: "What is a typical day like for you as a professional runner? What do you do with all your time?"

Well, I'll give you a run down of a very typical day in the life of a Hansons-Brooks runner. I think that most of you would be surprised to find out that it is not glamorous at all, but rather tedious in how monotonous and simple it is. Like I mentioned earlier, there is no soaking in mountain river streams, and no high-speed motion photography gait analysis in a lab. No underwater treadmill or yoga; no elaborate core drills or gym session routine; no regular sessions with sports psychologists to practice visualization tactics. Just a lot of plain running, recovering, eating, running, driving, and some working.

Obviously I'm probably not fully appreciative of how much free time I have to train, and the general lack of responsibilities or demands of real life have yet to perpetrate my somewhat twisted view of reality. Having time to sometimes take a 2 hour afternoon nap is a luxury that I never thought I'd get to indulge in. So, objectively as possible, this is how a normal day would go for me:

7:20 AM: Alarm goes off (at the start of 2010 we decided as a team to meet and run from the duck pond at 8 instead of the usual 7:30, which allows us to sleep in a little more and allows for better visibility in low-light winter days). I hobble downstairs to my favorite bathroom in Bloomer next to the kitchen. It serves as a laundry room, and the furnace room, so it is the warmest room in the house.

From 7:25 to 7:40 AM: I prepare some coffee and sip it, check the temperature outside, check my email, and put on my running clothes.

7:48 AM: We are off and running towards downtown Rochester to meet the rest of the guys.

8:00 AM: We arrive at the duck pond downtown and stop for a couple minutes to bullshit, go to the bathroom, etc.

8:05 AM: Off running down the Paint Creek trail at 6:20/ mile pace, heading out towards Lake Orion for a 12 mile run. The older guys take off and open up a gap on me. I choose whether or not I want to close the gap…sometimes it depends on what my other teammates do. If everyone goes fast, I go with them. If not, I hang in the back and avoid the continuous battle of one-stepping.

9:10 AM: Arrive back at the Bloomer house.

9:10-9:25 AM: Stretch and do some core-work (basic sit-ups) on the floor in the Bloomer house living room watching VH1 Top 20 Countdown music videos on TV. Usually this involves repeats of some Lady Gaga or Miley Cyrus videos… in the spring, Katy Perry's "California Gurls" comes on and I become thoroughly intrigued.

9:30-9:35 AM: Quick shower.

9:40-10:30 AM: Prepare and eat breakfast: get out a mix of Hungry Jack buttermilk pancakes and make a short stack. Soak in butter and syrup. Fry up a couple scrambled eggs and drink a cup of milk. Take a cocktail of pills (my own choosing) with B12, zinc, magnesium-potassium, and Vitamin D. Watch TV while eating.

[Note: half the time I work the earlier shift at the store from 10:45 to 3:45, which is not as convenient as this day's schedule because I don't have the luxury of taking a nap and I must leave the house by 10:10 to drive to work.]

10:30-11:30 AM: Clean up dishes, go on computer to check email again, check LetsRun.com, Flotrack.org, RunnerSpace.com, and Facebook. Write a little bit for this very book.

11:45 AM: Starting to get tired, prepare for afternoon nap with some light reading.

12:00-12:30 PM: Attempt to doze off. This usually takes a while as my window blinds let in a lot of bright light, and the noise of neighborhood construction, which seems to constantly be going on, is a bit distracting…as is the rumbling of the Bloomer house foundation whenever a truck passes by (also quite frequently). Sleep lightly.

1:45 PM: Alarm goes off again…I feel like I've barely slept and that I just finished running. Legs are usually still stiff, and I feel drowsy and groggy. Not enthused to do second run.

1:50 PM: Change into running clothes and get iPod Shuffle ready for some music on my second run (I usually run alone and need music as a distraction to break things up). Usually my teammates are at work or not running at this particular time because they have the day off, are injured, or are running later on their own schedule.

2:00 PM: Head out the door for a 30:00 run…usually have 4 miles scheduled (but do closer to 5). I head up the road to Bloomer Park and loop around a couple times on the wooded trials (if not covered in snow). The run is uneventful, except I usually get run off the shoulder on the quarter mile stretch of road between our house and the park by one of the 5-10 cars/oversized trucks that always seems to be speeding down our residential street.

2:30 PM: Return to Bloomer and stretch for a couple minutes. Chug water or juice and take an iron pill. Grab some chips or cookies.

2:40 PM: Jump into the shower again.

2:45 PM: Change into regular clothes, check email.

2:55 PM: Prepare a couple sandwiches (usually PB& J or cheese and mustard) and put in Ziploc bags to take to work. Pack another small snack of chips or cookies for later at work also.

3:10 PM: Gather shoes that need to be transported for customers to the store in Royal Oak. Usually a pile of 3-6 pairs that a housemate brought in from the previous night from a different store.

3:15 PM: Load shoes into car and leave Bloomer house for afternoon/night shift at the store in Royal Oak, a 13 mile distance that usually takes 25-30 minutes because of traffic.

3:25 PM: Stop at Starbucks for a grande Pike Place roast (time permitting).

3:45 PM: Arrive at Royal Oak Hansons Running Shop, inevitably spilling coffee, while trying to carry in several boxes of shoes and backpack of sandwiches simultaneously.

3:46-8:00 PM: Work at the store, fitting customers with shoes, answering questions about Gu and fuelbelts, talking about layering clothing to stay warm, taking special orders, re-stocking inventory in the garage, and un-stuffing wads of paper out of shoes. Answering an absurd number of phone calls asking for directions to the store.

8:00-8:30 PM: Close the store down, vacuum, and take out the trash. Patiently wait until 8:30 to check-out.

8:30 PM: Check for shoe and product transfers, load up car, leave Royal Oak, and drive straight home.

9:00 PM: Arrive back at the Bloomer house.

9:02 PM: After unloading a pile of shoes, walk straight to the refrigerator in the living room and grab a cold one (you need it especially if having dealt with an unruly customer in the store).

9:05 PM: Put a pot of water on the stovetop and bust out a bag of pasta.

9:15 PM: Cook pasta, heat up some tomato sauce, and sip choice beverage.

9:20-10:00 PM: Eat pasta and watch TV. Converse with teammates.

10:01 PM: Empty out some laundry, do dishes, retire upstairs to room.

10:05-10:25 PM: Check email, Facebook, write or read a bit.

10:30-11:00 PM: Prepare for bed, set alarm clock extra early (if workout the next day), push a mess of clothes into piles in the corner of my room, wash Albuterol inhaler, brush teeth, go to bathroom, and lights out!

I usually am quite tired and ready to fall asleep around 10, but some nights my mind is racing and it takes until after

11 to stop tossing and turning. The house is conveniently peaceful and quiet as teammates are on the same schedule and have also retired to bed.

There it is, a very typical day. Unfortunately, things really don't vary much from that. It was actually kind of downer for me to write such a detailed routine out...my life is so boring! Of course there are some days where I go to the grocery store to buy food, go out to eat dinner with the team, or play my guitar for significant amounts of time. There also are a couple days each week where I don't work at the store. On these days off I usually nap longer, do my second run later, and buy groceries. Overall, we do have a lot of free time compared to most of the real world, and I cherish every minute by staying busy blogging, writing this book, or doing some other hobbies of mine like playing music or filming.

* * *

The following is the start of another day (a Saturday), described a little differently (see video "A Day in the Life" at www.Vo2maxProductions.com for reference):

Just another day. I woke up with my CD alarm clock crescendoing into the song "I'm in Miami Bitch" by LMFAO. Where am I? Oh yeah, very far from Miami. I'm stiff and cold...like freezing crazy cold. I sleep in a long-sleeve sweatshirt under 3 blankets because the insulation at the Bloomer house is very minimal, and we keep the furnace low to save money on energy bills. I suddenly realize that I had a nightmare last night where I was shot and a bullet had ripped into the back of my left hamstring. I grip my leg instinctively. Whew! It was only a dream; just a bad dream. But I digress. It's dark and cold throughout the house. I do not want to get out of bed. I let my alarm clock play the full song and then throw off my blankets and quickly grab another hooded sweatshirt.

It is 6:53 on Saturday morning, and all I can think about (besides how cold I am) is working an 8.5-hour shift at the Utica store and cramming in my two runs in before and after that shift. Coffee. I NEEDED to get downstairs to the kitchen and get that coffee maker brewing. My mind in a fog, I stumble down the stairs, each quad nearly buckling. I can feel all the tight, swollen tendons in my legs protest a bit from the effort. Careful. Don't trip and fall. I have to concentrate even though my mind doesn't feel like it's working yet. I pause and limp like an old man, short-stepping some stairs and gripping the handrail to stay balanced. After about 10 minutes my coffee maker gets the coffee (AKA the lifeblood: a warm liquid of life) hot enough so that I can enjoy its energy and warmth. I have something sweet with my coffee; a kid-sized Clif bar. After that indulgence I stumble into the bathroom; yeah, those cheesy enchiladas and 3 beers last night at the Sagebrush Cantina constipated me (that was a special meal for a Friday night though).

7:05…time to get dressed. We are running from the house at 7:20 sharp to meet the rest of the team at the duck pond by 7:30. Time goes by quickly when I am stumbling around in the morning.

I grab my Apple iPod Touch to check the weather: 7 degrees Fahrenheit outside. If there is any wind this run is going to hurt. I'm thinking of wearing 3 layers on top, my warmest Brooks hat, Brooks Paradox Mittens, and Brooks Equilibrium Windbrief Boxers with my Brooks Podium Pants. I also wear a Brooks Nightlife Jacket to top it all off and fend off the freezing wind. Christian puts strips of duct tape on the exterior of his shoes to add insulation. Such is the inventiveness that runners come up with while living the simple, frugal life in the frozen tundra that is Michigan.

Luckily in the winter we do get a couple opportunities to travel to Florida for 7-10 days at a time, and a trip out to the city where our next marathon is to be held (this year it is Boston). These breaks from working in the store are quite refreshing, and escaping the winter weather in Michigan is a huge plus. The times we spend in Florida are pretty much centered around running and watching TV, and are very relaxing. I wish I could go there more though.

After hearing about the obscene amounts of snowfall hitting the DC area, winter has finally pounded the Detroit area with a merciless series of cold-hearted punches. There is a little blizzard going on outside all day today. My solo afternoon 4-miler involved squinting through a stiff wind of snow flakes and slip-sliding my way through residential loops around the Driftwood house. Boston marathon training is finally in full-swing now: 3 weeks in and this week I'll crack 120 miles hopefully. Last week I was at 114, with our first two workouts of 5 by 2 miles downhill in Florida, (and then 3 days later) 3 by 3 miles on the first three miles of the Boston Marathon course. I had never been on the official Boston course, and driving over it several times with Keith was a real eye-opener. There are no totally flat parts on the entire route. I had heard that Heartbreak Hill was a joke, and people who had run the race told me it was nothing but just a little bump in the road basically. Well, it was anything but a bump to me; it was a giant hill. I think people who downplay such inclines are the ones that don't have to run up it at 5:15 pace. Anyway, doing a 20-miler on the last 20 miles of the Boston course in 1:56 was a good training stimulus the day after our 3 by 3 mile workout, because it pounded our legs to a pulp. We actually saw Ryan Hall running out on the course so that means we must be doing something right, huh?

In Boston, we got to watch the Reebok Indoor Games because Desi was competing in the 3000m. Of course, the most entertaining race of the night for Drew and me was the men's 5k. I got out my little Cannon Powershot and started filming on video mode while simultaneously attempting to give split updates to the LetsRun.com message board. I felt compelled to be the first to let the fans who couldn't see the games live on TV know what was going on with the race. Rupp, Lagat, and some Kenyans were in the lead pack most of the way. Seeing their skinny legs and fluid strides always made me a little jealous. Man, if I had skinny legs and hip mobility like that. If I just had that poppy stride and ran like I was floating above the surface of the track…it must feel amazing to be that light and fast.

The 5k turned out to be a fast one. After stringing together some 31 to 32 second laps on the 200m indoor track, the athletes were formed in a line and running a consistent, blistering pace. The leaders came through the first 1500m in 3:56. After that the pace slowed to a projected 5k time of 13:20, and just when it looked like there wouldn't be an American record, Rupp turned up the heat. Making a strong move with 800m left, Galen shot to the front with a 28-scond lap. It reminded me of back in the day when we were both juniors in high school. I ran at a small, decently competitive meet called the French Prairie Invitational in Woodburn, Oregon, and Rupp toed the starting line for a 3k workout. I was running an all-out 3k race, but there goes Galen running a 30-40 workout (alternating 30 second and 40 second 200 meter splits) and then kicking it in to run an 8:40 as a total fartlek workout on the track. Anyway, unlike Lagat who stuck to the back of Galen on that 28 second lap, I was totally dropped by Galen's surges way back then.

The race was on! Eventually Lagat and a couple Kenyans outkicked Rupp in the last 300 meters. Lagat finished with a new American Record of 13:11 [see video at Vo2maxProductions.com, "Boston Indoor Games"]. The crowd was excited and on its feet. Rupp still ran a PR of 13:14, breaking his previous best mark by 4 full seconds. Supposedly Salazar had said that his young athlete had a cold also. (Rupp always seems to have some health ailment.) I was impressed with all the track speed that had taken place in that instant. I missed track; the raw, blazing velocity, the steady coast around the curves, the grip of sharp spikes digging into a hard synthetic surface. I always grimaced with the pain of running so fast and intensely. There is nowhere to hide on the track; you are always exposed to the competition and the crowd. Some of us just never had that lethal combination of fast-twitch muscle fibers, a high Vo2max, and a large anaerobic capacity to post the kinds of times these guys just did. I know now my days on the track are pretty much over. I was never the guy sitting and kicking; I never had that smooth form and gear-changing ability. Alas!

In the women's 3k Desi ran a PR of 9:00. Imagine, a marathoner mixing it up with the likes of Sara Hall and company? I don't know how Davila does it! We don't even train on an indoor track up here in Michigan. Just 4 hours before the races we ate lunch at a Pan Dolce and saw Bernard Lagat getting some soup. Lagat asked Chad what was good there, and then proceeded to get a cheesy cheddar soup that Chad recommended. Ballsy. And to think, some elite athletes are so religious about pre-race meals that they have gone to such extent as to pack pasta in Ziploc bags to make sure what they are eating is safe. And here's Lagat, chowing down on some cheddar soup as his last meal before demolishing the indoor 5k American record. Desi also had a full sandwich and a relatively large shortbread cookie half dipped in chocolate. Man, I could not stomach that kind of meal before such a high quality 3k or 5k.

See video "Boston Indoor Games highlights" at www.Vo2maxProductions.com for footage of Desi racing on the indoor track.

Single Awareness Day
February 14th, 2010

Today is going to be a long day. One of those days where you stare at the clock with tired eyes and become frustrated by how slowly the minutes seem to tick by. We now live in a fast-paced society where time should be valued more; you should want time to always slow down so you can enjoy every moment. Well, on this Valentine's Day I was not cherishing or appreciating the minutes of my life. Actually, I wasn't appreciating what I had in general very much. If I was in love it might have been a totally different story. For Valentine's Day I worked a 6.5-hour shift at the Grosse Pointe store alone, save for a couple hundred pairs of fresh smelling shoes.

Chad, Drew, and I woke up extra early this morning to drive to the boat launch for our mandatory Sunday community run, which no one else on the team (or Kevin or Keith or Don) showed up to for some reason. Don't get me wrong - I'm all for meeting Team In Training and other community charity runners and members. I love to support the local running scene, the Stoney Creek Running Club, the Oakland University team, and other various high school and kid-runner teams. However, the 20-minute drive out to Stoney Creek Metropark has an opportunity cost in terms of my time and my gas money. The '98 Chevy Prizm has only so many miles left on her old, ragged, oil-leaking engine. So this morning we started at the boat launch in the park and did a relatively easy 16 miler in about 1:45. Yesterday, I finished my 4th week in this Boston training segment at just over 120 miles. Also, yesterday we had a downhill workout of 10 by 1 mile repeats on a negative slope with a three to four percent grade. We easily averaged around 5:10 per mile repeat - something that any 2:40 or better marathoner could keep up with. Since we had a 4-minute recovery that involved driving up the hill between each effort, the workout took a significant amount of our morning. We started the repeats at 7:30 AM and weren't done until after 9:00. Chad and Drew had 8.5- and 7-hour shifts respectively at the Royal Oak store immediately afterward. Luckily, I had the day off, and upon completion of the workout I drove home and promptly crashed in my bed. The workout was easy aerobically, but it made my quads quite sore (which succeeded in completing the goal of trashing our legs again). I really need to work on my downhill running form. I tend to heel strike, and this causes a braking reaction that slows me down, costs more energy, and increases the impact on my legs. There doesn't seem to be a whole lot I can do to make downhill running smoother except lean forward a little more and try to let gravity do the work.

Last night we thought it sounded like a good idea to go out and get a drink and perhaps (wishfully) meet some single girls who were looking for a Valentine's date. Fail. Shall I say epic fail? We went to this bar/restaurant called The Red Ox, which was near the local Oakland University on the northwest side of Rochester, hoping to meet some college girls. At 10 PM we were greeted by a bunch of more mature adults in their late-30s and 40s. Almost all were couples, and many were dancing (or trying to dance) to some cover band performing renditions of classic '80s songs. The place reeked of smoke as it had not become state law quite yet to prohibit smoking in public indoor places. I got a tall Sam Adams seasonal brew and drowned my sorrows. By 11 I was thoroughly exhausted and feeling like an old man myself. We reminisced about the glorious college days of the past when we actually had a social life, and felt sorry for ourselves in the present situation, where we were dateless and low on energy before midnight. This isn't my scene. I want to go back to college. With our heavy training schedule this kind of simple night out is a risk because of the physical toll that is placed on your body. Drew said he's feeling like he is getting sick with a cold. I started to worry that being out so late would make me extra tired for the morning workout. We left a bit disappointed. However, there appeared to be no young, single females in the bar worth talking to anyway. At least the music was good!

Living the full-time running lifestyle means having consistency not only training, but also in terms of sleep and diet. Our bodies respond best to developing a routine. Unlike the rest of the world, we have trouble adapting to the demands of real-life in terms of partying late, sleeping in on weekends, or even eating out. The stress of not being able to do things that are considered normal slowly eats away at your soul. There aren't many outlets to cope with this dilemma, and so we indulge in unhealthy, self-destructive habits (which unfortunately often becomes the case with many semi-obsessive distance runners).

For example, my diet has taken a turn for the worse. I started a food log to keep myself more accountable for everything I ingest. I lack the discipline to restrict my food intake and successfully drop the 5 to 10 pounds that may (or may not) be hurting my running performance. The following is what I've been eating for the past week or so:

2-19-10:

coffee
a slice of sourdough bread with peanut butter

40 oz of Gatorade

a kid-sized Clif bar (peanut butter)
30 g of whey protein drink mix

banana pancakes (5 small ones) with honey
hot cocoa

an avocado/cheese quesadilla…3 tortillas, with fresh salsa
half a cup of orange juice with liquid iron

a large Dunkin' Donuts coffee with sugar and cream
non-fat blueberry Greek yogurt

a large serving of pasta with cooked carrots, onions, tomato sauce, and
peppers
a packet of Annie's fruit snacks
an apple

mixed greens, a whole avocado, half a red pepper, and balsamic dressing
2 pieces of wheat/seed bread
12 oz choice beverage [beer]

2-18-10:

kid-sized Clif bar
coffee
bowl of oatmeal with a glob of peanut butter and two tablespoons
brown sugar
2 cups of hot cocoa

a couple saltine crackers
a lemon poppy seed muffin
coffee

a big bowl (2 servings worth) of Amy's lentil soup
a slice of wheat/seed bread, 2 slices of sharp cheddar cheese

a large salad
two more slices of wheat bread with cheese

20 oz choice beverage

2-17-10:

cup of coffee
kid-sized Clif bar (blueberry)

PB and J sandwich on sourdough (large)
Banana
Gatorade and Red Bull mix – 16 oz

hot cocoa
2 eggs
3 wheat/flax frozen waffles with globs of peanut butter and syrup

Annie's packet of fruit snacks
half cup orange juice with 1 teaspoon of liquid iron (nasty)
1000 mg of vitamin C

my usual pill cocktail of magnesium, vitamins D and B-12

2 large jelly-filled doughnuts and a large coffee
100 calorie packet of almonds
Sharkies fruit snacks
1 carton of mac and cheese with extra butter and milk added
1 flatbread wheat lavash
1 banana

6 oz of Greek yogurt with a handful of Honey Nut Cheerios and jam
hot cocoa

2-16-10:

2 Taco Bell bean burritos
3 cookies
2 cups of hot cocoa
1 choice beverage
1 pintos and cheese cup from Taco Bell put inside a wheat flatbread, 4 packets of hot sauce
3 oz of extra cheddar cheese

(forgot to keep track the rest of the day…ate some chocolate)

2-15-10:

1 cup of coffee
1 kid-sized Clif bar (peanut butter)

1/2 can of Red Bull and 16 oz Gatorade

1 chocolate mocha Balance bar
2 eggs
2 large pancakes with syrup and extra butter
2 cups of hot cocoa

1 cup of tomato soup
8 saltine crackers
1 oz of cheddar cheese
1 bag of Sharkies fruit snakes

1/2 cup of orange juice with 1 teaspoon of liquid iron and 1000 mg vitamin C

large salad with carrots and balsamic dressing
1 individual-sized frozen pizza, plain cheese
1 choice beverage

1 sheet of lavash flatbread with 1 oz fresh salsa
1 choice beverage (20 oz)
1 cup of hot cocoa with choice seasoning
2 oz chocolate toffee bar with almond topping
1 Pepperidge Farm Milano chocolate cookie

2-14-10:

1 peanut butter kid-sized Clif bar
1 cup of coffee

2 large jelly-filled doughnuts
1 cup of coffee

3 eggs scrambled with 1 oz cheddar cheese

1 chocolate mocha Balance bar
1 bag of small fruit snacks
1 bag of 100 calorie Emerald almonds
1 cup of green/white herbal tea

2 Taco Bell bean burritos
1 Taco Bell bag of cinnamon twists
1 16 oz grande Starbucks coffee

1 bag of Sharkies fruit snacks
1 cup of tomato soup
1 large bowl of spinach pasta with tomato sauce and 1 oz of Parmesan
cheese

1 apple
1 bag of 100 calorie Emerald almonds

After writing down everything you eat for a week you start to notice some unhealthy patterns. I definitely could improve the balance and nutritional content of my diet as well as lose weight by adding more fruits and vegetables and reducing my high carbohydrate intake. I love Taco Bell too much though! To rationalize any not-so-healthy food item I eat, I think of guys like Bill Rodgers, who was said to have a notoriously bad diet. I think of times when I made big sacrifices and went dry on drinking soda for two months only to have a horrible season of track (not that there is even a cause-effect relationship between those instances, but you get the point). I'm a relatively young, active male who can get away with eating over 4000 calories a day and still only have five-percent body fat. Damn right, I'm going to take advantage of that. If anything, I just like to make sure that I get some blood work done a couple times a year to make sure my iron isn't too low and that I don't have any major vitamin deficiencies.

As intelligent, thoughtful beings we have developed the curse of rationalizing our actions so that anything and everything we do can seem right or justified in our own minds after we think about it long enough. For example, I'll justify eating a less-than-healthy diet because I am "stressed out," "am enjoying my youth," or "because I'm a guy and cooking isn't what I do." The fact of the matter is, yeah, we can all improve something in our lives, optimize our performance and give closer to the 100% effort that it takes to reach our goals. But do the ends justify the means? Are you willing to make those big sacrifices and still risk failing in the end, when all is said and done? Is it worth it to fully invest yourself in reaching a destination, when in fact you may end up regretting that you didn't just enjoy the journey in the first place? All these thoughts. I guess when you are single on Valentine's Day, and you are amazed to see these couples out spending hard-earned money on over-priced material items you start to think about your own self-actualization. Heavy stuff, but such is the burden we carry in our heads and on our figurative shoulders (the burden is more on our legs) for being solitary, lonely, and (at times) frustrated distance runners. We are like nomads…but nomads on a mission.

Nick Left
February 16th, 2010

At Hansons, athletes are usually bound to a 12-month contract. The contract ensures several things - most notably that you can't leave abruptly and sign with another program or shoe sponsor without a major financial penalty. The contract also details how you need to keep the houses tidy, how you are reimbursed for health insurance benefits, and that you'll volunteer up to 50 hours a year to "promote the sport." Historically, athletes have always been coming and going in the program. Some have been kicked out and banished. Others became injured, depressed, and couldn't take it anymore. However, more recently athletes have been leaving right when their contract ends. With each departure and new arrival the team chemistry changes a little bit. A different, often younger, dynamic develops. It is sad to see a teammate and friend that you have trained hundreds of miles with decide to move on to another program or give up on the dream altogether. After becoming the 3rd fastest marathoner in Hansons history, Nick Arciniaga decided it was time to move on.

Nick's career at Hansons involved several notable highlights, and his development as the next star was evident in his progression from being the top American finisher at the Boston marathon to running an epic 2:13 at New York just a year and a half later. Nick never seemed to get hurt. He had run so many 140-mile weeks since I arrived in Michigan that I had lost count. Tall, skinny, and blessed with near perfect form, Nick had finally transformed himself into one of the best marathon runners in the country. A far cry from a mid-14:20s 5k runner in college. He was ready to move on, to explore a new training stimulus at altitude with McMillan Elite, based in Flagstaff, AZ. And who could blame him? At Hansons he had been tied to the stores too much. He often didn't have time to nap because he was manager at the Royal Oak store and worked immediately after morning runs most days. I vividly remember him coming home from work after 4 PM, exhausted. He would sometimes lie down for 20-30min, change into his running clothes, and just sit on the Driftwood living room couch. He'd say something like, "I'm trying to get up enough energy to do my second run." Late in the fall it gets dark and cold out at 4:30. He'd vanish off into the dark, no doubt running at least 6 miles after putting in a solid 14 miles in the morning. Tough stuff. Perhaps in Flagstaff he could become more of a full-time runner and not worry about selling shoes for 25 to 30 hours a week.

So Nick left yesterday. I couldn't go to his good-bye breakfast because I had to work. He joined us for one last morning run on the roads around Avon Circle…a 10.5 mile run that pounded pavement the whole way and seemed to take forever. He had just returned from Spokane, WA where he was 15th in the USATF Cross Country Championships - not bad considering that he hadn't done any speed workouts specific to the demands of such an event…no cross country or fast track workouts at race pace or faster. I watched the race unfold on Flotrack. Notre Dame grad Patrick Symth led most of the race with Scotty Bauhs and Ritz with him. Ritz put it into high gear the last 2.5 kilometers or so and easily won. It appeared to be a nice February day for Spokane… much warmer than back here in Michigan and not nearly as much snow.

* * *

This morning I got up at 6:48 AM for a 20-mile long run with Chad and Drew out at Stony Creek Metropark. It was snowing on the 20 minute drive there as I sipped my coffee out of a dirty ceramic mug. The sky was dark and visibility was limited. I nibbled on a blueberry-flavored, kid-sized Clif bar. I had brought a couple 24-ounce plastic

bottles with squirt caps filled with a Gatorade/Red Bull/
water mixture to drink on the run. We arrived right at 7:30…
almost late. Keith was waiting for us in the parking lot.
Within two minutes we were out and running around the 6
mile paved path that circumnavigated the lake. A thin layer
of snow covered the rolling route as we ran. It was a rather
balmy 25 degrees out and there wasn't much of a wind. Chad
shed his jacket after the first 2.5 miles when Keith handed us
our first fluid bottles. We started easy at around 7:00/mile
pace for the first 4 miles. It felt faster than that, but after
taking mile splits around the park it is easy to figure out your
exact velocity.

"It's going to be hard to bring it down," I exclaimed.

"I thought 2 hours [flat] would be good today - but
not in these conditions," Chad reassured, implying that a
6:00/mile average would be too tough on the slippery path.
Like in Boston, I tailed the guys. Drew is a "one-stepper,"
always edging slightly ahead and pushing the pace. Five
miles into the run we were already under 34 minutes on the
stopwatch, and we were speeding up. We agreed that each
6-mile loop we did around the lake would become a faster,
negative split. I pulled even with my two teammates going up
the largest hill on the route.

"On the last loop this is going to be like Heartbreak,"
Chad chimed in, referring to the incline at about 20 miles
into the Boston Marathon. Since we were running a full 3
laps and then an extra mile out, plus a mile back (for a full 20
miles), we decided that the last mile would be a cool-down
mile. Suddenly, in the middle of the run the guys really start
to speed up. I am content staying back, trying to drink at
least 8 ounces of my fluid mixture every time Keith swings by
in his car and hands out our bottles. I am not thirsty at all in
the cold, but I force the liquid down. We come through 10
miles in about 63:15…starting to drop sub 6's. Chad knows I
can grind uphills well, and it seems like he put in a little surge
before every hill. 5:40, we split our 12th mile, which involved

some heavy drinking. I charge up a hill. Drew's breathing is heavy. I open up a little gap. Chad counters my move at the crest of the hill...oh! It's ON! We are really flying now. I'm in the hurt box at this moment, revisiting my good friend of long-run-specific-marathon pain! Chad and I surge back and forth...27:20 for the last 5 miles...we are dropping 5:30's now. The snow picks up and blinds me. Drew wore sunglasses in anticipation of such a blurry snowfall. Chad tucks in behind me and drafts; he later recalls: "I just stared at the logo on the back of your jacket...if you had run off the trail into the bushes, I would've followed you..."

The visibility was horrid. I could only look down at my quads. The snow accumulated during the run, so we were slipping around in about an extra fresh inch of the fluffy white stuff. Finally, we complete three full laps around the lake and are 18 miles into the run. Chad has stuck to me, but I am happy he isn't going to try to kick past me going into the last couple miles. We run the 19th mile close to 5:40 because it is a net uphill. Drew is about 200m back and struggling. In our last mile Chad and I "jog" it in at about 6 flat pace and Drew catches us. The long run was a success, and I finally feel hardened not just to the winter elements, but also to the intra-team competition and Hansons long run intensity. This is how you really prepare for a marathon: show some blood and guts on a long run. Little did I know that such high-end efforts on my part would come back to haunt me.

Drew's Training Log comments on the workout:

"Long run at Stony with Chad and Sage. Snowy and slippery. We started out pretty slow (7:00 pace), then continuously dropped the pace well under 6:00, which took a solid effort in the slippery conditions. Sage and Chad actually dropped me on the third lap when they accelerated up a hill and I couldn't really match it. It was a little frustrating, but I am not too concerned. I am in the middle of a cold right now which I

think has weakened me a little. I wore the heavy [Brooks] Glycerins when I probably should have gone with the lightweight Launches like the other guys. The last 6 miles or so were tough, but I didn't completely go to the well, so I'll live to fight another day. Good to get a solid long run in at least."

Drew's positive attitude would pay dividends in the near future.

Downhill
February 19th, 2010

8.5 weeks out from Boston. Today we had our last downhill workout on a hilly gravel road called Drahner. The road ends close to the Palace [Piston's basketball arena] out in Auburn Hills, which is Northwest of Rochester. Drahner is a narrow venue, and on a winter day like today it was filled with some slick ice patches. The workout was "7 by 1.5 miles" at 5:17 per mile pace with a 5-minute rest between reps (or however long it took to drive back up to the top of the hill). It was a cool, clear day as Chad lead us down the first rep as we twisted around blind turns trying not to slip.

"2:40...2:41..." Kevin called out the first half mile split. Slow! Damn. This was the steepest downhill section on the road. I was surprised at how fast the pace felt. Usually you want marathon pace to feel a little more comfortable early in a workout. We finished the first 1.5 miles in 7:50. After that we warmed up, and the effort actually got a lot easier. I led some reps faster than our target pace and split 7:43 and 7:45 (average mile pace of 5:10 to 5:08).

The downhill twists of the road proved to be not only fast, but also dangerous. In the middle of the workout, when we got to the top of the hill to start our 5th rep of the workout, a near-disaster struck: Carl (a local, former Hansons runner, and national class masters marathoner who trains with us) made an attempt to open the side door of Keith's vehicle to jump out onto the road, but luckily Keith still had the automatic lock engaged. This probably saved Carl from a trip to the hospital. At that very moment I was sitting in the middle seat, crammed between Carl and Drew with no seat belt on.

"Car back," Keith blurted. A half a second later there

was a wham sound accompanied by the shattering of glass. I flew forward as Keith's Suburban lurched ahead despite having its parking brake on. A rusty old pick-up truck had plowed into the back of us. I heard a crunching sound as we slid forward on the slick gravel road, and the whiplash nearly knocked the wind out of me. The driver of the pick-up had sped up the hill and apparently couldn't stop. It was obvious that he was either drunk (or on some other drugs), talking on a cell phone, and/or driving without his eyes on the road. It was a straight stretch of road, and the visibility of our large vehicle shouldn't have been an issue. Carl's one-second hesitation kept him from getting totally creamed. My neck and back ached. Drew and Chad were pumped up on adrenaline also.

"That's like the 2nd accident I've ever been in in my life," the thirty-four year old Chad recalls. Keith was surprisingly calm; his vehicle only had a minor dent in the back fender. The junker that hit us, on the other hand, had dropped rust flakes and debris all over the road. A somewhat creepy guy, pretty much a stereotypical backwards hillbilly, creaked open the truck's door and stepped out. His old truck's front fender had busted down near his front wheels... it was all bent out of shape. Keith had us go ahead and start on our next rep.

"You guys are going to have to time yourselves," he lamented.

Shaken and jacked on adrenaline we charged down the hill...2:29 for the first half mile! I felt like I had another lease on life. It reminded me that we in fact weren't invincible. The workout finished a little faster because of that incident. My body became extra sore from the ordeal, but luckily no one was injured.

Our little "training bubble" actually existed in the outside, real world and most people wouldn't understand why we were charging down a snow-covered hill early in the morning. Danger looms around every corner, and when you are running on the roads you have to always remember how bad some drivers are. Ah, the risks of running!

Determined to get health insurance, I headed down to the local DMV that very afternoon. Supposedly I need a Michigan Drivers License or State ID in order to apply and qualify for the health insurance program that the Hansons set us up with here. I had finally straightened out my car insurance for coverage in Michigan. Unfortunately, since I had recently moved from the Driftwood house to the Bloomer house, my proof of residence in Michigan papers didn't match since the addresses were different. Shit, why does my W-2 still have me living at Driftwood? Frustrated, I took my passport, my Oregon driver's license, insurance forms, and various other employment papers and left the DMV a little flustered. Because of incidents like today, I am actually kind of worried about not having any health insurance right now [Unknowingly, I was still covered under ObamaCare since I was younger than 25 and could still rely on my parent's plan]. A lot of the guys on the team go uninsured. What if I got seriously hurt or sick? What if I got toasted by a car like Rizzo did two years ago while he was training for Boston? I couldn't imagine the hospital bills as they'd bankrupt me and my family! There were a lot of things on my mind besides just training for Boston now. I was feeling a little heat. To make things worse, I had just found out that my Grandpa had been rushed to the hospital with serious health problems. He had been a major supporter of my running for the past several years, and was patiently waiting to hear about my next race. Distraught, I laced up my shoes for another run.

Often, on my solo, afternoon runs I try to clear my mind of such worries and stressors. Some say running is like a form of meditation. When one examines what place aerobic exercise has in their lives, they often overlook the psychological benefits. As a stress reliever or coping mechanism, running is therapeutic. Although originally seen as a "flight" response for survival, the act of running itself (in my opinion) does not figuratively represent the cowardice of escaping from one's problems. Rather, I'd like to think of running as an opportunity for the brain to think about how to solve problems (perhaps even if this occurs only on a subconscious level). So I haven't just been running to train for Boston; I have been training my brain with feelings of well-being. Another good reason to keep running.

Florida
March 3rd, 2010

Two to three times a winter we travel down to Florida for 7 to 10 day stints to escape the snow in Michigan. The warmer weather and secure footing allows us to pile in the miles a lot faster. It is a great opportunity to improve one's fitness. My first week in Florida was last week, and I ran 130 miles. It felt manageable.

This morning I had a "magical run." This could be a turning point.

"I've never felt so good on a training run," I excitedly exclaimed in the van ride back from some orange groves where we had run entirely on dirt roads. When Mike had stopped to take a dump I took advantage of the situation and surged away because I was annoyed that we were already going 5:40 pace due to his one-stepping.

"Let's see if we can make him [Mike] work to catch us!" I told Drew and Chad as we pressed the pace down to close to 5:10/mile. I knew Mike never let anyone beat him on an easy run, and that he'd want blood if it looked like we were trying to drop him. We were over halfway into a 12 mile run, and when we hit a mile-long uphill stretch Drew had had it.

"WHAT ARE YOU DOING?" he angrily shouted at me.

"I feel good" I shot back.

This was my day. I never lead easy runs. I had all this pent-up energy from always hanging off the back, never pushing the pace and challenging my teammates. Today, I was determined to hold the lead and fend off any challengers. I charged up the hill, and Chad stuck to me like it was a race. I felt my breathing quicken, and my legs felt the effort of the pace, however I couldn't seem to dial in to my lactate threshold. It was like I had no threshold to limit me! My legs churned; I dropped Chad with a mile to go. There was no pain, no burning lactic acid. I knew Kevin would be waiting for us in the van. He had been watching the whole drama unfold, and hadn't said a thing. Chad told me later that Keith and Kevin love it when we get competitive on our easy days and long run days. During these workouts, pace is never restricted, and whoever feels good can go for it. Guys who don't feel good feel obligated to stick with the leaders, guys like Drew who don't want to feel like they are getting dropped. I knew Mike was really going to try to catch me; he didn't. I ran the last two miles of the "recovery" run in about 9:40.

During the hour-long van ride back from the run Chad, Drew, and Mike appeared to be annoyed with me. I had a smugness that never left my face. In retrospect I should have been more concerned; such reckless training often has a backlash effect. The damage may have already been done. I was on fire! It was still over a month away from the big race.

On this morning run in Florida, I was reminded of the few times in college when I used to rip a workout and no one could stay with me, a rare occurrence that only happened a couple times in five years. I would feel invincible, untouchable. These feelings in running are dangerous though, because your fitness can only be at this high level for so long…you can only pay the price a certain number of times before you become in debt. You dig your own fitness grave.

"You can't burn out until you catch fire" was something I used to tell my teammates to justify why I did 400m track repeats all summer before cross country season. Keeping things aerobic, keeping the mileage easy and relaxed with a few faster, alactic, turnover sessions never did any harm. However, the cumulative fatigue, the manipulation of several training variables like intensity and volume simultaneously is like playing with fire. Once you cross that delicate line, that internal balance of adapting and super-compensating, your body goes straight to overtraining and failing. When this happens within a season, your fitness can be in jeopardy. If I keep running these competitive easy days like I did today, I will burn out before Boston; best not to leave my marathon race out on the training runs. I must save up for the real event, 6.5 weeks out. Fuck, I can't wait.

* * *

Additionally, Drew and I are calloused in our battle to under weigh each other. We compare our weights on a near daily basis - on any scale we can find at any time of the day. We are both near the 150-pound mark. Chad is too, but he isn't obsessive about it like we are, and he shouldn't be since he is about 3 inches taller than me. For breakfast most mornings Chad has two boxes of Kraft Mac and Cheese with 3 eggs, scrambled. Drew likes his milk/banana/peanut butter protein shake that he mixes up in a blender. I just started supplementing with some extra Vitamin E and D. I think such supplementation will help with my deficient diet. I also still need to check my iron level again before it's too late. We are running so much that the toll of the miles can really mess your body up. You lose a lot of nutrients through sweat and running impact force. This could be a monster week...Chad is going for 140...Drew and I might just do 130. However, I am eager to put in those 20-mile days back to back again and again.

More cautious in his approach, Drew frets about all the cumulative fatigue vocally, later recalling that so far during the Boston segment: "I felt like [I had been] running as hard as I could...the workouts were much faster than anything that I could do by myself..."

Drew says that everyday he feels tired, yet he still hammers out every easy run with the lead pack. Some days he admits that he'd wake up in the morning and not be sure that he'd finish the hard workouts. For me, the workouts aren't very tiring. Things almost feel too easy...so far.

Chad "Nails" Johnson

Chad's middle name is really Niles – however, we call him Nails. It's not that Niles isn't a cool name to have, but rather Nails fits his personality as a runner better: he is tough as hell! When it comes down to a kick or surge at the end of races and workouts you'd better look out. At 6'2" and 155 pounds, he is tall, lean, and muscular (or at least as much as a long distance runner can be). He regularly lifts weights at the gym because he "likes the way it feels." Included in his workout routine are leg presses and the bench press. All this, on top of 140 mile weeks and his assistant coaching duties at the local high school (where he runs workouts with the kids in the evenings even after mornings he has workouts with us). Not a stranger to the camera, Chad appeared on the cover of *Wired* magazine in 2002. Despite his model-like good looks and talent in running, Chad is bashful. It seems as though his worst fear is to make people upset or mad, and he often glances down at the ground when he is talking to you. He speaks in a smooth, diplomatic way, but is quick to trail off if interrupted. At 34 he is the oldest guy on the team, but he fits right in when hanging out with teammates that are a decade younger.

Outside of running, Chad enjoys collecting coins. He is on the look-out for Wheat Pennies and is always talking about Buffalo Golds. Aside from being a collector, Chad is intrigued with games and challenges ranging from cards to jump roping. However, over the last decade Chad has solidified his identity as a national class runner who has made multiple US World Teams, and qualified for the Olympic Trials in 2000, 2004, 2008 and 2012.

As an athlete, Chad is a strategic racer who likes to sit and kick. He is the most accomplished track runner on the team with a 5k PR of 13:36 and a 3:43 1500m to his credit. When he was in the original Nike Oregon Project he ran workouts with Galen Rupp (a high schooler at the time), but also trained for a debut in the New York City Marathon. Chad runs up on his toes, with a pop in his stride. He can dunk a volleyball on a basketball hoop, a testament to his overall athleticism.

With his running career winding down, Chad's work ethic still remains surprisingly strong. Perhaps it is the remnants of the mindset that he developed from doing such eccentric workouts as 30 mile long runs on treadmills at 6:00 pace, to running to and from work at the Royal Oak store (12 miles each way). The stories Chad has of putting in 150-mile weeks, and doing 20 miles in under 1:40, make one realize that this guy is not only tough, but also very talented.

* * *

"It feels so good to sit down it brings tears to my eyes," says Chad as he rests his weary legs for a couple minutes at a rare time when there aren't any customers in the running store. At points during the summer, we make fun of Chad for only bringing Twizzlers to work to eat (when he had a solo, 7 hour shift). After a hard morning run, Chad worked at the store on his own and it was quite busy.

"I bent over to pick up a shoebox, and I got so dizzy I almost fell over," Chad recalls. Many of us can relate to that low blood sugar feeling as it is the same kind of marathon-induced fatigue that makes your thoughts cloudy in the latter stages of the race. But Chad was used to this pain; he had endured thousands of miles and hundreds of races. This Boston was going to be his last big one, he claimed.

Left to Right: Chad, Chad's Fiancé Melissa White, and Me.

Brian Wore Shorts Today
March 3rd, 2010

Back in Michigan. Drew and I flew back from Florida yesterday night with Mike Morgan. On our way back from the Detroit airport we drove straight to Antoniou's for a pizza dinner. The drive from DTW airport on the west side of the city to Rochester takes about an hour, and we were starving by the time we got to the restaurant. Morgan's wife Kelly "Yacho" Yacevich Morgan and her friend Brittany (who is training with some of the women's team for the USTAF 25k in Grand Rapids) met us for pizza, beer, salad, and bread sticks. It was awesome as usual, but unfortunately the women didn't want to stick around for one of the excellent homemade desserts (Drew, Mike, and I did...but we had already made the women wait for us, so we left with them). Drew and I split a "dinner for two," which probably sounds kind of unmanly for single bachelors - however, we were both trying to keep our weight under control (also not the most masculine thing to do).

This morning the team met at the boat launch in Stoney Creek Metropark for a community group run. Drew and I were out by 7:30 to get in some extra miles beforehand since he had to work at Grosse Pointe all by himself from 10:45 to 5:15. I was also scheduled to work all day at Royal Oak. It was a tiring and busy weekend day as usual. I had slopped together a stack of small pancakes as my late breakfast and lunch, put them in a Tupperware container, and soaked them with peanut butter and syrup. I didn't get a chance to eat that mess until 4:30. Man, I get so hungry during the height of marathon training! I ran 140 miles last week and this week is going to be around 130.

* * *

We recently heard the status of our teammates Luke Humphrey and Christian Wagner, and their disastrous indoor results from the Iowa State 5k. They ran 14:29, when we all expected them to be flirting with the 14-minute barrier. The meet supposedly had no competition, and their mindset was destroyed going into the race because Keith and Kevin couldn't get them into the indoor track at Notre Dame, where they were supposed to run. Instead, because of last minute plans, they flew out to Iowa the day of the race. Usually flying and running within a couple of hours is a bad idea if you aim to run fast.

* * *

It actually got above 40 degrees here. Could things be warming up? Brian met us in shorts for our morning run. The weather is now like a typical Oregon winter day; wet and damp, but great for running. I thought back to the days when I ran all winter in high school wearing baggy basketball shorts and a hooded sweatshirt that said "Newberg Track." I was so proud to wear that shirt because it made me feel like a jock when in reality I was more of a nerd. Sometimes I'd wear my track sweatshirt to class all day at school before practice. Years may come and go, girlfriends come and go, and classes change; however I've found that competitive running has been a single constant in my life ever since I told my mom I was "going out for track" in the 6th grade. The road has been long and tiresome since then, but worth every step of the way.

How I Caught The Running Bug

I vividly remember the first time I felt that I had a natural inclination to really excel at distance running. I remember thinking, "Wow, you may really be on to something here!" It all happened in 7th grade track. I had been running mid-to low-5:00s for the 1500m, and it appeared my progress was slowing down over the course of the short spring season. "Training" consisted of 5 to 10 miles a week, some 2.5-mile weekly long runs, and various sprints, drills, and games. I didn't think about structuring my workouts or care for running slow and easy.

One sunny, hot day at Athey Creek Middle School (a private school near Portland, OR), I had a breakthrough performance that came as the most pleasant surprise. It was the last meet of the season, and I had entertained the idea of maybe sneaking under the mythical 5:00 (1500m) barrier that day. In a race loaded with these big-looking, stud 8th graders (whom I had heard mention they were going to run a crazy 4:50 pace!), I started off conservatively, just off the back of the lead pack. My old school, all-black, size 6.5 Nike Zoom Rival D's clicked as I plodded around the first lap. It was hot enough that the dark track radiated an extra wave of heat. You could almost smell the surface melting; the odor of tar and ground tires. Two laps into the race I caught the lead pack of 8th graders, who were starting to slow down. Ignoring my splits and just racing, I tucked in behind them for another 200m before deciding that I could keep running at a faster pace. The last lap was always a blur. I actually referred to it as a dream because I wanted my vision to be hazy from the pain. I then started my kick early down the backstretch, unknowingly extending my lead. With 200m to go I remember feeling like the veins in my forearms were filling with corrosive lead. I thrashed my way around the turn and squinted at the clock at the end of the homestretch. As usual, I snuck a peak behind me - a move that almost made me lose my balance. I closed my eyes in the last 50m and sprinted as hard as I could. The pain was intense. When I crossed the line and the clock read 4:47, I was in shock.

"Surely the track was short!" I thought to myself. Within a couple hours I placed in the long jump, recording a personal best of 14 feet, 4 inches (which is still my best), and then led wire-to-wire in a 6th/7th grade open 800m, which I finished in 2:24. To this day, it was probably one of the greatest athletic performances of my life. The euphoric feeling of winning and smashing my PRs entered my blood stream and soaked into my brain, planting a seed of competitiveness that has driven me to still compete in distance running today.

* * *

By the end of high school five years later I hadn't really improved that much. I had taken only 38 seconds off of that 1500m time, and although I proved to be much better at cross country and the longer distances, there was never any chance of making Footlocker nationals or any elite-caliber high school event. Despite being the top freshman in my class at the Oregon state cross country meet, I never placed better than 13th in the state in cross country. Some guy by the name of Galen Rupp decided to quit soccer and run cross country our sophomore year...he got pretty good pretty fast. By my senior year, we had guys like Rupp, Ryan Vail, and Stuart Eagon dominating Northwest Oregon, and other guys were popping 8:20 3ks and 9:00 2-miles like it was nothing. The Oregon high school class of 2004 was perhaps one of the most competitive classes in state history, and I really didn't feel like a part of it because I wasn't mixing it up with any of those guys.

Frank Shorter was once quoted as saying, "Everyone ran 4:30 for the mile in high school." Well, I actually did run a 4:30 full mile in high school. I did have a 4:09 1500m to my credit though, which might be worth something a tad faster… but not by much. Anyway, I felt I was a decent high school runner, but not great. I never made states in track, and I never placed better than 4th at my district track meets, despite winning the district cross country meet by 30 seconds against a larger field of runners. My track times, the quantifiable personal bests that represent speed and aerobic power, were not up to par for most DI college recruiters. In fact, since I regressed my junior year in track, I only had sophomore PR times to my name for a long time. Running in college was not something I had even planned on doing until my senior year at Newberg High when college applications became due. However, that passion for running, that spark that ignited one fateful day on a hot track in 7th grade, slowly generated a flame that eventually turned into a bonfire. Not only did I run in college, but I kept running post-collegiately! You never know how one day, one event, can influence your life for years to come.

Clint's Comeback?
March 16th, 2010

Clint unexpectedly walked in through the front door of the Bloomer house at 7:48 this morning. Drew and I were just getting ready to leave for our morning run at the duck pond. We found out that he is running about 4 days a week now and biking on the remaining days. He is thinking about jumping into our 8 by 1000m track workout tomorrow. These steps in regaining fitness are impressive, given the multiple surgeries that the former 2:14 marathoner has recently endured.

Clint told us old stories about how the Bloomer house was different way back in '99. He mentioned that there was a raccoon family living up in the attic and that he had built large traps to capture them (and then release them unharmed into the wild). Hearing the wisdom of a guy that got 10th at Boston and got 5th in the 2004 Olympic Marathon Trials is reassuring. Drew and I had both recently been to Clint's office (Clint Verran Sports Medicine) in Lake Orion for scripts to get our blood work done. My red blood cell count and hemoglobin were surprisingly low, but Clint said I was overloading on iron. I knew my ferritin (one rough measure of iron) was 79, which is pretty decent, but for some reason my iron-binding capacity and ability to make new red blood cells is hampered. I'm guessing that that 140-mile week down in Florida has taken something out of me. Foot strike hemolysis anemia, or the fact that the pounding force of your feet against the ground ruptures red blood cells. Damn, at least I am hitting the right pace on all the workouts and feeling fit.

As usual on today's easy morning run a deep conversation occurred. With Mike and Clint leading the way down the Paint Creek trail, Drew and I tucked in the back with Chad as we clicked off 6-minute miles. I wasn't "feelin' it" this morning. Typical. Everyday feels like the pack is running just a little too fast for me to be comfortable.

"I was watching the Olympics several weeks ago," Clint exclaimed. "You know, the perfect sport for me might've been cross country skiing. Those guys are aerobic monsters."

"Yeah, but usually they are like 6' or 6'2" and 160 lbs," Mike chatted back, all 110 lbs of him bouncing up and down as he slapped his Brooks Glycerins (heavy cushioned, neutral training shoes) into the ground and pumped his arms.

"They say that a lot of the energy to drive forward comes from your arms - your lats and triceps," Clint said, explaining his reasoning. Clint was one of the more muscular guys on the team, and his heavier frame contrasted with Mike.

Drew put a new twist on the topic: "With his background, Brian would probably be really good at the biathlon. Racing and carrying a gun!"

* * *

The past week or so has been tiring. I only ran 125 miles in the last 7 days, but I had to work at the store every single day - 39 hours for the week. And business is booming: Drew and I probably sold close to 60 pairs of shoes on Saturday alone. When work is like that at the store you never get a chance to sit down or eat. My brother came up from Cleveland to visit for a couple days on spring break, so I dragged him to work with me (sounds like an awesome spring break, right?). Luckily, he was generous enough to drive over to Dairy Queen to get me some fries and a chocolate malt to devour. I get so hungry sometimes and just crave the fat and simple sugars of ice cream!

On Sunday the 14th (two days ago), we had our most difficult workout yet, down at the boat launch. My brother filmed the workout, and commented on how smooth we made 5:00 pace look. [The workout can be viewed at www.Vo2maxProductions.com under the heading "1-2-3-4 Workout"]. It made me confident that I was fit, and running 5:07 mile pace in cold weather on tired legs while drinking 10 ounces of fluid during each of the efforts was surprisingly manageable.

Desi

(Editor's note: this chapter was written long before Desi's stellar finishes at the 2010 Chicago Marathon (4th place) and 2011 Boston Marathon (2nd place), which further highlights her meteoric rise to the upper echelons of the sport.)

With the support of Brooks in 2003, the Hansons-Brooks Women's Team was formed, and a 3rd house was purchased to expand the program. At the time it seemed like a lot of promising female college runners were ending their competitive running careers immediately upon college graduation. There was a lack of opportunity available to them, and finding sponsorship for a post-collegiate running career was daunting at best. Given the initial success of the men's program, the addition of a women's team was an obvious next step in attaining the Hansons' goal: improving the competitiveness of American distance running on the international scene. Melissa White was an initial member of the team, and she quickly led the program by making multiple US championship teams on the track and the roads. The number of athletes and talent on the women's team has grown steadily over the years. One of the most notable additions has included California native and Arizona State alum Desiree Davila.

Desiree Davila may only be slightly over 5 feet tall, and less than 100 pounds, but rooted deep inside her petite frame is the fierceness and tenacity of a 500-pound tiger. When she competes, her eyes flash with a strong intensity, a fearless desire to drive the pace and pass her opponents. Desi is tough. Desi is talented. However, her flashy, but not phenomenal college career, capped by earning All-American honors in both cross country and track, pale in comparison to her ability to compete on the world stage in the marathon. Desi is now one of the few elite woman marathoners in the country to make the short list of contenders for the 2012 US Olympic Marathon Team. She just placed 11th in the world with a 2:27:53 at the 2009 IAAF Championships Marathon in Berlin (5 seconds and closing from the fading Nike poster athlete Kara Goucher).

In workouts Desi is often accompanied by her boyfriend (whose marathon PR is very close to hers). Through her progression and racing prowess she has earned herself the lucrative 6-figure salary guarantee from Brooks and Hansons - something that only Brian Sell had been able to pull off. She doesn't live in the women's team house, unlike many of the other members of the team. She doesn't work in the shoe store. When she first joined the program, she wasn't the star female of the program like she is now. In fact, others mentioned that initially she appeared out of shape, slow, and took time to adjust to the program. In her first marathon, a stormy Boston in 2007, she coasted in an Olympic Trials qualifying time of just under 2:45 (finishing several minutes behind teammates Dot McMahan and Melissa White). In the 2008 US Olympic Trials she went for a top 3 finish with Melissa and faded to finish 13th in 2:37:50 (the last spot to make the team was Magdalena Lewy Boulet in 2:30:19). Teammate Dot finished a stellar 8th to lead the Hansons-Brooks women in 2:35:02.

Fast Forward to March 2010:

Desi's most recent performance breakthrough just occurred at the World Indoor Track Championships. Yes, I said "indoor." The LetsRun.com staff and many message boarders (including myself) were surprised that she even had made it all the way to the championships in a 1.8 mile race of pure foot speed.

The race occurred a couple weeks ago in Doha, Qatar. In the prelims Desi ran in the faster heat and clocked an amazing 8:51 3k PR to qualify for the finals. Incredible, considering she "only" has 4:43 mile speed. Desi's American teammate Sara Hall was in the other, more tactical heat and wound up with a non-qualifying 9:04 performance. We just couldn't believe Desi knocked a solid 9 seconds off her PR just in the prelims! In the finals, Desi ran 9:07 and placed a respectable 10th in the world in a race won by Ethiopian's Meseret Defar (8:51).

The latest *Running Times* magazine has Desi ranked 2nd in the country for US road racers last year…Kara Goucher is ranked 1st. Desi's range is pretty incredible - none of the guys on the team could pull off world rankings in the 3k and marathon. The women's team, with Desi, Melissa, and Dot leading the way, continues to build the Hansons' tradition of strength and depth that will be a major force in the 2012 trials.

With both men's and women's sides to the program, the national rankings of US distance running often list multiple athletes all hailing from the snow-covered grounds of Rochester Hills, Michigan. In the *Running Times* year-end rankings for 2010, Nick Arciniaga was ranked 6th, and Brian Sell was ranked 8th, due to their respective performances in the NYC and Boston Marathons. In the end, however, the rankings, the media hype, and the predictions are useless. Desi may be an emerging Olympic athlete who has the potential to medal on the world stage, but she has so far managed to fly under the radar and avoid all the hoopla generated by her competitors. Unlike Kara Goucher, who makes media headlines on a regular basis, Desi slowly and steadily improves her racing performances at various distances. There is almost a direct contrast between the two women. While more media exposure might be a good confidence boost now and then, many Hansons runners simply just let the race results speak for themselves!

Desiree Davila: One tough competitor.
[Editor's note: for additional information
about Desi, including more recent interviews
and training runs, please visit
www.Vo2maxProductions.com and look under
"videos."]

Night Before The Simulator (10:21 PM)
March, 21st, 2010

Tomorrow I will rise at 6 AM, down 2 slices of toast with a little peanut butter and a cup of coffee. Then Drew and I will drive north out towards the hills of Lake Orion… to the top of Drahner Road for the start of a 26.2 kilometer "Boston simulator" workout. This is a major staple of the Hansons marathon training program, and it has been known to be the best indicator of marathon fitness. I am a bit nervous and prepared for some real pain.

The roads will be gravel and hilly, with a downhill start just like Boston and a series of uphills at the end just like the Newton hills. Our target pace is 5:17 per mile (marathon race pace) for the entire workout. For a run of over 16 miles all at once, that is no joke…I am prepared for some serious effort on my tired, un-tapered legs. We are to wear our racing singlets and flats (for me and Drew, the Brooks Green Silence). We are also to drink all 5 bottles of our race fluid. I have decided on 10-ounces of Gatorade mix (watered down 50%) for each bottle, as well as a Gu packet and a 200 mg caffeine pill, which I will take somewhere in the middle of the run.

As far as workouts go, tomorrow will be our biggest test to date. Like the long runs, I feel like it is most specific to the demands of the marathon physiology. We haven't done any long tempo runs, so this will be a first. I have no idea how I will feel, but I did not rest up for it - we ran 18 miles today and I'm coming off a relatively high 130 mile week. I am a little nervous the pace will feel hard early and I'll struggle. I don't know if Drew or Chad will be with me or not at the end - there might be a little competition between us! I don't even know the exact route we are running tomorrow. However, I've heard that traditionally Keith and Kevin come out with roadside signs that highlight real, historic landmarks, that are on the Boston course, like "Wellesley College" or "Citco." In any case I am prepared to dig deep and bust one.

Uff da!
March 30th, 2010

The simulator turned out better than anticipated. I was last to finish. I ended up 8 seconds behind Drew and Chad, which I didn't expect, but I'm not worried about it because it wasn't a totally all-out effort and we killed the pace anyway. The 16.28 miles (26.2 kilometers) was run on hilly terrain, and half of it was on gravel roads. Each little up and down somewhat mimicked the Boston marathon course, and I did pay a bit for storming up every hill, including the infamous "Heartbreak" where I split my slowest kilometer of 3:30. We averaged 5:11 per mile for the effort, which equates to a 2:16 marathon pace. This was significantly faster than 5:17 mile pace, our goal marathon pace to crack 2:19, which also works out to about 3:17 a kilometer. The effort was the most tiring workout to date for me, but that wasn't a surprise. Overall, the simulator was a success. Our confidence is high.

Last Long Hard Effort
March 31st, 2010

2.5 weeks until Boston - just about taper time. I feel as though the hay is in the barn now. Today's rather hard 20-mile effort will basically be the last workout that I can actually gain fitness off of…from now until race day we can only screw things up and overtrain. All the remaining workouts, (including the infamous 2 by 6 mile coming up) in my mind, will be for maintaining fitness and to keep the metabolism revved up. I still plan on running 130 miles this week because I think tapering is overrated. When you are used to this volume, 100 miles a week feels like nothing. Mileage figures are all relative though.

Since our simulator last week we had a solid 3 by 3 mile effort out at the boat launch, in which we ran 15:17 to 15:15 for each interval with an easy 7-minute mile recovery in between. I got down all my fluids and a caffeine pill in the middle of the fast running sections, so that was good practice for what we'll have to do on race day. Drew said the effort was harder than the simulator for him. I didn't feel great in this workout, but we were all running on really stiff and tired legs from the simulator. Cumulative fatigue has built up from running such taxing workouts.

Our very next workout three days later (on March 27th, 2010) was 5 by 1600m on the track. I had had some ankle tendonitis for the last couple of days and was kind of worried that I wouldn't be able to do the workout (there was one dark moment in my mind where I thought I might not be able to race because of the pain). However, much to my relief (and after the purchase of some new Brooks Adrenaline GTS 10s for training runs), my ankle felt decent through the workout even at 4:55 mile pace around the turns of the track in the Green Silence racing flats. I had bought the Adrenalines because Clint said that the stability shoe's posting (the grey part on the inside) would keep me from pronating and therefore alleviate the strain on the post-tibial tendon. I don't know if it was my religious icing, the switch in shoes, or the 8 or so Tylenols I took over the last couple days, but the pain is under control now. If it were my Achilles tendon instead, I would be screwed right now. I'm pretty sure I jacked my ankles up running down the gravel roads in racing flats at 5:00/mile pace at the end of the simulator though.

* * *

Last night was rough. Just as I was slipping into bed at a rather late 11 PM, a couple of my housemates came back from the bar. They are on a break from running now and finally wanted to have a little fun, so they went out drinking. They had a friend at the bar/restaurant drive them back to Bloomer because they were hammered. Anyway, they were pretty rowdy, and Drew and I were pissed because we couldn't sleep until after 1. Let's just say that they had a little fun with some golf clubs, our plastic table out on the deck, some matches, golf balls, and a BB gun...

So on 5 hours of sleep Drew and I rolled out of Bloomer at 7 this morning and drove to the boat launch to start our 20-mile long run. We had on the schedule 3 go miles at sub marathon goal race pace for miles 16, 17 and 18.

On the last half mile I was starting to really wish the run was over. There was some tightness in my stomach, I was breathing hard and coughing. There was some lactic acid, and my form was painfully breaking. Chad surged a little on a 100m downhill stretch and opened up 15 feet or so on me. With a quarter of a mile left we flew past Kevin and Don.

"You've got a head wind and a hill!" Kevin excitedly taunted us, with a big grin on his face. My pain and suffering was enough to make me think to myself, "Shut up." I

powered up the final steep incline before the paved bike
path evened out the last 300m and pulled even with Chad. I
looked over into his eyes and said, "I'm hurting"

Chad grunted for the 50th time on the run and
blurted out, "I'm at ninety-eight percent all-out right now!"
I tried to laugh, but I was too tired and too deprived of
oxygen. On the final straight we could see Mike about to
finish ahead…he was about 15 seconds up on us. I pursed
my lips and grimaced simultaneously. A sudden rush of
pressure had hit my lower intestines and I had the urge to
defecate into my shorts. Hold it in! Chad and I finished side-
by-side. 5:04 for that last go mile, not bad considering it was
a net uphill. We had run 15:12 for the last 3 miles, and about
54 flat for the last 10 miles or so. We still had 2 miles to go
to finish off our 20 for the day, but those were treated more
like cool-down miles. We waited 15 seconds or so for Drew
to finish (he had dropped off slightly) and then jogged it in
together. Overall, with our last 2 miles near 14:00 (relaxed),
we had still run 20 miles in 114 minutes. This was with
our first 10 miles in about 60:20, a relatively steady pace for
warming up. From miles 11 to 15 we dropped some 5:25s
to 5:17s in there, followed by the 3 go miles close to 15 flat.
So there was a 10 mile stretch in there when we hit a really
strong rhythm.

* * *

But then again the little skeptic inside of me
questions the workouts a little: "Do you have the endurance
to finish strong in the last 10k? Why didn't you get to do a
22 mile long run? Why didn't you do a 25-mile long run?
Maybe you should have done another week at 140 miles?"

In all my past marathons the actual velocity of the
marathon race pace was never an issue - my lactate threshold
is trained well enough, and 5:15s will feel like a comfortable
speed. It won't feel like a sprint. But can we hold the pace

after 20 miles? What is going to happen in those critical final miles when your glycogen is running low, you're dehydrated, and your muscles as well as your mind are failing? I never want to blow up again in a marathon. I hate to run positive splits. Only time will tell, and right now I'm going to focus on recovery. It's naptime before my night shift at the store today. Sometimes when I sleep, I dream about Boston; these visions occur a lot more often now.

Taper Time
Early April 2010

In the final weeks leading up to a marathon you start to obsessively think about your reasons for racing and training. You have to justify all the time you spent running, and you attempt to quell your anxieties as logically as possible. The following is a blog that I posted on Flotrack.org for the public to see and as a way for me to share my prerace thoughts:

"Almost Taper Time: Reflections before Boston"

It's hard to be patient when you are young. As one of the youngest guys on the Hansons-Brooks team I have had to constantly remind myself that my older teammates (guys like Chad, Mike, Luke, and Brian) are essentially the "old and wise" ones when it comes to the marathon. They have been there and done that - whereas I haven't really done anything (yet.) So I follow them on runs, I listen to their stories and I learn. I have always believed that you should respect your elders - and I respect all those guys anyway because they also have run significantly faster than I ever have...and many of them ran fast at Boston.

In just over two weeks I will be toeing the starting line in Hopkinton looking down the first descent, and waiting to put months of hard work into the 26.2 miles that leads to Boylston street. That day cannot come any sooner! Sometimes at night when I close my eyes I visualize running by the fire station turn at mile 16 and looking up at the hills...my heart races as I imagine grinding up Heartbreak (the last big one) just after the 20 mile mark.

I'm confident - we've done the (down)hill work and I'm strong on the uphills anyway. I've never been so prepared for a marathon in my life. I've run miles and miles of workouts at 4:57, 5:07, 5:12, and 5:17 mile pace (all marathon race pace or faster). I've done the long runs, the 20 mile days. I've averaged 128 miles a week for the last 8 weeks - that's record high volume for me. Before I set my marathon PR of 2:21 three years ago (as a junior in college), I had only run over 120 miles a week a couple times. Back then I was training by myself, with no one to push me in workouts or help keep me in check during the race. I was younger and more naïve. For Boston this year I will have two teammates with similar goals and fitness levels. In the last 10 weeks we have basically run every step of training together...through the snow and ice...against the wind. There is a lot of synergy when you have a training group like that...we feed off of each other in tough workouts, and we ultimately support one another in all facets of life.

My teammates and I would like to run under the 2:19:00 Olympic trials standard at the bare minimum. I am confident that I can hit that time - despite the rolling hills of Boston and the threat of adverse weather. Ultimately, in my mind this is not a "do-or die race." I am not particularly worried about the Olympic trials standard - it is merely just there for a goal reference. What is more important in my mind is that I execute a good race, and that I run to the best of my ability within the context of this training segment. I already put enough pressure on myself for every race - and when you're racing a marathon you must be fully invested.

I've learned long ago to be able to mentally let go of things that you can't control; things like weather, what your competitors do, whether or not your fluid bottle has been knocked over, etc. I may worry a little about those things: getting the swine flu, having food poisoning, getting hit by a car - but ultimately I know it is more proactive to focus on the things that I can control: what pace I run on race day, what I eat before the race, and how well I've run in my workouts for the past three months. So in these last couple of weeks when I become more and more anxious, I will also be constantly reminding myself (as cliché as this sounds): Patience is a virtue.

Finally, it is phases like these in training and in a running career that you can really start to reflect on what you are doing. Why are you running? I mean, distance running is one of the most selfish things to be doing right now. As an act of self-centeredness and as a lifestyle, it's like you are "checked out" with the reality of the world around you. Sometimes I ask myself: "What am I running from? What am I running towards?" In the grand scheme of things, running may be a way of life, it may be a method of coping - or it may just be a way to keep from getting a beer-belly. But the "sacrifice" of time (your most precious commodity) and energy towards what others may see as such fruitless endeavors can't be totally meaningless. Like anything in life running is a process, not just a means to an end. The point of the matter is that if you value something in your life (be it running or some other hobby) you can't forget the influence and importance that activity may have on other individuals who are close to you. And I think that any positive impact you can have on other people's lives is going to be enough to justify finding some meaning in your life - even if it is as simple as just continuing to put one foot in front of the other.

All we have time for now is to wait and worry - or, maybe we can build ourselves up with positive self-talk and the confidence derived from the past 3 months of killer mileage and tough, mind-bending workouts. Often I have trouble sleeping at night because I am visualizing the race, heart palpitating and all. As long as nobody gets sick, nobody gets in a car accident, and nobody has overtrained we are in the green to "go!"

One Week Until Go-Time
April 12th, 2010

In exactly one week we will be running the full 26.2 miles into Beantown. I can't wait! In fact, it is the wait that is killing me. When you have trained for months leading up to one race; when you have dreamed about that one race for years; when you realize that a potential defining moment in your whole running career boils down to the day April 19th, 2010; you may start to get anxious. "Is that scratch in my throat the first sign of an impending illness? Does that gassy pain in my stomach mean I got food poisoning from eating that cold sandwich at that restaurant?" Thoughts like these always surface in my mind. They are the rare, potential spoilers that threaten to wreak havoc on this one messy race coming up: The Boston Marathon.

Chad, Drew, and I sit and wait in a luxurious Florida house condo now. It is so relaxing to kick back, get on my computer, take naps, eat, and run without worrying about work or dealing with cold mornings up in Michigan. We get the next 5 days down here near Clermont, Florida to basically just do nothing but rest up, train in a little bit of heat, and taper. It gives you almost too much time to think. The peace, quiet, and privacy is mind numbing. I am never bored though, and I don't consider myself to be a mental runner. I know exactly what to expect, exactly what can happen, good or bad. I've run New York, I've started the Olympic trials, I've crashed and burned and walked, humbled by a lack of respect for the distance. I ran my PR 3 years ago in 75 degree heat. I am confident. I am prepared. I am ready to give my best.

We will probably run about 85 to 90 miles this last week leading into the race. This is a pretty decent taper, but it still sounds like a lot of volume. Most days we still run twice a day. Kevin came down here to Florida first with us for several days, and then Keith replaced him. We each had individual lunch and dinner meetings with them separately to discuss pacing, our final preparations, and what to expect. Everyone (our teammates, friends, and family) is excited to see what we can do. Both Kevin and Keith stressed the importance of even pacing: going out around 1:09:30 for the first half and bringing it back from there for a 2:18:xx. I am a little skeptical about that strategy only because Boston is so hilly in the second half. I would rather not be at the top of Heartbreak thinking to myself, "Okay, I am now behind 2:19:00 pace because I lost some time on the uphills, and it looks like I am going to have to run 5:0x miles for this last 10k to negative split it and barely qualify." No, I'd rather bank a little bit of time before 16 miles, grind the uphills, and just "coast" in at 5:15 pace for the last 10k. Drew and I are looking to hit that first half in 1:08:45 to 1:09:00 instead, weather permitting. Looking at splits from the top 50 males last year, everyone significantly positive split. Kevin and Keith suggest I am in 2:16 to 2:17 shape right now. I am willing to take a little risk and go for it (running a sub 1:09 first half). Unlike Drew, I don't see the downhill parts in the last 10k aiding me to a negative split.

In my more inspirational meeting with Keith, he told me that I could be like Nick. I basically had the same credentials coming out of college (minus the 1:55 800m speed). Now Nick is a 2:13 marathoner. [Editor's note: Nick is most recently a 2:11 marathoner at the start of 2011] with a shot at making the Olympic team in the 2012 trials. Keith said that in 2012 I could place like Nick did in 2008 (top 20), and by 2016 I could have a shot at making the team. I just thought to myself, "Damn, I will be 30 years old in 2016!" He had me read a little short story, "The Precious Present," and it reminded me to live in the present time, enjoy the process, don't worry about the future, and don't hold on to regrets from the past. I am very happy right now in Florida. I am in the best shape of my life, and I want to prove it come

Monday.

    Every morning when we come back from our 10 AM run (to get used to Boston start time) Chad makes his same tried and true dish: 2-3 scrambled eggs with a box of Kraft mac and cheese. His plate filled with yellow, he sheepishly grins, grunts, and laughs simultaneously, and then and sits down on the couch in front of the TV. Yesterday he made himself a cheeseburger for lunch, and then another burger and sweet potato fries for dinner. I made fun of him for such an indulgent diet. Kevin likes to make jokes and poke fun at all of us. I get picked on for being the vegetarian mainly. Such shenanigans rub off on me: I made fun of Drew by illustrating his high school nickname, "T. Rex." Using my basic Photoshop skills I made the following illustration and promptly posted it and tagged it on Facebook for all to see.

Drew "T.Rex" Polley, complete with his favorite Brooks Paradox Mittens and Brooks Green Silence racing shoes.

I've been doing some reading with all of my free time. Right now I am ¾ of the way through the book *Born to Run*, which is becoming a cult classic for minimalists and barefoot runners. It is thought-provoking, but some of the arguments about shoe companies having this "conspiracy" makes me somewhat skeptical. The literature itself inspires me to write. Right now I am in deep thought regarding the whole biomechanics of the foot, and the transformation of our country's society. Just thinking about the science behind the minimalist movement and the marketing campaigns of not only shoe companies, but also the Vibram brand and certain individuals, motivate me to write and film more on the topic. I think a lot of the debate between wearing cushioned running shoes and running barefoot could eventually be solved with video analysis and more long-term, scientific studies. The Tarahumara (the tribe discussed in the book) definitely have something figured out - not just in running, but running as a lifestyle surrounded by living off the land and leaving a (pun intended) near invisible carbon footprint on our great planet.

Beantown
April 17th, 2010

We arrived to a barrage of rain, wind, and cold at Logan Airport last night. Coming from the humid, 80-degree sun in Florida was quite the contrast. After checking into the Fairmont Copley Plaza Hotel near the finish line in downtown Boston, we caught a light dinner at a bar/grill called Whiskey's Smokehouse. It was a Friday night, and the BU students and other 20-somethings were out having a good time and drinking. Drew and I eyed a table of hot, young co-eds ordering liqueur to dunk in their beers. Darn, it was so tempting - if only we could go back to the carefree college lifestyle and party. I ordered the only vegetarian thing I could find on the whole menu: a vegetable fajita. Keith got his typical, greasy burger. Drew and Chad also were not thrilled with the meal (it wasn't a healthy enough place for Drew), but mainly waiting late until after 8 PM to eat made us grouchy. Worse still, when Drew and I retired back to our fancy old room at the Copley Plaza hotel at 10, we suffered from insomnia most of the night. I guess the excitement of being in Boston, the anxiety of the upcoming race, and the change in weather (as well as indigestion from my late meal) may have played a role.

* * *

This morning we forced ourselves up at 7:30 to grab some bagels and fruit before our 70 minute, 10 mile morning run. The run involved inserting three 2-minute "pick-ups" at a steady effort just for leg turnover. Drew and I couldn't find directions at the front desk for any elite athlete suite so we wandered around on a floor below the lobby and found a special media room that had some bagels, coffee, fruit, muffins, custom omelets, and cereal laid out with milk and fresh-squeezed orange juice. Only a couple people were there so we sat down and grabbed some grub. Honestly I thought it was the elite athlete suite.

"Did it stop raining out there yet?" A tall, wispy figure that I immediately recognized as Boston Billy (AKA Bill Rodgers) asked as he approached our table. He seemed very busy and on the move so I didn't bother with any "OMG!" statements or hasty introductions that would end with "Can I snap a picture of you with me in it because you are one of my running idols" kinds of moments. It was inspiring to see the great Boston runner in the flesh to say the least though. Later in the day we met Marc Davis also, former American 5k record holder. The greats of the sport were all coming out of the woodwork in such a running mecca!

* * *

In the afternoon we ate pizza at a California Pizza Kitchen and then attended the Brooks booth at the expo for a couple hours. At the expo we handed out Brooks cheering posters that said "Run _____ Run!" and "Run Happy _____" for spectators to fill in names of those running in the race. It was the biggest expo that I've ever seen at a marathon, and the crowds were packed into every conceivable corner of the multi-storied building.

A couple friends of mine from Cornell came up to the booth, including LetsRun.com's "Employee #1" who had run a 2:24 marathon in the fall and was my older teammate on Cornell's 2004 and 2005 cross country teams. Brooks was selling an assortment of spring clothing, and the colors behind us created a collage of red, black, blue, and pink. Runners in their bright colored, Boston Marathon BAA jackets were speckled everywhere throughout the crowd. Every now and then a fan would recognize our team and ask us what kind of time we were aiming for. Chad would say something like, "Uh, oh, like 2:18 would be good." Most people would exclaim something along the lines of, "Oh, that sounds fast!" We didn't have to sell anything, but people questioned us still just like we were working at the running store back in Michigan.

* * *

So now it is 9:28 at night and I am sitting in the room with Drew watching crappy television. We are contemplating going to bed soon and then trying to sleep in until 8 tomorrow morning. Little things, like when to mix fluid bottles and whether or not I should eat a Powerbar and a bagel with my coffee the morning of the race, are dancing in my mind. It is rainy, cold, and windy now, but the experts are predicting that it will warm and dry up on Monday. So we sit with our fingers crossed. I have already let go, knowing you shouldn't try to control the uncontrollable. I would, however, hope that we don't get a headwind. Temperature extremes and a little precipitation I can deal with, but a strong headwind might wreak havoc on getting our trials qualifier times in. I'd still go for it though.

When I realize we are in the final 30 hours until showtime my heart skips a beat and I get a rush of scared and nervous waves. However, then I remember that I have also been waiting for this moment, this day, this race, to come for years…maybe (in a sentiment I adopted from finishing the book *Born to Run* on the plane flight over here) I have been waiting for it my entire life.

Boston Marathon
Reflecting on the 19th of April, 2010

"Kiss me now, Fuck me later…" Drew was in an observant enough mode to read that statement on a sign held by one of the hundreds of girls at Wellesley College as we flew by their screaming wall of sound at close to 12 miles per hour. The sight and sounds brought a smile to my face. We were 13 miles into the Boston Marathon, and we were coming up to a 1:08:43 half marathon split…right were we wanted to be. Drew and I were leading a large pack of wannabe trials qualifiers strung out for the next quarter mile behind us, probably about 20 guys in tow. Chad was about 10 seconds back. Every mile Drew and I would take turns in the lead to block the cross wind (it felt like a headwind) for each other. We had been drinking all of our fluid bottles. I was feeling decent, not great, but getting more and more confident as the miles clicked off. We had started the downhills a little slower than expected with a couple miles over 5:20, but had slowly eased into a string of 5:10-5:16 mile splits for the last 10 miles or so on the relatively flat parts of the course. It was exhilarating…so far.

* * *

It was a beautiful day in Hopkinton when we arrived near the starting line around 8 earlier that morning. For the first time in 3 days, it wasn't cloudy and raining. The sun was out, and a slight wind was coming in from the Northwest, which was promising enough since the course mostly ran northeast. The temperature was perfect in the low 50s. We were escorted off the bus with the other elites. I quickly recognized Meb, Hall, and many of the elite African runners as we walked into a Korean church (the elite hospitality facility) about 50 yards away from the front of the starting line. Keith, Chad, Drew, and our friend Chris Lundstrom took refuge in a small classroom, decorated with 1st grade ornaments, posters, and Korean writing. We sat down in little chairs, and when that became uncomfortable, we moved to the floor and tried to relax. I made several pit stops to the bathroom, ensuring my intestines were totally clear. Thank God I got my Starbucks this morning. Drew mentioned he couldn't shit at all. There was some tension in the air with all the elites hanging around in the same building, but at the same time there was a stimulating level of excitement and anticipation. I could feel some nerves, but I was in a relaxed enough state to notice that a lot of the volunteer BAA girls looked to be about my age (college students?), and some were pretty cute. I saw this girl eyeing me down, and I'm pretty sure that I'll regret for a long time that I didn't go over and talk to her at that very moment. But I had a marathon to focus on…no time for flirting! Damn. I finished half of my second bagel for the morning and sipped some Gatorade. At 9:15 the elite women were called to line up outside of the church and walk to the starting line. That meant that we would be heading out soon. I was getting pumped. Outside the church there was a little 200m long, 20 ft wide pathway that all the elites started jogging on for a warm-up. I tucked in behind a large group of Kenyans and Ethiopians and puttered around for 7 to 8 minutes (maybe 1 mile) on that little gravel driveway behind the church. We were fenced off from the masses warming up in the surrounding neighborhood.

      Twenty minutes before the start we were escorted out of the church to the elite, front corral. We jogged through the throngs of runners waiting in the other corrals, our path a narrow tunnel through the masses. Cheers erupted with applause. So this is what it feels like to be a rock star? I shyly waved, soaking in the attention. With 15 minutes to go until gun-time we nervously jogged about, having the luxury of doing strides in front of the starting line. Hundreds of spectators on both sides of the narrow road watched us, as well as dozens of cameras.

"Man, I didn't get to go to the bathroom one last time," I said with concern to Drew as we watched Ryan Hall come out to the line a little later (apparently he had to take a last minute bathroom break as well). I expected this: as usual I was extremely hydrated before the race, and the thought of having a totally empty bladder when the gun went off really appealed to me. It wasn't that I was afraid of pissing myself on the run if I really had to - but rather the idea of carrying around any extra weight or possible discomfort annoyed me. So, planning ahead, Drew and I had each thought to bring some plastic Ziploc bags in our racing shorts to the starting line with us, just in case. Well, after standing around another 10 minutes we both decided to whip 'em out. In retrospect, we learned wide-mouth Gatorade bottles would've been a better choice to bring to the starting line to piss in.

The thing is, the Ziploc bags lacked ample volume and structural integrity. In an effort to not blatantly expose myself in front of several hundred people (and on TV), I attempted to urinate into my bag while holding it between the inseam of my shorts. Usually I would take a knee; at most races you have a little space to do such maneuvers. However, at the starting line of Boston everyone can see exactly what you are doing, so with both hands in my shorts I stood like a bashful fool and let loose. Drew did the same, even though I thought we had communicated that one would at least stand and block the other while urinating. I looked down and saw the dry asphalt of the road quickly form a puddle that started trickling down the hill in the direction of the first mile marker.

"Ohhhhahhh! I pissed myself!" I looked over to see Drew having even more difficulty holding onto his baggie as it filled and overflowed with piss. Kids on the sidelines were most likely pointing and laughing. It was embarrassing, but also kind of funny. I saw Drew's bag drop to the ground, visibly filled with a yellowish fluid. Some of it trickled down his leg, his shorts visibly dripping. I tossed my fluid-filled bag off to the side of the road on the curb under a video camera tripod. Spectators were only a few feet away! This whole process would have been a lot better without the bags.

Relieved and still laughing, Drew and I lined up with Chad on the front line. There weren't very many of us in the elite corral, and I was surprised to get such an ideal position. After watching the wheelchair racers fly down the hills ahead of us, we were ready to go!

I could feel my heart in my throat. I thought about how the last 3 months had been an experience, an epic journey for me. This was the icing on the cake. I felt like I had to prove myself to everyone who had followed my running that I was worthy to be here. Perhaps I had to validate myself? I had to qualify for the 2012 US Olympic Trials today. I was confident that I would beat Drew and Chad to the finish line as well. The gun fired and we took off controlled, tucking behind the wake left by a lot of the Africans and Ryan Hall as they launched into the first mile. Gaps formed early, but we stayed back in a relatively crowded pack running consistently around 5:20 per mile early on. I couldn't wait for the pack that formed behind us to dissolve. The fear of being tripped or losing a shoe due to the mass of churning legs induced some anxiety. The downhills bothered me, and I couldn't wait for the flatter portions of the race after the first 10 kilometers.

Things were relatively uneventful, until the college girls at Wellesley. Drew and I had taken over pacing duties and we had sensed that the pack of 20 or so runners that started immediately behind us were dropping off into no man's land. My hip flexors felt strangely stiff…probably from the downhills, I assured myself. Our breathing had been steady and our fluid intake was consistent. Each one of my plastic squirt bottles was filled with 12 ounces of 50% watered down Gatorade Endurance Formula. Drew only drank 8 ounces of the same thing. Both of us carried 200 mg caffeine pills in our shorts' pockets that we planned on consuming around the 16-mile mark. Drew seemed like he was on a mission to push the pace just a tad faster every time he took the lead from me.

About 10 miles into the race, Drew tucks in behind me as the pack has thinned out.

"Too fast!" There was frustration and stress in my tone as I scolded Drew for leading us on a 5:09 mile split for the 16th mile. Suddenly I wasn't feeling so good, as the tightness in my legs had intensified and my thoughts were in a fog. I was feeling some pain. It was way too early to be fighting with the pace! Drew was antsy; he kept speeding up a little…I let the pace sag. "He's trying to gap me before the uphills," I thought to myself. I'll just let him go and run on my own. Too many miles under 5:10 were going to kill me. I just needed to hold 5:17s, damn it.

We made a sharp, right-hand turn at the old fire station corner and started up the first significant incline on the course which was a turning point that defined many a Boston race. Well, it was a critical juncture in our race too, as Drew dropped me hard on that uphill (and I had so deeply believed in my heart that I would be grinding the uphills strongly at this point). Drew just kept running the same pace up the hill. I significantly increased my effort (or so I thought) and split a 5:18 at the mile. Shit! It was right on pace - but my heart sank a bit; things were getting shaky and tough. The pace was suddenly hard to hold. I watched Drew pull away. 50m…100m…I was all alone.

The Newton hills punished me. I tried to keep my head up, and despite all the pre-race course preparations I had trouble processing exactly where I was on the course. "Is this heartbreak?" Nope, not yet. The hills were confusing me. My pace was faltering, a 5:24 on the next mile split.

I heard footsteps stalking me…Chad!

"Go Chad." I muttered as Nails flew past me going up Heartbreak hill around the 20-mile mark. His stride was strong and poppy. He grunted in acknowledgment as he flew past me. I glanced at the cumulative split times I had written on my forearm in permanent marker to gauge pace at major junctions in the race. For 20 miles I had run almost exactly 2:19:00 pace (which was a time of 1:46:00).

I remember thinking, "It's just not fair. I trained

so hard." It was something I had heard the speedy Boaz Cheboiywo say after failing in a marathon. I felt sorry for myself, staring up the hills in Newton, my legs puttering out so prematurely in such a crucial stage in the race. I thought I was strong, resistant to the fatigue of carbohydrate depletion. Things got hazy; I staggered at the next water stop, dizzy from hypoglycemia and craving the sweet nectar of full-strength Gatorade. At this point pure sugar cubes wouldn't have saved me. Even fast-acting carbs take too long to kick in, to fuel the brain and regenerate coordination. I was hopelessly plodding at the ground at what felt like a slow jog (in reality I was still going 6:30/mile pace). Other runners blew by me like I was the frozen statue of George V. Brown at the starting line. They ran like they were still newly minted, fresh and full of energy. I thought about dropping out. "No. You have to finish. You owe it to the race! Keith and Kevin would be so disappointed in you. We need three finishers to score for the team title." I scolded myself for considering the infamous DNF, and squinted for the next mile-marker sign: Mile 23. Are you serious? I still had over 3 miles to go, and I felt done, totally done. It's like when you are sleep-deprived, but you are forced to stay awake: all you want to do is close your eyes and give in to the fatigue. The passing of every second became more and more tortuous. Drew and Chad were out of sight. Man, I was really the slowpoke on the team today.

The remaining miles of the race were hazy, but I remember being in a lot of physical and emotional pain. Emotional pain because I knew that the clock was going to assign a time to my name that wasn't even close to my pre-race expectations. The end-result was quantifiable, and it was going to feel like I was letting down not only myself, but my teammates, my coaches, my family, and anyone who was following my race that day. Physically, there is really not much to do at that point as it's much like the last 50m of an 800m race when you are going full-tilt. Everyone has heart in the final 50m, it's really just a matter of the body locking up, feeling like you are running in quicksand, and like in a bad dream you are losing ground. I attempted to speed up on the final quarter mile stretch at Beacon Street as a couple more runners flew by me - great! While most Boston Marathon finishers seem to throw their arms up in pure ecstasy when crossing such a historic finish, I staggered across the line with my head down, somewhat dizzy, and not the least bit proud.

In the finisher's tent I spotted Drew and Chad already wrapped in foil blankets and sipping Gatorade.

"How'd it go?" I questioned my teammate. Drew's response caught me totally off guard; his result was so good, so much better and faster than we had anticipated:

"I ran 2:16!" he exclaimed.

"What!" I stammered, shocked that he could do so well when I did so poorly considering our training had been nearly identical. "What place did you get?"

"Like 15th." (He actually got 16th, one place shy of getting any money, although the BAA did provide us with a generous stipend for food and expenses that weekend.)

I was quite dizzy, and my quads began to stiffen. Instinctively I grabbed a bagel and consumed it. And then another…and another. I ate 3 bagels in 10 minutes and downed a 32-ounce Gatorade. There were not enough carbs in the world to satisfy me.

"Where did Chad end up?" I wondered out loud about my other teammate, who had broken my heart by flying past me on Heartbreak hill. Surely old Chad didn't sneak under 2:19?

"Chad ran a 2:17!"

"Wow, you guys did really well."

* * *

Why did I suck so much? I didn't want to confront Keith and Kevin. I didn't even know if my finishing time and place were good enough to win us the team title. No Olympic Trials qualifying time for me.

"Did you hear what the winner ran? He broke the course-record!" Drew informed me.

Damn, it was a fast day. So many guys busting a good one. I felt self-pity, like I had been wronged. There was a lot of frustration; the whole experience was somewhat of an emotional rollercoaster. Yeah, I felt sorry for myself. I was pissed. Why even bother with this bullshit? I wanted to curl up into a ball and disappear. But with Drew and Chad's success I knew I couldn't just sulk. We left the tent as a team and hobbled back to the hotel press conference room, which was conveniently only about a quarter mile away.

In the press conference room there were more snacks, and elites who actually placed in the top 10 were hanging out giving interviews and congratulating each other. I hid in a corner chair, but stood up to get a drink.

A vice grip tightened on my shoulder and pulled my whole body to the side. Kevin's face was inches from my ear, his grip crushing, his gaze intense: "You just didn't get paid today...today wasn't your day...but it will be next time..." His voice was hoarse. I was worried he was going to ream me out, yell at me for not making the cut...but he didn't. I was actually a little caught off-guard and surprised. Of course Drew was getting all sorts of praise for such a brilliant race (and it was!). Why couldn't I be more like him?

* * *

When Drew reflects on that day in Boston, his story almost directly contrasts with mine: "15 miles in I realized that 2:19 pace was going to be pretty easy...I started speeding up in the Newton Hills...I felt really strong." Drew notes that the early miles were enjoyable and seemed to fly by.

"By the top of Heartbreak I knew that I was going to run under 2:19 by a good margin...I was smiling and high-fiving people," he remembers, apparently not having felt much of the pain that usually consumes you in the last 10k. Such confidence and elation is the result of executing a perfect race on a perfect day. However, Drew feels that he has room for improvement.

"I feel I have more left in the tank," Drew reasons, given that a side-stitch from drinking too much slowed him down in the final miles. Both Drew and Chad ran negative splits despite the hills. Drew's mile split up Heartbreak hill was right around 5:20, and he dipped under 5:00 pace on a couple of the downhill miles after that.

Such a positive experience in a marathon is seemingly rare, and when I look back on the four marathons I've finished, none of them have had me feeling very good in the last 10k. Drew's body seemed to handle the training segment leading up to that fateful day much better than mine, considering our training was nearly identical [See "Boston Training Log" in Appendix for Drew's exact training for all 3 months leading up to the race]. Could it be that I was overly fatigued from the efforts, while Drew was ideally super compensated? Later, I reasoned that I simply had over-trained, while Drew with his higher mileage background had ideally trained. Such is the fine line between ultimate success and miserable failure. It's ironic because I was so confident before the race, and I hit all the paces in the workouts during the segment. However, once you over-fatigue your muscle fibers you shoot yourself in the foot and dig your fitness into a hole that you don't realize you are in until it is too late. On race day you must show all your cards, and when you are over-trained you face the reality of being dealt a bad hand.

After Boston I felt like I was in a depressed fog. It's like having had a significant other you are hopelessly in love with just break up with you. It stings hard, and you know the mental carnage is going to be something that will make you suffer for a long time. When running is your "girlfriend" (as famous Japanese marathoner Toshihiko Seko once said), when you build your life around running like we do at Hansons-Brooks, that is all you seem to have. And right now I don't have it...I don't have her. So it is painful to feel like the walls of the Bloomer house or the running store are caving in on me. Not to vent and complain too much, but with Drew's huge breakthrough and Chad's success comes additional frustration and even a little jealousy (I can't help it). Maybe more envy. To complete my significant-other-breaking-up-with-you analogy, think now that your ex just left you for someone new - maybe someone you kind of know and thought was a friend. Yeah, see how that feels. It's going to really sting for a while...this separation from Running. I liked her so much and she dumped me! It's going to be something that bothers me (at least a little bit) for the rest of my life.

Also see video at www.Vo2maxProductions.com:
"Hanging Out Before The Boston Marathon."

26:59!
May 1ˢᵗ, 2010

Mayday 2010, the day American distance running changed forever. Chris Solinsky, a Stevens Point, Wisconsin runner of Badger collegiate fame, ran a 26:59 10000m at Stanford to break the American record by 14 seconds. He is currently representing the Nike Oregon Track Club. Everything is changed now! The whole field was stacked with PRs, with other Americans running under 27:30 also. Galen Rupp (who had all the pre-race hype) still broke the old American record by a couple seconds and set a PR at 27:10.

Things are finally looking up for American distance running again. It seems like the whole last decade has slowly gained momentum as records are being broken, and the fields assembled for US Championships and the Olympic Trials have come a long way since 2000. Brian Sell puts it in perspective:

> "I think it's huge…you look across the board [from the 10k to the marathon]. You got Hall, Meb, Ritz, and Gotcher…there's going to be 10 guys capable of a 2:10 or better. It's good to see. That's where we need to go."

When asked if he thinks the Internet and media have influenced the influx of improvement, Sell is quick to comment: "I think it's mostly these guys just popping times…a couple guys get better and it drags everyone up."

I watched the 10k track race on the streaming video on Flotrack.org. The pacing was relatively good, with the first pack hitting the mile in around 4:25. By 5k they were putting strings of 65- and 64-second laps together to come through in about 13:35. From there the excitement built with each lap. Solinsky hung back just behind Rupp until about 2 laps to go and then The Rocket (as per his nickname in high school) just took off. His stride was so smooth and relaxed, and it was unusual to witness a relatively tall and heavy distance runner (contrasting with the little Sammy Chelanga) still hanging on Rupp. At close to 160 pounds, Solinsky outweighed the entire field. On the bell lap you could tell he had the record in the bag. With 200m to go the excitement grew as the clock revealed that he would need to close in around 27 seconds to flirt with the 27:00 mark - a quick last 200m for the end of such a long, hard race. I was skeptical that he would have enough in the tank to crack the seemingly impossible barrier. But he dug down real deep and kicked with his compression socks hard enough against the track to do it! The sight gave me goosebumps and tears formed in my eyes. This race was brilliant! When The Rocket hit the tape and the large digital clock by the finish flashed "26:xx," the fans in the stands just went nuts. There was an audible roar.

I think the fact that he broke 27 in his 10k debut, and that it shattered the American record by a whopping 14 seconds, made this a pivotal night in US distance running history. Not to mention, Galen still finished with a great PR in 27:10 to also break the pre-existing record by Meb. Chelanga set a collegiate record, throwing his arms up in the air as he crossed the finish in 27:08. In his Flotrack interviews, Solinsky hinted he had been doing more marathon type training with his teammates Bairu and Nelson (who are running NYC this fall). He mentioned hammering 8 mile tempo runs at 4:40 pace on a hilly route as one of his key indicators of fitness - but stressed that the race surprised him. He wasn't really chasing the time, he didn't have a PR to break; he just decided to compete, and he decided that above all, he wanted to win. When you run like that, you know good times are bound to come.

May 2010: Spring

"Saturday is the worst day of the week." Drew looks down towards a patch of bushes as he makes this statement.

I had mentioned how nice it was today, a Thursday where we both had a day off from work. It was a sunny day, perfect for outdoor activities. Drew and I had taken advantage of the weather and our free time and were walking through Stony Creek Metropark hunting for the valuable and delectable Morel mushroom. I was exhausted from hammering 16 miles (averaging 5:32 per mile earlier in the morning), but refreshed and optimistic to be doing something with my friend besides running or selling shoes.

The fact of the matter is, weekends in the program are generally worse than weekdays. Saturday means you have to wake up extra early, like 6 or 6:30, roll out for a longer run or a fast workout, and then work a longer shift at the store than usual (8.5 hours straight in the worse case scenario). Not to mention, the store is always busier on the weekend - you are standing up, bending over, and stacking shoeboxes constantly. Friday nights in college used to be fun outings of shenanigans and parties. Now, it is a direct contrast where we sit at home watching TV (if you're lucky and not working on Friday night also) and then retire to bed extra early. 10 PM is late on these nights.

I don't mean to complain about the strict regimen we have chosen in order to live the life of a serious distance runner. It's just you don't value the luxury and flexibility of a college lifestyle and the freedom of inconsistency that your body can handle in youth until it is too late. We have the luxury of choosing the amount of sacrifice we are willing to make in order to excel in something as trivial as running in circles or for 26.2 miles at a time. Sure, in college there were weeks at a time where we'd go dry on alcohol, try to sleep more, and rise early for Sunday morning long runs. There was some major schoolwork, 3 hour class lectures at night after practice, labs, project sets, papers, and the most stressful exams. But it didn't happen every weekend. It didn't happen for 6 to 8 months at a time. There was always light at the end of the tunnel in the monotony and loneliness that consumes the life of the long distance runner. More importantly there were girls. Girls to meet at parties; girls to meet in classes; girls running on the team. Cute, educated young women with a sense of humor flocked about waiting to laugh, joke around, and party. And in college you could socialize with them all the time. Sure, there would be some late nights, but those pleasant occasions never spoiled a season of running.

Here in Rochester there are some cougars, and there are also some mid-twenty-somethings with deep pockets. Most of them are the opposite of me on the political spectrum. They would laugh at my beater of a car. I am even embarrassed by it, only because I'm in the Motor City though. Going out on dates in the Prizm is out of the question. I need to get my act together. They'd question:

"What, you make $10 an hour working part-time at a shoe store? And you are 24 years old with an Ivy League Degree?"

"But I'm a professional athlete. I run marathons for money," I'll come back. "I'm sponsored by a major shoe company (true, really!)." Which, by the way, is awesome to be able to say and mean it.

But the non-running naysayers come back with the killer: "But you can't do that for very long…you'll be old someday…you won't make very much money…you just have enough to scrape by?" One serious injury, one accident, and I'm done. Heck, within 5 to 10 years my body is going to be done in terms of being able to run a national class marathon time. I already hobble down the stairs like an old man, feet blistered, tendons swollen, and muscles banged up. The body can only take so much before it breaks down. We seek to capture our youth, cherish it and utilize it to our advantage.

But is this what it really wants?

Going the Distance
May 18th, 2010

"I hope you decide to give it one more shot." Mike Morgan's words were like a warm blanket comforting my cold, indecisive thoughts. We are running down the Paint Creek trail together, and Chad asks me if I am planning on staying another year in the program. I had paused and muttered "I don't know" quite indecisively.

Lately I've been at a crossroads in what I want to do with my life. If the Hansons offer me the opportunity to re-sign for another year, I'm not sure if that's a good choice. After my disappointment at Boston, I am now only a 2:24 marathoner who hasn't qualified for the 2012 Olympic Trials. Maybe my body is finally revolting, wearing down from all the high mileage training over the years? Am I mentally losing it? No. I am more determined than ever to improve myself as a runner. But to improve as a person, to set myself on a career path...I'm not so sure. Perhaps it is time to apply for some 9 to 5 jobs or internships, something more along the lines of my college degree? Perhaps I should hang up my racing flats, call it a good competitive career, and move on? Running is such a time-consuming, energy-consuming, and selfish endeavor. What am I doing to make the world a better place? How am I contributing to society? At various points in my life I have looked in the mirror and asked these questions. I'm sure most people have them. It's weird, at these different transitions like freshman year of college and now, I really begin to wonder about my place in the world. When you turn 18 you are young and ignorant and feel like the world is yours - but then in a few years you start to realize that the world can tear you down at any minute and that most other people don't really care about what you say and do. It reminds me of a quote that a runner once said: "When you are in high school you think you are fast and smart, but then when you get to college you realize you are slow and dumb." Not sure who said that, but it's applicable to such transitions.

I'm not really fast enough to even deserve to be here right now. However, I am confident that I have the potential to run a sub-2:15 marathon, to maybe sneak into the top 15 or so at the Olympic Trials one day. That is a lot easier said than done though. I've always tried to be a realist. I've attempted to see things objectively as they are, and when it comes to chasing your dreams and goals you must constantly pinch yourself with a dose of reality. But what does a 2:15 marathon get you these days? Not much if anything in terms of financial incentive. I guess it is a matter of self-exploration, curiosity derived from trying to find out where your body's limits are and then testing them. Despite what many people might think, I didn't come here with the goal of running in the Olympics like Brian Sell eventually decided on. I came here to be the best runner I could be - something that I feel is worth chasing after, even in the prime of my mid-20s youth. To go the distance, to challenge yourself to the utmost brings out an instinctual component of human nature that connects us with pain, life, death, and joy. I think that's why we keep doing this shit.

I Puked up My Steak Dinner from Last Night
May 20, 2010, 7:30 AM, Medium Long Run

As runners we have learned to endure discomfort in many forms. Often, the physical stress of a race or hard workout causes our body to rebel, to protest. It is in these moments that we use our mind to override our body signals, to continue pushing through preconceived thresholds. This demands mental toughness, discipline, and a depth of character. Some say it is one reason why we partake in such a masochistic and crazy sport.

Today was one of those days when I tested my body and it resisted. In my time at Hansons I had yet to experience a workout hard enough for my stomach to give out and cause me to puke. I pride myself on having an iron stomach. Well this morning, my stomach was having a queasy day, and 15.6 miles into our 16-mile medium long run I puked up a frothy mix of steak bits, Gu, and gulps of water. I finished the run in 1 hour, 28 minutes, and 42 seconds, an average pace of roughly 5:32 per mile. The guys (Mike, Luke, Chad) dropped me hard, and Desi was not far behind me!

To put the effort of the run in perspective, I'll rewind to the previous night, when I came home tired from working a solo shift at the Lake Orion store until 8:30 PM. I was hungry and craved carbs, but in my new diet regime I have made an attempt to limit my extremely high carbohydrate intake and instead focus on eating more protein and fat. I fired up Luke's grill on the outside stoop at Bloomer and put on a 7-ounce cut of NY Strip Steak. Now I've been a pretty strict vegetarian for the last 24 years - and this was going to be the second steak I had ever had in my life. After my marathon disaster at Boston I've decided that getting some more natural sources of iron and a plentiful blend of amino acids might do my body some good. I can't stand that synthetic ferrous sulfate (liquid iron), as the stuff really does taste exactly like an amalgam of metal drink. Plus, over-dosing on iron is easy and fatal. Beef has a relatively generous amount of heme-iron, a natural source of iron that the human body absorbs a lot better than non-heme iron (which is from plant sources). So I swallowed my vegetarian pride and choked down my steak, over-cooked and burnt on one side and near raw and bloody on the other (I don't know how to grill very well yet either!). By then it was 9:20 and Drew and the rest of the guys were getting ready to retire to bed. We had received an email from Keith stating that Luke had an 18-mile long run the next morning - and we were going to meet at his house by 7:00 AM sharp for a "drive and drop." I figured I'd probably have to run somewhere between 12 to 18 miles as I didn't have a training schedule yet. Surely nothing more than usual since I haven't done any workouts and it was my 3rd week back to running post-marathon. So I poked around on my computer, updating various training logs and wasting time on Facebook. I downed a Corona with a fresh lime wedge in it. All of a sudden it was 11:20, so I rushed to bed and set my alarm for 6:30, my stomach and intestines still working on the carbonation, alcohol, and slab of poorly cooked beef.

      I arrived at Keith's house at 6:57 AM with Luke and Christian pulling up along the curb in front and behind my Prizm respectively. We waited 5 minutes or so for the rest of the women to show up. Mike Morgan came out of his car skinny and shirtless. Kevin made a crack that all the high school students driving by on their way to class probably thought Mike was waiting for the "special short bus." The nine of us piled into the back of the old, gray Hanson passenger van. Kevin and Keith sat pilot and co-pilot, and we took off on a bouncy ride over mostly gravel roads around 28 Mile and the end of Rochester Road. After slowly driving for 30 minutes the odometer finally clicked 16 miles. We piled out and started running almost immediately. No bathroom break! Good thing I was dehydrated and constipated. I remember feeling my left hamstring become tight and almost seize up the first 100m or so as we launched at 6:45/mile pace from the gun. The women were right behind us! After a couple miles we decided to take a piss break. Desi and Dot flew past us. The chase was on.

The older guys weren't going to let the females hang around us at all. Mike and Luke surged with a 5:15 mile just 3 miles into the run to break things up. I got strung off the back with such an effort as I was caught off-guard, and was still loosening up. Five seconds back, I clicked my watch and confirmed that I felt like shit because the pace actually was pretty fast. I looked behind me and was shocked to see the women not far behind. Oh, they're going hard today! I could clearly see Desi was trying keep the gap minimal. And I thought the guys' team was tough, cutthroat, and competitive; the women's team is even more so. Not only did Desi want to chase me down - she also wanted to prove to Dot and Melissa that she was in phenomenal shape.

8 miles in and I'm just wishing the run were over. Luke, Chad, and Mike have broken me, and I'm running 5:20s and 5:30s in a desperate fight to keep Desi from catching me. Christian, who only had 10 miles scheduled for the day (he is about to race a track 5k in a couple days), has dropped back and essentially been caught by Desi. We come through 10 miles in 55 minutes. It's hot, I'm thirsty, and my legs are stiff. At 13 miles in I almost walk up a hill because I feel like I'm hitting the wall and my stomach is tied up in knots. I can sense Desi is still close to me (and she was!), but I dare myself not to look back. In order to save my manhood, there is no way in hell I'm letting myself get "chicked" in a training run. The guys would make fun of me forever. I should be kicked off the team, although I have learned that historically guys in the program have bombed workouts and Desi has rolled them up. In the final mile I put in a closing effort, and the result yields the aforementioned vomit. As soon as I

finish the 16 miles I click my watch and look back, calculating the time that I had before Desi came storming past…did I mention she was also running a full 18 miles?!

Today, Desi was tough. She wanted some young blood, and if I had packed it in she surely would've caught me. I'm pretty sure that any competitive guy is going to be determined to not get "beat" by a female at the sport they excel at. I mean, we are supposed to be professional runners here - I don't want that many guys in the country to be able to beat me. When I looked back and saw Desi rolling me up this morning I became determined to hold on to 5:30s, even though my body didn't want to. To put in it perspective though, Desi could make the next Olympic team, and I wouldn't be surprised if she eventually ran a marathon close to 2:20 flat…faster than my current PR. She ran her first 25k split of the run faster than Katie McGregor had raced to recently win the 25k USATF national championships. Desi can make most distance runners, including DI college guys, die in oxygen debt during these long workouts and races. I know Paula Radcliffe ran a 2:15 marathon, which is just unbelievable - but right now Desi is at a level that surpasses almost all the female marathon runners in US history…she obviously can compete on the world scene. I think that the rest of us guys on the Hansons team felt our masculinity threatened a little bit today by how close and how fiercely Desi ran behind us. She dropped Dot, who got 8th at the last Olympic Trials and was surely focusing on taking me next. We were all pushed by her charge. These are the kinds of group training runs that ignite the competitive edge that separates us marathoners from the masses. We are united, men with women, as one team of American distance runners.

Most of the guys team at a Tiger's game before a night out in Detroit (left to right: Drew Polley, Me, Mike Morgan, Luke Humphrey, Chad Johnson).

Lily's Birthday
May 23rd, 2010

"It doesn't get much better than this, Lil," Brian says, holding his daughter in his lap. She smiles back at him, face covered in melted chocolate from her first s'more. We are sitting in the backyard of Brian's house out by the fire pit. It is a pleasant, warm Sunday night. The festive occasion is Lily's 3rd birthday, and Brian had invited us all over to help celebrate. By now the party had dwindled down to just me, Drew, Ryan Sheehan, Sheehan's wife Taryn, and Luke.

"I heard you can play the guitar, Sage," Brian's wife Sarah prompts me with a little grin. I remembered Brian had asked me to bring my guitar to the party for a little campfire singalong. In college I used to love to play with my teammates around a campfire. I guess I like the attention even though I can't really sing (some of us were just not born with a very resonate voice).

"I'll get your banjo out of the car too, Drew." I gave Drew a nudge and he sighed bashfully. We could really only play one song together - a cover of Old Crow Medicine Show's "Wagon Wheel." It wasn't a very good cover, but we played with lots of emotion so I guess that counts for something. We tuned our instruments and strummed over the orange flames that flickered off of everyone's faces. My voice was flat I'm sure. Brian watched gleefully. It's not every day that you get to play the guitar and sing in front of an Olympian.

When the singing ended it was basically Lily's bedtime. Drew and I were gorged on Sarah's banana cream cupcakes, s'mores, and the earlier food spread including various cheeses, vegetables, fruit, casseroles, potatoes, and adult beverages. It had been a refreshing party, which started in the evening when 20 or so guests arrived at Brian and

Sarah's comfy suburban home on the other side of Rochester. It was a dwelling that concerned Brian because he had purchased it before the real estate bubble burst, and selling it was going to be a considerable loss for the young family. I had arrived several hours earlier to find Brian happily manning the grill, cooking up hot dogs and burgers. I helped myself to a cold one.

"You want to try out the 'Lunch Box?'" Brian asks, handing a remote control transmitter to me. He pulls down an R/C monster truck and sets it down on the garage floor. "I've had this thing forever."

I somewhat nervously gun the throttle, not used to the mini steering wheel on the transmitter. The Lunch Box quickly accelerated out onto the driveway like it was possessed. The moving object startled Brian's golden retriever, Toby, who was sitting out in the front yard. Like Brian, I love remote-control vehicles. Some other little kids at the party around Lily's age were drawn to the Lunch Box like little magnets. After several wheelies and quick turns into the grass I scooped the vehicle up. "Don't break one of Brian's favorite toys!" I thought to myself. I put the Lunch Box up on a shelf behind Brian's motorcycle. There, safe and sound now.

During the party, Brian and Sarah take turns entertaining their guests and running into the house to check on baby Levi. Levi is at a tough age where he likes to cry at the top of his lungs fairly often. I can't imagine Sarah or Brian get much sleep at night.

"You want to see my new plane?" Brian says with a twinkle in his eye. He has been taking about his new remote control bi-plane during our morning runs.

"Sure," I respond, eager to see his newest project.

Brian's hobbies are confined to a small basement beneath the ground floor kitchen in the house. The basement has a couple rooms. In the main one, there is a small desk covered with various nuts and bolts. Beside the desk rest two sets of wings and a large fuselage. Brian proudly shows me his workspace and where he keeps his tools of assembly. I am surprised that he can put together planes in such a small, makeshift area. A smaller connecting room off of the main basement space houses a treadmill and a total body workout machine. The rest of the room is mostly bare, white space. On the wall directly in front of the treadmill is a Hansons-Brooks poster showing images of Brian, Clint, Chad, Melissa, and Luke that says "Banded By The Run." I have this same poster taped to my wall in front of my bed…it is usually the first thing I see in the morning when I wake up. The poster always motivates me to get out of bed and run. I remember hearing Brian mention that he doesn't really like running on the treadmill - except that one winter he "spread-eagled" on an icy sidewalk and realized that having a warm, dry surface to do night runs on might be a good idea. Plus, he could watch the kids and run at the same time.

"What kind of engine are you going to put on it?" I sheepishly inquire about the new plane.

"Probably a .60 or a .67," Brian answers, knowing that even though I've only flown electric, I know very well that the small, internal combustion engines are rated at cubic inches of displacement. A .60 is relatively large and powerful. It is typical for Brian to put on something like that to ensure that there would be lots of power. That's exactly what he did with his own running - he ran the high mileage and intensity that ensured he had the power and strength to get the best out of himself, when it mattered the most.

* * *

Brian would be leaving the Hansons Distance Project very soon, following in the footsteps of previous Hansons alums. Runners that eventually decided to move on to other stages in their lives, to live out their dreams and goals in other aspects of adulthood. In the end though, these former athletes, former teammates, life-long friends and retired competitors are what made a dent in revitalizing the depth of American distance running at the start of the Millennium. We'd like to think that we were part of something greater than just ourselves; we were (and are) a part of a movement that embodies the competitive spirit of hard work, sacrifice, and self-discipline. A movement that every runner who trains full-heartedly with the fiery desire to improve, attain goals, and compete participates and contributes in. Through this, this simple act of putting one foot in front of another, we figuratively move forward, abandoning our differences, and strive towards the light of progress.

Dedication

This book is dedicated to my Grandpa, R. Burton Canaday (1923-2010) who generously supported my dreams and closely followed my running endeavors.

Press Release

The end of 2010, the start of 2011, and the Future of the Hansons-Brooks Distance Project

By the start of 2011 there have been several new additions to the program. This new, young blood at Hansons is full of diversity, talent, and a strong work ethic that will carry the team into the upcoming 2012 Olympic Trials:

Tim Young, a former athlete at James Madison University, joined the team in the summer of 2010. Tim only ran 2 years in college because they cut the men's cross country and track teams there before he had fulfilled his eligibility. Not willing to give up on the dream, Tim continued to train on his own as a junior and senior, often logging up to 140 miles a week. Before joining Hansons, Tim had run a 49:04 for 10 miles at the Cherry Blossom Run where he was the top American finisher. He also had debuted with a "disastrous" 2:25 marathon. All this with college sophomore track PRs of 14:36 for 5k and 31:09 for 10k.

Robert Scribner, an MBA graduate from Mississippi State, also joined the program in the summer of 2010. Scribner, an intellectual, has never run (or driven) in snow. Often the comedian full of witty remarks, Scribner is not only my book editor, but also a minimalist that likes to primarily train in the Brooks Green Silence. Teammate Drew Polley describes Scribner best:

> "Robert Scribner was the first person to make me realize that not all southerners speak with heavily exaggerated drawls. After a collegiate career at Mississippi State University, marked by 5k/10k

PRs of 14:14/29:07 and an individual berth to the NCAA Cross Country Championships in 2008, "RL" Scribner continued to train individually in Starkville as he completed an MBA degree. His early post-collegiate racing career included a disappointing Chicago Marathon experience followed by a promising half marathon performance of 1:05:43 at the Rock and Roll New Orleans 2010 event where he claimed the top American place. Upon completing his MBA in the spring of 2010, the Tupelo, Mississippi native decided to take his talents and greater road racing ambitions north to the Hansons ODP where Keith and Kevin recognized his potential as an elite marathoner. Scribner's spontaneous personality immediately made an impact on his teammates, who can always count on him to cook up activities, projects, and outings for entertainment. His roommate and teammate Paul Hefferon quickly awarded Scribner the nickname DJ Bob E Scribzz, which ironically became more relevant as he helped form a band as a drummer with teammates Sage and I, including a rap/electronica side project, despite no musical background. He is a longtime enthusiast of music and film however, and is constantly armed with new album and movie recommendations. An example of Scribner's creativity and commitment can be found in his creation of a mixed drink, the "RL," which is now recognized at a surprising number of bars (and websites) throughout the world due to persistent word-of-mouth networking. Obviously, his range of talents extend to writing as well, as Sage called upon the one-time Mississippi State student newspaper Opinion Writer of the Year to serve as the main editor of this book. Watch for Scribner as he works with the Hansons program toward translating his success at shorter distances to the marathon."

RL Scribner, book editor

Paul Hefferon, from The University of Kansas, joined the program in the summer of 2010 as well. Paul is a 2-time All-American (once in the 5k on the track and once in cross country). A big talent, Paul ran a 13:59 5k on the track, and earned a silver medal at the 2005 Junior Pan American Games as a sophomore in the same event. The last couple of years before joining Hansons, Paul has struggled with injuries and has not been able to push very many 100+ weeks.

Zachary Hine, one of my former teammates from Cornell University. Zac joined the team in the fall of 2010 after finishing up grad school at Cornell. After running a 29:09 10k on the track as a senior, he stuck around Ithaca and raced for a year on the roads wearing the LetsRun.com singlet and being coached by Robert "Rojo" Johnson (co-founder of LetsRun.com and distance coach at Cornell). During this time he ran an impressive 1:04:14 at the NYRR New York City Half Marathon in March after already running a 60:46 for 20k at the New Haven US Championships (where he placed 13th in the fall of 2009). Zac looks to debut at 26.2 miles in the 2011 Boston Marathon.

The Women's side of the program also saw major changes as **Nicole Blaesser** (Indiana Univeristy of PA), **Lavenna Mullenbach** (Adams State) and **Molly Pritz** (Bucknell University) joined the program in the summer of 2010 as well. Most notably, Molly, who primarily cycled in college at Bucknell, is a willful talent with a lot of speed and potential. She has trained under Jack Daniels in Flagstaff, AZ, and has posted a 32-minute 10k on only a slightly aided road course.

Finally, the addition of a Hansons-Brooks Satellite Distance Program, involving several talented athletes from around the country who train with different coaches, was born late in 2010. Brooks Sponsorship supports these athletes as well, and they also sport the colorful Hansons Olympic Development singlet and represent the program while training and racing on their own terms. Recent additions to this group include **Jeremy Criscione** (University of Florida), **Brian Medigovich** (Adams State), **Ryan Sheehan** (Saint Francis University), **Mattie Bridgmon** (Eastern Washington, University of Oregon), and **Andrea Pomaranski** (Miami of Ohio).

The most recent athlete to move out to train in Rochester, MI with the group is St. Norbert College's **Jenny Scherer** (AKA "knightrunner22" on Twitter) from Wisconsin. Jenny joined the program in January 2011.

Combined with a roster that already includes standouts **Erin Richard** (Clarion University), **Emily**

Mortensen (Adams State), **Dot McMahan** (University of Wisconsin-Milwaukee), **Desiree Davila** (Arizona State), and **Melissa White** (SUNY Geneseo), the future of the Hansons-Brooks women's team is full of talent and depth heading into the 2012 Olympic Marathon Trials.

Rick Moody, co-founder of the popular "Warrior Running Camps," has joined the program as coach of the Hansons-Brooks South Distance Project team. *(Editor's note: Coach Moody recently led Florida-based athlete Jeremy Criscione to a 2012 Olympic Marathon Trials Qualifier with a 1:04:28 at the NYC Half Marathon in March 2011).*

Corey Kubatzky (Washington University of St. Louis) has joined the program as a new assistant coach. Corey ran at Washington University before attending graduate school at the University of Colorado-Colorado Springs (where he was an assistant coach of both the men's and women's cross country and track teams). With already a couple years of experience guiding elite post-collegians as well, Corey balances his coaching responsibilities with being the new Hansons Running Shop Store Manager at the Royal Oak location.

* * *

Finally, a recap of the 2010 Chicago Marathon:

Chicago
10/10/10

The Windy City heated up quickly with unseasonably warm temperatures for marathon race day, as the thermometer quickly spiked in the mid-morning sunshine.

For the second half of the race, the Fahrenheit reading exceeded 70 degrees. The heat took its toll on many runners, and the chances of many PRs and a world record time quickly vanished. However, despite the heat, 2008 Olympic Champion Sammy Wanjuri won with a time of 2:06:24 in a thrilling and gutsy race over Tsegaye Kebede that involved many surges over the final 10k. It was known pre-race that Sammy had been battling some health problems and had not trained well leading up to the event. In a record 35,000 + field of runners, the Hansons-Brooks team did surprisingly well, highlighted by having 5 men place in the top 18 overall, with the best placing from the team coming from the performance of Desiree Davila getting 4th (top American) in 2:26. Desi's time is currently the 4th fastest marathon ever run by an American woman! On the men's side, Mike Morgan led the Hansons with a new PR, 2:14:55 for 11th overall in the race. In order to crack the 2:15 barrier and beat his 4-year-old personal best, Mike soiled himself in the final mile. The smell in the elite athlete tent later was horrendous, but that's what it takes! Mike was followed by Luke Humphrey's 12th place, 2:15:49 finish; newbie, 23 year old Tim Young's 2:19:01 and 16th place (7th American); my 2:19:18 17th place finish; and Chad Johnson's 2:19:31 for 18th place. Other teammates placing in the race included females Melissa White in 16th in 2:35:02 and Dot McMahan in 17th with a 2:36:01 for the women.

For me the race was a bittersweet PR that I am extremely proud of. I finally cracked the 2:20 barrier, I placed in the top 20 (partially due to the large number of elites dropping out), and I won $2500. However, I failed to qualify for the 2012 Olympic Trials by running an average of 0.4 sec/mile too slow for the 26.2 mile distance. More heartbreaking was my teammate Tim Young (newest member of the team), who ran a gut-wrenching 2:19:01 (gun time) and missed the standard by a single, agonizing second! We ran together much of the race until the last 3 miles when

Tim pulled away *(Editors note: Sage and Tim would both earn their qualifications four months later at the 2011 Rock 'n' Roll Mardi Gras Half Marathon).*

Mike Morgan and Luke Humphrey had trained the entire segment to run 2:12 marathon pace, or 5:03 per mile. Many of our classic workouts like 3 by 3 miles, 5 by 2 miles and 2 by 6 miles were done at 5- 10 seconds/mile faster than marathon goal pace, or 4:55-4:58/mile for them. Through the autumn leaves in Rochester, MI we had done 20 mile long runs where Mike and Luke would pull away with a 5:30 mile from the gun, and end up running that pace the entire way, often surging close to 5:00 pace at times. They stacked on many 140+ mile weeks. Tim, Robert Scribner, and I trained more conservatively, by running less mileage, taking easy days easier, and being restrained to do workouts no faster than 5:07/mile pace (10 seconds faster than marathon goal pace). By the start of fall, I realized I had done nearly the exact same build-up as I had done before Boston, except I ran slightly less with more 120-mile weeks (instead of 130). More importantly, I realized now that I had become more accustomed to the heavy volume and relative intensity of Hansons-style marathon training that most likely overtrained me before my disaster at Boston in April 2010.

* * *

The future of the Hansons-Brooks Distance Project is as strong as ever with funding for the program by Brooks secured to at least the 2012 trials. Both the men's and women's teams are full of depth. Front runner Desiree Davila is looking like a favorite to follow in the path paved by Brian Sell in earning a US Olympic Team berth.

Training Advice for Developing Runners

Brian's career as a professional distance runner was more or less a fairy tale of progression, but that doesn't mean it was attributed to good luck or chance. You don't just go out and run world-class marathon times on a whim. His consistent, grueling regimen of high-mileage training piled for eight consecutive years gave him the strength to perform to the best of his ability. He used the pre-race pressure on himself to fuel his performances; he defied the odds by not getting injured and by pushing himself (in some mental or physical aspect) *every day*. At times he ran alone in workouts, ahead of the pack.

When asked what a developing high school runner or college runner should do in order to improve or make the varsity squad he states:

"Find the balance between over-doing it and doing enough. Guys come up to me and want to know 'The Secret'."

Sell doesn't have any training secrets - the balance of optimal stress and recovery is the essential, key component. Sell elaborates:

"The big thing with me was slowing increasing the mileage and intensity as I progressed…you kind of have to walk that thin line…that is the key [between overtraining and optimally training]."

Looking back on my personal training segment leading up to the 2010 Boston Marathon that is highlighted in this book (the same program that Drew Polley flourished with) I can tell you that it was too much too soon for me. I could handle the workouts and I didn't get injured - but come race day I was fried. Clint reiterates some similar concepts:

"I'm 35 now, and have run 20 marathons…if I had

to go back and do it again [I'd look out for]...overtraining...
it's out there and it happens to a lot of runners, especially the
more motivated runners...there is a breaking point and it's
easier to cross than I thought."

Clint reemphasizes that there is a fine line between
overtraining and ideally training. It's not cookie cutter, it's
not black and white - it is a gray area that differs for individuals at different stages in their careers. Clint continues on with
the wisdom he has gleaned from a decade of being a professional:

"It's easy to burn through your legs." Your structural strength and integrity (bones, tendons, muscles) fry
way before your cardiovascular system (heart and lungs). He
references how elite cyclists in the Tour de France can wail
on their bikes, often training 5-6 hours a day. That is a lot of
hard, aerobic stimulus! Compare that to the pounding forces
of running that many hours a day - it would give you a stress
fracture! Although Clint is a physical therapist, he strays away
from precisely defining specific training efforts for individuals:

"It's hard to explain overtraining with proven science...there is so much individual variation. When I was
24-33, it was physiological 'staleness' from overtraining...you
have this 'dead leg feeling." Sometimes going by qualitative
measures of effort like "feel" are the only ways that athletes
can truly gauge the correct pacing and workout intensities. In
other words, listen to your body!

Clint summarizes his reflections on his years of toil,
injured from the kind of shit he did to run a 2:14 marathon:

"If I had to do it over again I probably would've never run 150 miles a week...I would run 100 miles a week and
supplement with other things like biking so that I'd get over 3
hours of aerobic training a day. Your heart and lungs can take
a pounding...and you can't tax that system all the way even

when running 140 miles a week." Such is the enigma of the human body.

Drew Polley's Exact Training Log Leading up to a 2:16 at the 2010 BAA Boston Marathon:

Notes: Drew was coming off a slight ankle injury after running sporadically following his previous marathon in November of 2009 (a 2:20 at the San Antonio Rock 'n' Roll Marathon in hot, humid conditions). He arrived in Michigan during the first week of January and officially started training for Boston then. The first couple weeks were more of a transition period of easy mileage, a couple easier long runs and even some cross-training in the gym (which Drew did because his foot pain still bothered him).

Drew's mileage totals for his 15 weeks leading up to Boston went as follows:

95
90
87
82.5 (+ 20 miles biking)
112
124
127
129
132
127
135
133
129
117
83

Training Log:

January 3rd, 2010
AM: Easy 18 miles in 127minutes (7:03min./mile pace)

January 4th, 2010
AM: Easy 12 miles + 45min on stationary bike

January 5th, 2010
AM: Easy 10 miles…driving from Washington to Michigan in the snow

January 6th, 2010
AM: Easy 12 miles in Billings in the snow

January 7th, 2010
AM: Easy 12 miles on a treadmill

January 8th, 2010
AM: Easy 12 miles in the snow. Finally in Rochester, MI!

January 9th, 2010
AM: Long Run 19 miles
Comments: "long run, starting out with the guys (going easy) and adding with Tim [Friend from Washington]. Went slow and it was still snowy but much better than yesterday. Foot still bothering me but doesn't seem to be getting worse."

(Weekly Total: 95 miles)

January 10th, 2010:
AM: Easy 6 miles
PM: Easy 10 miles

January 11th, 2010:

AM: Easy 12 miles
PM: Easy 6 miles

January 12th, 2010:
AM: Easy 10 miles

January 13th, 2010:
AM: Easy 12 miles

January 14th, 2010:
AM: Easy 12 miles

January 15th, 2010:
AM: Easy 12 miles

January 16th, 2010:
AM: Easy 10 miles

(Weekly total: 90 miles)

January 17th, 2010:
AM: Long Run 20 miles (2 hours and 4min)
Comments: "Ran with Brian for first 10 then added on. Actually felt really good despite a lack of sleep. Foot is still sore but holding up"

January 18th, 2010:
AM: Easy 11.5 miles

January 19th, 2010:
AM: Easy 12 miles
PM: Easy 5.5 miles

January 20th, 2010:
AM: Long Run 17 miles

Comments: "Kind of a medium distance run from Stony, finishing back to Bloomer by myself. Started pretty fast with Morgan and Luke and slowed down for the second half. Planned on going a little shorter but wasn't sure how far it was back to the house. Foot is sore."

January 21st, 2010:
AM: Easy 10 miles

January 22nd, 2010:
AM: Easy 11 miles

January 23rd, 2010:
(took a day off...foot in pain)

(Weekly total: 87 miles)

January 24th, 2010:
Biked for 60min at 20mph effort

January 25th, 2010:
AM: Easy 13 miles

January 26th, 2010:
AM: Easy 11 miles
PM: Easy 5 miles

January 27th, 2010:
AM: Easy 12 miles

January 28th, 2010:
AM: Easy 10 miles
PM: Easy 5 miles

January 29th, 2010:
AM: Easy 12 miles

January 30ᵗʰ, 2010:
AM: Easy 10.5 miles
PM: Easy 4 miles

(Weekly Total: 82.5 miles)

January 31ˢᵗ, 2010:
AM: Long Run 18 miles (1 hour, 54 min)
Comments: "Felt surprisingly good despite cold, length of run, and lack of sleep. The lightweight Ravennas [Brooks Moderate Stability Shoe] seemed to have contributed to this. Feels like I am running in flats. Foot was pretty sore afterward though. Rushed to airport for Orlando flight afterward."

February 1ˢᵗ, 2010:
AM: Easy 12.5 miles in Florida
PM: Easy 4 miles

February 2ⁿᵈ, 2010:
AM: Easy 12 miles in 75 min
PM: Easy 4 miles

February 3ʳᵈ, 2010:
AM: 5 by 2 mile repeats at Marathon goal pace (downhill) 6min rest between efforts:
Comments: "5 x 2 mile, mostly downhill, at MP in FL with Sage. We struggled to find our pace a little, especially with the hills, and tended to run a little too fast. Shooting for about 5:15 pace. They were something like 10:25, 10:22, 10:26, 10:24, 10:27. This was actually a pretty easy, relaxed workout. I was nervous for it though and glad to have my first real workout in 3 months in the bank."

February 4ᵗʰ, 2010:
AM: Easy 12 miles in 78min

PM: Easy 4 miles

February 5th, 2010:
AM: Easy 10 miles (flew from Florida to Boston)
PM: Easy 6 miles...last 10k of Boston Marathon Course!

February 6th, 2010:
AM: 3 by 3 mile repeats at marathon goal pace (downhill) on first 3 miles of Boston course (8 min rest between efforts)...15 miles total for the day
Comments: "Boston: 3 x 3 miles on the first 3 miles of the marathon course, which is once again largely downhill. Drove back to the start for recovery between each. Aimed for MP around 5:17. Hard to find the pace with all the hills and we tended to be a little fast. Overall it was a pretty easy workout though. Legs are sore from the last few days however."

Weekly Total: (112 miles)

February 7th, 2010:
AM: Long Run 21 miles (just over 2 hours) from mile markers #6 to #25 on the Boston course.
Comments: "Last 20 miles of the Boston course with Sage and Chad. Dropped the pace down to a pretty good effort for the last 10, especially on the hills. Felt good overall but was feeling beat up by the end of course. We did miss a turn and add an extra mile so we slowed to a jog the last mile. We think we ran about 1:56 for the 20 miles, around 56 for the second half. Forced down fluids every few miles which was not comfortable. Boston training has officially begun.

February 8th, 2010:
AM: Easy 12 miles
PM: Easy 4 miles

February 9th, 2010:

AM: Easy 12 miles
PM: Easy 4 miles

February 10th, 2010:
AM: 10 by 800m on an indoor soccer field
In around 2:28 each with a 2:30 rest/jog between each.
Comments: "10 x 800 on the indoor soccer field, aiming for
2:28s and starting every 5 mins. Most of them were a couple
seconds too fast. Had problems getting to the facility so
unfortunately my warm-up was inadequate but I settled in
after a couple. Very snowy outside so it was great to get inside
and run a little faster. Solid workout, legs were having to work
a little on the last few but it was still pretty controlled. I was
worried about my tight hammy but it felt much better after I
took care of it yesterday. Foot felt fine."
PM: Easy 6 miles on the treadmill

February 11th, 2010:
AM: Easy 12 miles in 76 min
PM: Easy 5 miles on treadmill

February 12th, 2010:
AM: Easy 12 miles
PM: Easy 6 miles

February 13th, 2010:
AM: Downhill 10 by 1 mile around 5:10 average, about 8%
slope, 4min rest between (driving back up to the top of the
hills)
Comments:
"10 x 1 mile downhill with the Boston crew out Dutton Rd at
MP (5:17). Some pretty good downhill today on a paved road
which accomplished the goal of beating up the quads a little.
Aerobically, it was another pretty easy workout though and we
ran under pace on every one, probably averaging around 5:10.
I've been pretty tired lately but had no problems today. Keith

drove us back to the top after each one. Very long workout."

PM: Easy 4 miles on treadmill

(Week total: 124 miles)

February 14th, 2010:
AM: Long Run of 16 miles
Comments: "Run at Stony with Chad and Sage. Feeling pretty tired and quads are a little sore from yesterday. I think we were all feeling similarly, so we didn't get going too fast today, which was nice. Need a little recovery before the long run on Tuesday. Unfortunately I am coming down with a nasty cold, but I guess it's a good time to get sick now rather than closer to Boston, hopefully."

February 15th, 2010:
AM: Easy 12 miles
PM: Easy 5 miles

February 16th, 2010:
AM: 20 mile Long Run in 121min
Comments: "Long run at Stony with Chad and Sage. Snowy and slippery. We started out pretty slow (7:00 pace) then continuously dropped the pace well under 6:00, which took a solid effort in the slippery conditions. Sage and Chad actually dropped me on the third lap when they accelerated up a hill and I couldn't really match it. It was a little frustrating, but I am not too concerned. I am in the middle of a cold right now which I think has weakened me a little. I wore the heavy Glycerins [Brooks heavy cushioned shoe] when I probably should have gone with the lightweight Launches [Brooks lightweight shoe] like the other guys. The last 6 miles or so were tough, but I didnt completely go to the well, so I'll live to fight another day. Good to get a solid long run in at least."

February 17th, 2010:
AM: Easy 12 miles
PM: Easy 6 miles

February 18th, 2010:
AM: Easy 12 miles
PM: Easy 6 miles

February 19th, 2010:
AM: Downhill 7 by 1.5 miles at Marathon Goal pace (5:15 average)
Some uphill as well, but net downhill for the reps. Drive back up to the top rest (about 3 min).
Comments: "7 x 1.5 mi downhill at MP on Drahner Rd. Once again, not too hard aerobically to hit the 5:17 pace and we were a little fast most of the time. There was a little uphill though and the quads were feeling it a little by the end. Finally woke up feeling slightly better than the day before in terms of sickness but feeling drained still. A little ice on the dirt roads and we got in a car wreck! Keith rear ended by a distracted yokel. No one hurt."

PM: Easy 4 miles
(20 miles total for the day)

February 20th, 2010:
AM: 12 miles in 76 min
PM: Easy 6 miles

Week total: 127 miles

February 21st, 2010:
AM: Easy 12 miles
PM: Easy 6 miles

February 22nd, 2010:

AM: 5 by 1 mile repeats at indoor soccer field (artificial turf surface with coned off loop approximately 250m around). Most around 4:55 with a 4 min rest between each.

Comments: "This was actually really good timing as we got a shitload of snow this morning. 4 mins recovery between each. First was probably a little over 5:00 (distance was a little short) then we went about 4:57, 4:55, 4:55, 4:54. Definitely wasnt easy by the end, but stayed under control. The pace felt pretty fast after MP stuff, especially on the soft turf. Good workout though and it went by quickly. Still fighting off my cold."

PM: Easy 5 miles on treadmill
(16 miles for the day)

February 23rd, 2010:
AM: Easy 12 miles
PM: Easy 6 miles on treadmill

February 24th, 2010:
AM: 3 by 3 miles at goal marathon pace (5:17/mile)…15:51 each. With 5 min jog between. Ran on residential streets due to slick snow.

Comments: "3 x 3 miles at 5:17 MP with Sage, Chad, Steven. Ran the Bill Roney 5k course behind the Utica store to try to get some better traction with all the ice and snow. Roads were decent out here; a little icy but better than Stony. I wore Ravenna with sheet metal screws which seemed to help a little. Anyway, this was my most challenging workout I've done yet as a member of the team. I'm sure the ice and turns slowed us a little, but I was surprised at how tough MP felt today and pretty wiped out by the end. We had some trouble finding pace the first few miles (too slow then too fast), but settled in somewhat by the end. Good workout overall though. Tired from having to wake up so early. Happy to leave the ice and head to Florida tomorrow!"

PM: Easy 4 miles
(21 miles for the day)

February 25th, 2010:
AM: Easy 4 miles (Flew to Florida!)
PM: Easy 12 miles

February 26th, 2010:
AM: Easy 12.5 miles
PM: Easy 6.5 miles

February 27th, 2010:
AM: Long Run 21 miles in 128 min
Comments: "Long run in the orange grove loop (two 10 mile loops) with Sage. Fast miles 15-18. No coach today so we just had fluids at halfway. It was cold and rainy, and the dirt roads were pretty soft at some points, but at least miles 15-18 were pretty good. I felt much better than I expected, in fact this was about the best I've felt on a run since I've been here. Surprising since I've been so tired the last few days. We ran faster than we needed to on the "go" miles: about 5:04, 5:07, 5:07 (I was wearing my Garmin). I think we did have a slight tailwind though, and the effort felt about right. I still felt pretty good after that and actually found myself wanting to keep running farther at the end. Felt like I could have gone 30 miles at a good clip today. We were scheduled for 20. The extra mile was just to retrieve our bottles. I didn't want to drive the van through the muddy patch. I did take a caffeine pill halfway for the first time, which seemed to work great without any stomach distress, so I should keep that in mind."

(Week total: 129 miles)

February 28th, 2010:
AM: Easy 13 miles in 90 min

PM: Easy 6 miles

March 1st, 2010:
AM: Easy 12 miles
PM: Easy 6 miles

March 2nd, 2010:
AM: 4 by 2 miles downhill around 10:15 each with 5 min rest between.
Comments: "4 x 2 mile on the mostly downhill course in Florida. Aimed for 5:07 mile pace (MP - 10). Ran with Chad and Sage. Very humid. Our pacing was pretty inconsistant, a little fast on most of the segments. I think we got a little riled up by some certain cougars prowling up and down the road. I got a little tired at the end, but overall it wasn't too bad, especially considering the fast splits. Ankle wasn't a factor."
[editor's note, "cougars" being referred to as women, not actually wild cats]

PM: Easy 6 miles
(20 miles total for the day)

March 3rd, 2010:
AM: Steady 12 miles in 70 minutes
PM: Easy 6 miles

March 4th, 2010:
AM: Easy 12 miles in 76 minutes
PM: Easy 6 miles

March 5th, 2010:
AM: 3 by 3 miles in about 15:15 each with 7 minute jog between each.
Comments: "3 x 3 miles at 5:07 pace, on the overpass road in FL with Chad and Sage. 1 mile recovery jog between each. Running this pace here felt much easier than running 5:17s

in Utica last week. I guess that's because of the easier course, warm weather and lack of ice. Had to start working a little on the uphill segments of the last one, but overall I was able to stay pretty relaxed."

PM: Easy 4 miles
(18 miles total for the day)

March 6th, 2010:
AM: Easy 12 miles
PM: Easy 6 miles (Flew back to Detroit)

(Weekly total: 132 miles)

March 7th, 2010:
AM: 12.5 miles
PM: No run! Comments: "Unfortunately I skipped my afternoon run today because I got stuck at Grosse Pt pretty late trying to straighten some things out and felt terrible after a really busy day at work."

March 8th, 2010:
AM: Long run of 20 miles in 117 min. Miles 15 to 18 done in 5:10, 5:00, 4:57 (hard).
Comments: "Long run with Sage from Keith's house with 3 sub-MP miles at 15-18. I felt pretty strong overall and I think this went really well. It helped that we had nice weather and conditions in Rochester. We squeezed the pace down quite a bit before we got to our fast miles and then went about 5:10, 5:00, 4:57 or so for miles 15-18. Sage was a little stronger than me on the hills as usual but other than that I think we felt pretty similar. Slowed down a lot for the last two miles and still had a pretty fast average pace."

March 9th, 2010:
AM: Easy 12 miles

PM: Easy 6 miles + a few strides

March 10th, 2010:
AM: Easy 12 miles
PM: Easy 7 miles + a few strides

March 11th, 2010:
AM: 2 by 4 miles in about 5:10 mile pace average (20:40) with 1 mile jog in 7:30 between.
Comments: "2 x 4 miles at 5:12/mi pace (MP-5) at Stony. 1 mile recovery between. With Sage and Steven, and Morgan and Brian jumped in for a lot of it, too. Both Sage and I went a little too fast on a couple of the miles, but they were all between 5:07 and 5:13. I wasn't feeling very strong this morning to begin with but was able to power through it without too much struggle. Uphills started to hurt a little toward the end. In any case I am getting excited for Boston now that I'm starting to realize I'm in pretty decent shape already."
PM: easy 6 miles
(21 miles for the day)

March 12th, 2010:
AM: Easy 12 miles
PM: Easy 6 miles

March 13th, 2010:
AM: Easy 12.5 miles
PM: Easy 6 miles

(Weekly total: 127 miles)

March 14th, 2010:
AM: "1 mile + 2 miles + 3 miles + 4 miles" workout: first mile in 5:07, (half mile jog rest in 4min), 2 miles in 10:14, (1 mile jog rest in 7:30), 3 miles 15:16 (mile jog in 8 minutes), 4 miles in 20:24

Comments: "1, 2, 3, 4 miles at 5:07 pace at Stony Creek. 1/2 mile recovery between 1&2 and 2&3, 1 mile recovery between the 3&4. Rainy and pretty cold. Got off to a bad start as I was a dumbass and forgot my Green Silence, and had to run this in the big heavy Glycerin clunkers. I knew this would be a tough workout to begin with, and I was already pretty tired after a tiring last couple of days and losing another hour of sleep to daylight savings. Anyway, I was pretty happy that I was still able to hit the times overall, going about 5:07, 10:14, 15:16, 20:24. I did get dropped by the Sage, Chad and Steven on the second half of the last 4-mile interval on the uphills, but I still ended up being under pace which was reassuring. I had to work hard though; this was definitely the toughest workout I've done yet and my legs feel pretty thrashed.
PM: Easy 4 miles
(22 miles for the day)

March 15ᵗʰ, 2010:
AM: Easy 13 miles
PM: Easy 6 miles

March 16ᵗʰ, 2010:
AM: Easy 12 miles
PM: Easy 6 miles

March 17ᵗʰ, 2010:
AM: 8 by 1000m on the track at around 3:04 average with 400m jog in 2 min between each.
Comments: "8 x 1000m at 4:57 mile pace (3:05) on the Stoney Creek HS track, 400m jog between. Had a big crew of wily veterans today with Morgan, Brian, Clint, Carl, Chad with Sage and I. All of the 1000s were between 3:03 and 3:05. It was very managable, but actually felt a lot harder than I expected given the short distance and relatively slow pace. I guess the fatigue of the marathon training has been catching

up with me. Quad was pretty sore afterward. Chilly morning temps may have contributed to that."
AM: Easy 6 miles
(18 miles for the day)

March 18th, 2010:
AM: Easy 12 miles
PM: Easy 6 miles

March 19th, 2010:
AM: 5 by 2 miles at 10:10, 10:11, 10:14, 10:09, 10:10 with a half mile jog between.
Comments: "5 x 2 miles at 5:07/mile (mp – 10 seconds) at Stoney Creek with Sage and Chad. Half mile recovery jog between each. Something like 10:10, 10:11, 10:14, 10:09, 10:10. I lead the first and fourth. Tough but manageable workout. Felt pretty tired to begin with and quad is sore from Wednesday's workout. Uphills hurt but other than that it wasn't too bad. Much easier running in the Green Silence again instead of the Glycerin! I do like these types of workouts and feel like I'm getting ready to run well at Boston."

PM: Easy 4 miles
Comments: "Easy double to stretch out. Felt pretty crappy after workout followed by work."
(22 miles for the day)

March 20th, 2010:
AM: Easy 12 miles
PM: Easy 6 miles

(Weekly total: 135 miles)

March 21st, 2010:
AM: 13 miles

PM: 5 miles

March 22nd, 2010:

AM: "Marathon Simulation Run" 26. kilometers (16.3 miles) in 1 hour, 24 min and 34 seconds (5:12/mile average). On hilly road course. Practiced drinking fluid bottles. 4 mile warm-up/cool down.

Comments: "26.2K Boston simulator workout at Drahner. Every kilometer was marked, made to simulate Boston course by the mile, fluids every 5k, tried to simulate race routine and pacing. Our 5:17/mile pace equals about 3:17 per k. Sage, Chad and I took turns leading k's for the first half or so and were right around goal pace. Felt strong so started to pick it up slightly after that. I hurt struggled a little up the "Newton/Heartbreak" hills and Sage gapped me there, but I felt very strong again for the last 6k, caught back up and dropped the pace significantly without much trouble. Ended up finishing well under pace - about 2:16 MP without having to dig too hard. Sage and Chad were right there too, which is really encouraging for Boston. It was great to practice the routine, complete with fueling (watered down gatorade endurance and caffeine pill 10 miles from finish). Running MP or faster felt easier than I expected in the middle of this training block and got me pretty pumped for the race. Trying not to get too worked up about it. Ankle is a little beat up though and the sore quad is kinda thrashed again after finally feeling good before the run. Just need to keep going about business for another few weeks and hope things go this well on race day." (21 miles for the day)

March 23rd, 2010:

AM: Easy 13 miles
PM: Easy 5 miles

March 24th, 2010:

AM: Easy 13 miles

PM: Easy 5 miles

March 25th, 2010:

AM: 3 by 3 miles all at about 15:15 to 15:22, each with 1 mile easy jog between.

Comments: "3x3 miles at 5:07 (MP-10) at Stoney Creek with Sage, Chad and Steven. 1 mile recovery. Legs felt pretty tired from the start, so this ended up being a pretty tough workout for me. Able to stay on the pace, but it was a bit of a struggle by the end. Legs are obviously pretty fatigued from cumulative training, especially the simulator a couple days ago. Have some sore spots, but got a massage afterward which already seems to have helped a little. Suddenly I am feeling like I don't have too many more weeks of this training left in my legs, which I guess is pretty good timing."

PM: Easy 4 miles

(21 miles for the day)

March 26th, 2010:

AM: Easy 14 miles
PM: Easy 4.5 miles

March 27th, 2010:

AM: Easy 15 miles
PM: Easy 4 miles

(Weekly total: 133 miles)

March 28th, 2010:

AM: 5 by 1600m on the track in 4:56 average with 800m jog recovery between (1:45).

Comments: "5 x mile on the track at 4:57 (MP-20), 800m jog recovery. Chad, Sage and I took turns leading and we stayed pretty consistent in the 4:55-56 range. I felt very controlled during the whole workout which was nice after feeling pretty worn out coming into this. Didn't have as much trouble as I

expected turning the legs over today."
PM: Easy 6 miles
(19 miles for the day)

March 29th, 2010:
AM: Easy 14.5 miles
PM: Easy 4 miles plus some drills

March 30th, 2010:
AM: Easy 14 miles
PM: Easy 4 miles

March 31st, 2010:
AM: 20 miles in 116min (5:48/mile average)
Miles 15-18 at or under 5:13/mile.
Comments: "Long run from Stoney Creek boat launch, with
miles 15-18 at sub-MP, with Sage, Chad, Morgan and Carl.
Left the Stoney path for miles 2.5-10.5 and finished up on the
path. Feeling a little tired this morning from the start but got
through it ok. We were actually rolling at around 5:20 pace
from about 10 miles, so the 'go' miles weren't that much of
a shock, but I was already pretty tired by then and couldn't
quite hang with the other guys today after the first of the go
miles; ran about 5:03, 5:13, 5:13. Definitely a tough run today
but satisfying. Good to get one more out of the way. It's
definitely nice having such a solid training group in a similar
fitness range."

April 1st 2010:
AM: Easy 14 miles
PM: Easy 4 miles

April 2nd, 2010:
AM: Easy 12 miles
PM: Easy 4 miles

April 3rd, 2010:

AM: 2 by 6 miles in 30:50, 31:00 with 10min recovery jog between.

Comments: "2 x 6 miles at 5:12 (MP-5) or faster at Stoney with Sage and Steven. 10 min recovery between. I was a worried about this workout because of the length and with how tired I've been feeling, but it wasn't a problem. The first mile of each set were about the hardest parts, and I felt surprisingly strong once I settled into the pace. Just about all of our miles were between 5:09-5:12 and I felt pretty relaxed through the end. It helped that we had nice weather, but this was another good checkpoint to pass and gave me some more confidence."

(19 miles for the day)

(Weekly total: 129 miles)

April 4th, 2010:

AM: 14 miles in 87 min

PM: Easy 4 miles

April 5th, 2010:

AM: Easy 13 miles

PM: Easy 4 miles

April 6th, 2010:

AM: 8 mile tempo run, with first 4 miles at 5:15 average, last 4 miles at 5:04 average (one 5:00 split at the end).

Comments: "8 mile tempo at Stoney; first 4 at 5:17 MP, last 4 at around 10 sec faster per mile. Felt pretty good once I settled in to the pace. Wanted to stay controlled with Boston less than 2 weeks away. Still got a little excited on the second 'go' mile and went close to 5 mins, then started to feel it a little and slowed back down a little and let Chad and Steven go. Finished feeling ok still which was good. Iced in lake and got massage later. Legs are tired but I can tell I'm in a dif-

ferent realm of fitness I've ever been in and am getting very excited and nervous."
(14 miles for the day)

April 7th, 2010:
AM: Easy 12 miles
PM: Easy 4 miles + drills

April 8th, 2010:
AM: Easy 12 miles
PM: Easy 4 miles

April 9th, 2010:
AM: Long run of 20 miles in 127min (relaxed).
Comments: "Easier long run with Chad, Sage and Carl. We made sure to keep it well under control (which meant letting Morgan go) with Boston only 10 days away, and we had no 'go' miles. This was good, since I still felt pretty sluggish this morning. It did make the run go by pretty slowly though. Cold today with some snow falling. Pretty pumped to head out to Florida today and start gearing up to race."

April 10th, 2010:
AM: Easy 12 miles
PM: Easy 4 miles

(Weekly Total: 117 miles)

April 11th, 2010:
AM: Easy 14 miles

April 12th, 2010:
AM: Easy 10 miles
PM: Easy 4 miles

April 13th, 2010:

AM: 3 by 2 miles at marathon goal pace in Florida (all around 10:30-10:35)

With 5 min rest in between each.

Comments: "3 x 2 miles at 5:17 MP on the overpass road in FL with Chad and Sage. 1/2 mile recovery jog. Obviously this is kind of a final tune up for Boston. We all were pretty terrible at finding the pace today, part of which was due to some pretty strong wind. I was also a little surprised at how hard the effort felt, but I realize that I can't read into it much, with things being a little out of sync now with some extra rest and also the heat here. Enjoying the free time here and still feeling confident my legs will come around when it's time."

(13 miles for the day)

April 14th, 2010:

AM: Easy 8 miles in Celebration, FL

April 15th, 2010:

AM: Easy 8 miles

PM: Easy 4 miles + some strides

April 16th, 2010:

AM: Easy 12 miles (flew to Boston)

April 17th, 2010:

AM: Easy 70 min run including 3 by 2 minutes at a strong pace...around marathon race pace, with 2min easy between each surge.

Comments: "70 minute run from the hotel in Boston with Sage and Chad, along the river, with 3 x 2 minute pick-ups. Nothing crazy, kept it easy of course. Weather is shitty so its hard to feel too good out there but I expect to be ready Monday."

(Weekly total: 83 miles)

April 18th, 2010:
AM: Easy 5.5 miles

April 19th, 2010:
AM: RACE DAY! Boston Marathon:
16th place overall, 2:16:36 (5:12 per mile average)...came through first half in 1:08:43, ran 2nd half in 1:07:53.
Comments: "Boston Marathon; 2:16:36, 16th place. Temps around 50 degrees and North wind, which was anything from a head, side, to tail wind depending on the location. Overall pretty nice conditions though. Couldn't be happier with how well this went. I just wanted to run sub 2:19 like we trained for and get the trials qualifier out of the way, but I still felt very strong after going out on 2:18 pace for the first 16 miles or so and was able to drop it down as the course flattened out at the end. I feel like I might have even had a little more in the tank as my legs really weren't in that bad of shape at the end but I had a bad side cramp that was limiting my mobility. I wouldn't have thought I was capable of this yet, but now its nice to feel like I have a mark to back me up and put me at ease a little. The whole spectacle of finishing somewhat high at Boston, with all the insane crowd support, was unreal and I had fun the entire time. This was the highlight of my running career so far. I've had doubts about whether I can be an elite marathoner, but this was a huge confidence boost and makes me excited to get back after it. For now, 2 weeks off though."

A Training Manifesto:
an opinion of how to train for events ranging from the 3k to half marathon.

Principles I've learned over the years as well as basic definitions and ideas for designing performance programs. (Keep in mind my distance running bias towards those more high mileage, marathon types).

We'll start with defining training speeds/intensities that many sources and coaches over the years have proven are successful in improving distance-running performance at events ranging from the 800m to the marathon.

Think of all your running paces as progressing from left to right on a line. On the far left you are going at a slow jog/ walking pace and on the far right you are sprinting at top speed. While training at any speed (or "points" on this "line") can improve your fitness, there seem to be certain sets of points, or ranges that trigger more effective adaptation within the body. For example, as detailed by the diagram below, there are ranges of intensities/velocities that correspond with "V02max" and "Lactate Threshold."- terms that I will later clarify.

SLOW JOG-----Easy Aerobic Pace---Lactate Threshold-----V02max----Sprint

Which corresponds respectively (from left to right) with:
(recovery) to (conversation" training pace) to (tempo effort) to (aerobic capacity) to (all-out).

Note: Obviously this is an over-simplification of the

continuum, and the labeled ranges have more detailed pace/ intensities within them. It is not showing a scale, but is merely a basic visual telling how different training paces/intensities are relative to each other.

Confusion has stemmed from many different coaches and books using complicated definitions and terminology for training intensities that are *essentially the same*. For example, similar terms describing a "Lactate Threshold" and "V02max" are shown below:

Lactate Threshold:
LT, Anaerobic Threshold, AT, Tempo Pace, Threshold (Daniels), Anaerobic Conditioning (Coe)…also corresponding very closely to this intensity/pace would be the terms: Aerobic Threshold, Marathon Pace, Half Marathon Pace, Critical Velocity, Onset of Lactate Accumulation ….the list goes on.

V02max:
Aerobic Capacity (Coe), Maximal Oxygen Uptake (Benson), 5k race pace…etc.

The scientific processes associated with these terms is not worth going into at this point, however, the more technical definitions associated with the two concepts listed above would be:

Lactate Threshold=
the "point" when lactate concentration rises in the blood at a rate faster than it is being cleared…. Higher intensities beyond this point lead to the formation hydrogen ions and the result is increasing concentrations of lactic acid which leads to the burning sensation and tiring in the muscles

as well as a metallic taste in the mouth. This threshold corresponds roughly to 15k race pace or roughly 10sec per mile slower than current 10k race pace.

Vo2max=

milliliters of oxygen consumed per kilogram of body weight per minute of exercise. It is determined by several factors including left ventricle size (stroke volume), maximal heart rate (beats per minute), and the differential of oxygen content in your arterial blood and venous blood (Pfitzinger 18). This corresponds roughly to current 5k race pace for a well-trained endurance athlete.

Why are these two training intensities so important? Well, for racing lasting anywhere from 1500m to 10k, the **V02max is the most important determinant in your success**. For races 10k and longer, the lactate threshold becomes increasingly important (Pfitzinger), although it is also helpful at improving your ability to race distances shorter than 10k as well. Likewise, having an improved V02max can help you in races beyond 10k also.

In terms of training there are many workouts that can improve your lactate threshold and Vo2max. I personally believe in having specific workouts target exclusively one system at a time (either Vo2max or LT), although many coaches like to design workouts that evoke both systems within the same workout.

Furthermore, there are workouts that should target other systems above and below the paces/intensities of Vo2max and LT.

Paces/Intensities slightly faster/harder than V02max velocity/effort (but slower than all-out sprint speed) can and should be used to capitalize on gains in V02max by improving your muscle coordination (through the stimulation of neuromuscular pathways between muscle fibers and the brain), as well as by having the body adapt to clearing increasing concentrations of lactate at a faster rate.

To simplify things, I like to call workouts in this intensity/pace range **"Economy"** workouts because they are specific to developing a sense of race pace velocity and lead to adaptations of more efficient biomechanics and changes at a chemical level. (Daniels calls this "R-pace", Coe might call this "anaerobic capacity," *Run with the Best* calls this "Anaerobic power running" or "Lactic Acid tolerance"). However, it is important to clarify that the workouts in this pace/intensity range can be **easily manipulated** throughout the season to stimulate very different adaptations within the body. Changing one variable, such as decreasing the rest between intervals/repeats or increasing the intensity or total volume of the training session are **only appropriate at certain times and must be integrated into the overall training picture of complementing workouts and critical periods within the season.**

Paces/Intensities slightly slower/easier than Lactate Threshold velocity/effort but faster than an easy jog recovery pace can be used in Long Runs to capitalize on building strength and endurance as well as teaching the body to more efficiently burn fat as a fuel and increase glycogen stores (energy to be used by the muscles) in the liver. Perhaps more importantly, this **"Easy Aerobic Pace"** as I will call it, is what makes up the bulk of training mileage at any given season of the year. Improvements in capillary densities in the legs, the number and size of mitochondria (powerhouse of the cell) as well as burning fat and excess calories are important adaptations to make an athlete more fit over the years. (Daniels refers to this as E-pace or L-pace, Benson refers to this as a range of "Aerobic Power running, to Aerobic Endurance training.") It is important to note that this is a **large range** of intensity/pace, which could blend into "steady state" and near Lactate Threshold effort running down to an easy conversational pace that is employed on days between hard workouts.

To summarize the major terms listed above from slowest/easiest pace-range efforts to the more difficult pace ranges/efforts I have listed some example workouts below:

Easy Aerobic Pace:

"60min run starting at a slow shuffle jog and ending at marathon race pace"

"Long run of 20 miles or 2 hours….stop at whichever comes first." (note: this is applicable to any sub 2:30 marathon runner…others should just run for a steady 2 hours)

"AM: run easy 45min, PM: Run at an easy, but steady effort on hilly trails for 70min"

Lactate Threshold:

"6-8 mile run at current 10k pace + about 20 sec/mile"

"20 min 'Tempo Run' at current 10k pace + about 10 sec/mile

"3 by 2 miles at 10k pace + about 10 sec/ mile with a 2 min rest between each"

V02max:

"8 by 1000m at current 5k pace with 2 min rest between each"

"5 by 1600m at current 5k -8k race pace with 3 min rest between each"

Economy:

"16-20 by 400m @ current 3k pace with a 1:30 rest between"

"10 by 600m @ goal 5k pace with a 1:30 rest between"

"24 by 200m @ mile race pace (manipulate rest depending on goal of workout and time of season)"

4 by 400m @ fastest possible average w/5min rest between *

*note: this last workout is not applicable to merely building "Economy" like those others listed above, as it specifically targets the demands of a middle distance race and high concentrations of lactic acid which if performed too frequently or too early in the season will lead to burn-out by destroying aerobic enzymes. I only listed it because it falls into this pace/intensity range that I broadly defined above, although I do not plan to discuss workouts such as these any further because they are outside my personal area of training emphasis.

Finally, there are **two more main paces/intensities that should be noted:** All-out sprint speed, and a very easy recovery jog pace, which I will refer to as **Speed** and **Recovery** respectively as seen on the first diagram at the top. While these paces/intensities will be used the least in the training cycle of a distance runner during the year, they still may very well be emphasized one day each week.

Speed:

For example, a set of strides after an easy day can be slowly increased throughout the training cycle to reach velocities of a near-maximal sprint. When kept at workbouts of less than 15 sec and with plenty of recovery these efforts are short and intense and designed to work on speed. Combined with hills and/or drills and plyometrics these provide an excellent stimulus to the neuromuscular system…making all relative paces feel slower and more comfortable. In fact, famed marathon coach Renato Canova suggests even marathoners run 8 sec hill sprints at least once weekly to improve their performance…at the marathon (site: Mensracing.com interview)! There is no doubt that on the track speed often rules in the closing stages of a race. Being able to shift gears coming off the final turn of an 800m-10k race may be the difference in several places or qualifying for a final. As Peter Coe said: "Touch on speed every day." At the very least, some 100m strides at mile race pace or faster several times a week should maintain this stimulus to some degree. However, athletes already training 2 hours per day often ignore doing the little things that will touch on their speed. All this extra focus and attention to top end speed development may very well be the extra edge gained by 1cm in stride length or a 1/100th sec decrease in foot strike ground contact time - which can pay big dividends in all races (i.e. 30-40 sec in a 10k or several minutes in a marathon).

Recovery:

Running at a slow jog is appropriate on days after very hard workouts or races. Recovery runs are about regeneration and simply moving the muscles allows for blood to flow and in fact can speed the healing process for muscle damage and resulting soreness. Mentally allowing yourself to relax once a week, you can slog through an easy mileage day and still burn calories to hit your weekly total (while actually enjoying the scenery). This is equally as important as any hard workout because it allows you to absorb all of the harder workouts. At heavy periods in training, you may be on the brink of injury and these days might be the only thing that save you from coming down with more severe tendonitis or the dreaded stress fracture.

Different Training Considerations for Individuals:

Types of Athletes:

To oversimplify things I'm going to categorize the typical runner into one of three "types":

The "speed guy," the "born marathoner" and "the versatile runner." The book *Run With The Best* uses this idea of runners based on their PRs at various distances…they come up with more complicated classifications of type A, B, and C, C1 and C2 runners etc (Benson 103).

To give you a general idea of these types of athletes, I made up some hypothetical PRs for each type of runner. This would be some expected times for an adult male with a significant amount of training and mileage background (i.e. at least 4 years at 60mpw + on average).

-events-	400m	1500m	5k	10k	marathon
Speed guy:	50.0	3:50	14:45	32:00	N/A
Versatile guy:	52.0	3:50	14:20	30:00	2:25
Marathoner:	56.0	4:00	14: 25	29:45	sub 2:20

I might be going out on a limb, but I think most runners are born to be somewhat like the versatile type. Many of these guys ran the mile and 2 mile in high school as well as cross country, and tended to be decent at all three events. With decent 400m speed, they have the potential to gain enough endurance to run a very strong 5k and hold on for 10k. They can also move down to the 1500m and do relatively well.

The "speed guy" is most likely to be primarily a middle distance runner who may not even run XC, but would often contribute to running the 4 by 400m in high school.

The "born marathoner" is mainly a 2 miler in high school and they usually excel in XC as well, but not necessarily on certain courses or rough terrain.

A "speed guy" in high school may find that he is in fact a "versatile guy" in college, as his mileage increases and he gains the strength to move up to longer racing distances and excel. Furthermore, many versatile guys who were only decent at the mile- 2 mile in high school find that with increased training volume over the years they have dropped PRs in a wide range of events and may in fact be most successful at the 5k distance during their later college years.

Why stereotype? Because training a group of runners all as individuals is optimal in theory, but not practical in a team environment. Runners within each of these three categories will have individual strength and weakness variations that could undoubtedly lead to more classifications. However, for the sake of simplicity, it is best to generalize like this. What is important to note is that the training of each type of runner should be somewhat different in order to capitalize on genetic variations and to identify an optimal training stimulus that will allow each to reach their full potential.

For example, the speed guy is most likely going to do long runs and tempos at a slower pace than the marathoner - even if their 5k PRs are the same. Generally the speed guy weighs more and is more likely to get injured from running high mileage. Most importantly, the speed guy has fewer slow-twitch muscle fibers than the marathoner. The few slow twitch muscle fibers that the speed guy has are easily fatigued from high/drastic increases in mileage, and very long runs. However, because of their superior reservoir of speed, 6:20/ mile pace on Long runs may feel slow on the legs, yet after an hour it becomes somewhat of a chore due to the fact that their muscle fibers are tiring. On the other hand, the marathoner feels like his legs are moving somewhat fast, and yet he finds a comfortable groove with calm easy breathing and even feels progressively better after 90 min at this pace. The

speed guy may be running 75mpw and the marathoner needs
to be running in excess of 100mpw to fully reach their potential due to the specificity of what their main events are, and
determined by their physiological "strengths and weaknesses."

In the off season or base building phases of training,
nearly all runners should be developing their aerobic base
through increasingly high mileage weeks and lots of Easy
Aerobic Paced runs. However, mileage figures aren't end all
numbers yielding instant improvements. One should not
become a slave to hitting weekly totals merely for the sake
of maintaining a perfect average. The theory of LSD (long
slow distance) to build base endurance may have initially led
to great improvements for "speed runners," as they simply
gained some sorely needed endurance to carry their speed out
over further and further distances. However, performance
gains from an increase in mileage is a matter of diminishing
returns and eventually the speed guy will find that he needs
to keep moving up in race distances in order to keep getting
PRs. On a larger scale, this is exactly what may happen to
the versatile runner and marathoner after a period of about
5 years UNLESS a new, more intense and ever-changing
training stimulus is introduced. This may simply be a matter
of adding more quality miles to the weekly mileage figures
by not running LSD on easy days, or by adding an additional, higher volume track workout once per week. While
the "marathoner" should look to increasing both mileage and
intensity, the "speed guy" should look to mainly increase endurance through Lactate Threshold workouts, Speed sessions,
and perhaps a continuance of higher mileage totals (but at a
slower overall pace).

Since the human body is like any other organism, new
stimuli trigger it to adapt…and we must formulate specific
workouts for that adaptation to occur. This will result in
optimal improvement in race performances. This is where
Lactate Threshold, V02max, Economy and Speed workout
intensities come into play because for races lasting 800m to

the marathon, they are most specific to developing efficiency in race efforts. I will now discuss how these training terms/workouts illustrate principles of training that have historically been successful:

Principles of Training:

Training theory has changed over the decades and it is worth mentioning some historical achievements that have influenced the world of distance running. (Take into account that the following is my opinion).

1. To improve, to win, to reach your potential you have to work **HARD** (high mileage and appropriate intensity to back it up).

Back in the 1956, Olympics Emil Zatopek won the 5k, 10k, and the marathon. He revolutionized the way people thought about distance training by a) running high mileage and b) backing that high mileage with high intensity. He did single workouts in excess of 20 miles, such as 2 sets of 50 by 400m daily…for consecutive days! Jim Ryun and Gerry Lindgren both ran over 100 miles per week in hs. Lindgren claimed that he hit over 300 miles per week several times later, and Ryun repeatedly ran workouts like 40 by 400m.

Obviously these training volumes are a bit too much for any runner, but it goes to show that you have to sometimes be a little crazy in order to succeed in athletics. Frank Shorter averaged nearly 120 miles a week for an entire decade! (Bloom 22). Leading up to his gold medal in the marathon for the 1972 Olympics, Shorter said he ran weeks of 170 miles at 8,000ft of altitude in the mountains of Colorado (22). Alberto Salazar once told me that to improve I must be willing to train "haaaaaaard" and "really hurt"…the fiery look in his eye conveyed his message of masochism.

2. Periodize your training so that you never lose touch with your sprint speed or your base-building endurance:

When Arthur Lydiard developed what many would refer to as the "aerobic base building" phase in training a lot of people misinterpreted him. They watered it down to simply "running slow and easy for weeks on end while increasing weekly mileage totals by no more than 5% per week." While some of Lydiard's work is what I consider outdated, it builds the backbone of most successful training programs because it introduces periodization (read: changing training stimulus) which allows a runner to build on their levels of fitness through different adaptations week after week, season after season, and year after year.

Lydiard's general "base phase" was 10 weeks of 100 miles/week with a weekly long run of over 20 miles, and several runs at "¾" effort "steady state runs." He also incorporated hill workouts (running up and down hills as well as sprinting on the flats) to promote speed, strength and good biomechanics.

But, pure sprint speed on the track is also needed. While pure sprint speed is more specific to the 800m then say the 10000m, it is often ignored and underrated by distance runners. Top end speed however, is important even for marathoners because it allows all sub-maximal paces to become more biomechanically efficient and allows the runner to relax more at all race paces. *Run With the Best* advises a weekly workout of 10 by 100m at 400m goal pace for about 50 weeks out of the year. Therefore, as I defined "Speed" workouts earlier, these sessions can be done after easy mileage days and may consist of short sprints, drills, and pylos.

3. Different Paces and Intensities work together as complements (much like amino acids to form proteins …or ingredients in a cake recipe) in developing the program as a whole.

Think of the big picture. Where do I want to be a

year from now? 4 years from now? Your idealized progression in your mind is often not realistic. Set-backs occur, changes in the training program should occur (some for the best, some for the worst). Doing sprints, economy workouts, lactate threshold workouts, and V02max sessions build upon each other month after month. Coupled with high mileage you aim to become both stronger, faster, and more efficient to the unique demands of running what you consider to be your best event. Therefore, during many of your productive months training and racing you want to not only keep hitting on your sprint speed and base endurance - but also not stray too far from a V02max stimulus, a Lactate Threshold stimulus, and an Economy (read goal race pace or key race pace specific velocity) as well.

Coach Mark Wetmore at The University of Colorado is an example of a coach who utilizes many of Lydiard's principles without all the watering down. Most importantly, I think, is Lydiard's idea of "steady state running," combined with high mileage and single day each week where the athlete only runs once, but runs LONG at a relatively fast pace. What Lydiard's steady state runs were leading up to was the modern concept of "Lactate Threshold" intensity and progressing at increasingly faster and faster speeds on relatively easy efforts. This is much like how many African runners train…starting out at a slow shuffle, but eventually building into a pace that capitalizes on faster and faster aerobic development by closing runs at under 5min/ mile (which may only be marathon pace for them). Like a "random" fartlek these kinds of runs explore the pace range spectrum from a slow easy jogging pace all the way down to all-out sprint surges.

In more recent times, we've seen evidence of periodization in dividing training into specific periods or phases, for an emphasis on one type or stimulus/workout type or another…however, this does not mean that all those other stimuli can be neglected. Sometimes there are two or three sub-periods or sub-phases within a phase. Things get complicated with a 3-10 week block of training chunked off and devoted to the emphasis of different systems. However, this amount of detail is important because knowing that certain weeks of training are devoted to developing specific qualities of training is the cornerstone of appropriate planning for the overall season or "the big picture." What is more important is being able to see the system, the whole program and its phases, and to have it planned (roughly) ahead of time. This is best done by working backwards from the day of a championship race (end of season) and building the program around a time frame leading up to that culminating event. While some may call this a peak. I tend to think of it as being a time when the athlete is at a very high level of fitness. I don't believe in true "peaks," and I think that the athlete can perform at a relatively high level of fitness nearly year-round. This is done by integrating all intensities/velocities of training somewhere within each phase/period of training.

For example, American great Bob Kennedy was once quoted as saying:

"At any time during the year, there has to be an element of base, V02max workouts, and speed work in your training" (Pfitzinger 106). Coach Joe Vigil from Colorado State has mentioned having elite athletes do a session of 4-6 by one mile at 5k-10k pace with a short rest once a week nearly every week out of the year (Sandrock 36). Jack Daniels, who in *Daniels Running Formula* suggests having an early phase of training focus on R-pace (Economy Pace) or doing relatively fast speedwork early in the season, while maintaining it throughout the rest of the season/year. In the relatively simple "Summer of Malmo" (named after runner George Malley), the author suggests a summer devoted to doing 2 medium intensity workouts a week on the track. One of those workouts is a Lactate Threshold Tempo Run of 4-6 miles in length. The other two are economy based workouts involving repeats of 16-24 by 150m-300m at relatively fast efforts with a full recovery one week, and then doing longer, "pre-

Vo2max" workouts of repeat 1200m-2000m intervals with a lap jog recovery the next week.

Alan Culpepper and many Colorado runners would do Lactate Threshold runs of 8k-10k on the track on a regular basis, closely monitoring their progress with heart rate monitors.

So in my mind, the athlete should be training 50 weeks of the year (barring injury risk). Most of those weeks are going to contain track workouts and nearly all of them contain a long-run and a near all-out sprint/speed/ stride session.

Since most of the working world and the calendar year is based of cycles of 7days, I like to keep mileage totals in that kind of time span. However, I personally believe in the 10-12 workout cycle because it seems to be the most appropriate way to rotate enough variety in workouts while allowing adaptation and recovery to occur.

A sample "pre-season" training cycle for an athlete targeting a 5-10k track, road, or XC race might look like this:

1. **Easy Aerobic Pace:** AM: 5 miles, PM: 10 miles steady

2. **Speed day (Easy):** PM: 3 mile warm-up, drills, 10 by 100m fast (400m date pace) with 300m full recovery jog between OR 16 by 8 sec steep hill sprints with full recovery, 5 mile warm-down at Easy Aerobic Pace.

3. **Long Run:** 16 miles or about 95-100min….throw in fartlek surges of 30sec- 5min at a time or run Steady pace down to Lactate Threshold intensity.

4. **Recovery:** Easy 8 mile jog

5. **Lactate Threshold:** 6-8 mile Tempo run at about 25-20sec/mile slower than current 10k fitness. OR
2 by 5k at about 5-10sec/mile slower than current 10k fitness.
6 by 100m strides before and after.

6. **Easy Aerobic Pace:** 10-12 miles

7. **Economy:** 20 by 400m at current 3k race pace w/1:30 recovery.

8. **Recovery**: double if you have to, Easy Aerobic Pace if feel good.

9. **Easy Aerobic Pace** (steady) 12 miles + 6 by 100m strides

10. **VO2max:** 5-6 by 1600m at current 8-10k pace w/3min rest OR 8-10 by 1000m at current 8k pace or 2-3 sec/ 1km faster w/2min rest between.

Total: about 100 miles/ any given 7 days.

Repeat cycle 3-4 times, after reaching a period of peak mileage.

LSD, or long slow distance is what partially led to the demise of American distance running (along with low mileage, and overly intense anaerobic speed work on the track that was done at balls-to-the-wall effort 3 times a week). Several decades ago, there was not much science, but just a bunch of hard-headed coaches and athletes with egos to fill and time barriers to destroy. Successful training became an art - and it still is today. However, it has also become a science, something with biological adaptations and data that can't be ignored.

References:

Benson, T. & Irv Ray. *Run With The Best*. Tafnews Press, 2001.

Bloom, Mark. *Run with the Champions*. Rodale: 2001.

Coe, Peter N. & Martin. *Better Training forDistance Runners*. Human Kinetics, 1997. Champaign, IL.

Daniels, Jack. *Daniels' Running Formula*. Human Kinetics, 1998.

Pfitzinger P. & Douglas. *Road Racing for Serious Runners*. Human Kinetics 1999.

Sandrock, Michael. *Running Tough*. Human Kinetics, 2001.

Websites:

Beck, Kevin. "Summer of Malmo." Kevin Beck's Website on Running. online:
"http://www.kemibe.com/highschool.htm"

Men's Racing.com. "Interview with Renato Canova."
www.mensracing.com

Book References

Morgan, Mike. Personal interview. 11 May 2010.

Polley, Drew. Personal interview. 25 June 2010.

Sell, Brian. Personal interview. 3 May 2010.

Verran, Clint. Personal interview. 27 July 2010.

About the Author

Sage Canaday grew up in the backwoods of Sheridan, Oregon, where he started running seriously in 6th grade because his soccer coach told him that he was better off without a ball! A part of the very deep Oregon high school class of 2004 (Galen Rupp, Ryan Vail, Stuart Eagon, Scott Wall), Canaday's best cross-country finish was 13th at the Oregon State Cross Country meet (large-school division) his senior year of high school. Lacking natural foot speed, Sage was "just another 4:30 miler" who didn't even make states in track and never got to race at Hayward Field in Eugene.

At Cornell University, Canaday slowly developed as a distance runner under the guidance of LetsRun.com co-founder and Cornell distance coach Robert Johnson. After a disastrous freshman year of running sabotaged by iron-deficiency anemia and a poor diet involving the infamous "freshman 15," Canaday slowly built his mileage up over 100 miles per week. A gradual, but steady progression of improvement eventually resulted in a trip to the DI NCAA Cross Country Championships as an individual in the fall of 2007, and an Ivy League Conference individual title on the track for 10k in the spring of 2008.

Also in college, Canaday convinced his coach Robert Johnson that he should try to qualify for the 2008 US Olympic Marathon Trials. After receiving permission from his coach, Canaday trained between cross country and track seasons and debuted in the 2007 Houston Marathon with a 2:22:21, missing the trials "B" standard at the time by a margin of only 21 seconds. Determined to qualify for the trials (his dream since his sophomore year of high school), Canaday tried his hand at the marathon 6 months later at the 2007 Grandma's Marathon in Duluth, Minnesota. Despite racing in sunny temperatures over 70 degrees, Canaday succeeded in qualifying for the trials in his second marathon with a 2:21:43. He was the youngest participant in the 2008 US Men's Olympic Marathon trials at the age of 21.

Sage joined Hansons in August 2009 after graduating from college with a Bachelors of Science in Design and Environmental Analysis, and a concentration in Human Factors and Ergonomics. Most recently, Sage ran a 2:16:52 at the 2011 Rock 'n' Roll San Diego Marathon and qualified for his 2nd Olympic Marathon Trials.

ISBN: 978-0-9832941-1-5

Made in the USA
Lexington, KY
30 April 2012